The Best Stories Behind the

Top 20

Canadian Rock Pop & Folk Songs

The Best Stories Behind the

Top 20

Shania Twain, Bryan Adams, Alanis Morissette, Gordon Lightfoot, Joni Mitchell, Neil Young, Anne Murray, Leonard Cohen, Stompin' Tom Connors, and many more

FOX
MUSIC
BOOKS

Canadian Rock Pop & Folk Songs

by Jim Brown

Cataloging in Publication Data is available.

ISBN 978-1-894997-13-3

Edited by Bob Hilderley.
Designed by Susan Hannah.
Typeset by Laura Brady.
Copyedited and proofread by Ann-Maureen Owens.
Printed and bound in Canada.
Published by Fox Music Books, an imprint of Quarry Press Inc, PO Box 1061,
Kingston, Ontario K7L 4Y5 www.quarrypress.com

Contents

Canadian Songwriting

What makes a song great — melody, rhythm, tone, lyrics? Is it simply good timing, luck, or serendipity? Where do great songs come from — observation, imagination, talent, tradition? Or is it simply experience, tricks of the trade, coincidence? Every song has a story, and like songs, some are better than others. In some cases, the stories told about the genesis and enduring appeal of the song are as fascinating as the song itself. Knowing the origin of a song often enriches our pleasure in listening to it.

Telling the stories behind our favorite songs has become a popular pastime. Hundreds of stories about songs of faith and hymns are featured in publications like *The Heart of Worship: Story Behind the Song*, while popular music is covered extensively in books and websites like *1001 Songs: The Greatest Songs of All Time and the Artists, Stories, and Secrets Behind Them*. Even the Chicken Soup for the Soul editors have compiled *The Story Behind the Song: The Exclusive Personal Stories Behind Your Favorite Songs*. Whole books are devoted to telling the stories behind the songs composed by rock, pop, and folk stars – The Beatles, The Rolling Stones, Bob Dylan, and Neil Young, for example.

Which brings us to the stories behind songs composed by Canadians. The song-writing achievements of Neil Young, Joni Mitchell, The Band, Leonard Cohen, Barenaked Ladies, Shania Twain, Alanis Morissette, and other Canadian artists merit attention as a special group within the history of popular music. Besides producing most of the greatest hockey players and some of the funniest comedians, Canada is best known as the home of a distinctive cast of musicians. Despite being a relatively young country, Canada has a rich popular music history, as chronicled in *Oh What a Feeling: A Vital History of Canadian Music*, sponsored by the Canadian Academy of Recording Arts and Sciences

(CARAS), the agency that runs the Juno Awards.

Canadians have composed a wealth of lyrics and melodies that express the elusive Canadian identity. In the early years of radio broadcasting, Winnipeg-born and New Brunswick-raised Bob Nolan moved to Hollywood, where he formed the Sons of the Pioneers with Leonard Slye (a.k.a. Roy Rogers) and wrote the classic silver screen cowboy gems *Cool Water* and *Tumbling Tumbleweeds*. Before tasting success in the motion picture capital of the world, Nolan is said to have lived a hobo life riding the rails. Fellow Maritimers Wilf Carter and Hank Snow followed in his footsteps, also emulating the yodeling brakeman, Jimmie Rodgers. In 1951, Hank Snow's signature tune, *I'm Movin' On*, stuck at the top of the *Billboard* Country & Western charts for a remarkable 21 weeks and kicked off a superstar career in Nashville, where Snow was a regular Saturday night performer on WSM's *Grand Ole Opry* radio show.

Percy Faith's film score for a *Theme From A Summer Place* spent nine weeks at number one on the *Billboard* chart. Percy Faith also passed along to Tommy Dorsey a demo of a song by Canadian artist Ruth Lowe called *I'll Never Smile Again* that became Frank Sinatra's first hit record with the Dorsey band. Canadians were also there at the birth of rock 'n' roll, beginning with the Crewcuts' number one hit *Sh-Boom*, which topped the national charts in the United States for nine weeks in 1954. In 1957, 16-year-old Ottawa native, Paul Anka, became an international teen idol with the release of *Diana*, the first of his 33 Top 40 hits as a solo artist. Anka also has experienced many successes as a songwriter, including Buddy Holly's *It Doesn't Matter Anymore*, Tom Jones' *She's A Lady,* and Frank Sinatra's signature song, *My Way*.

Canadian artists owned the late 1960s and early 1970s – the Guess Who, Leonard Cohen, Anne Murray, the Band, Steppenwolf, Neil Young, BTO, Joni Mitchell ... the list goes on and on. These were high times for Canadian music, continued by mid-'70s and early '80s stars, including Bruce Cockburn, Rush, Loverboy, and Bryan Adams. By the 1990s a new generation was heralded by the happy-go-lucky lyrics of the Barenaked Ladies and shouted from the rooftops by Alanis Morissette, Shania Twain, and The Tragically Hip. The momentum has not let up in the new millennium, with exciting new singer-songwriters like Avril Lavigne, Diana Krall, Feist, and Michael Bublé joining the pantheon of Canadian stars who continue to scale the charts.

Enjoy these tales about the Top 20 Canadian rock, pop, and folk songs. Don't resist the desire to retell them. They deserve to become legendary. There's a touch of nostalgia in all of these stories, perhaps because we sometimes fear songs of this caliber will never be written again, but then we remember how consistently Canadian artists have given us so many great songs for so many decades now, we are thankful. It's those memories we celebrate in telling the stories behind these songs. And please join us at the back of the book to debate that thorny question, what is the number one Canadian rock, pop & folk song?

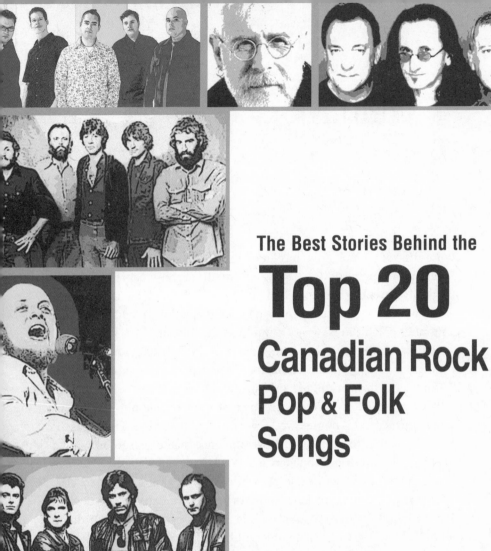

The Best Stories Behind the

Top 20

Canadian Rock Pop & Folk Songs

Diana

Words and Music by Paul Anka

© 1956, Chrysalis Standards

I'm so young and you're so old
This, my darling, I've been told

For a little guy, Paul Anka has an ego that some people find offensive. "I was pretty precocious," he has admitted, "a pretty aggressive kid. I think my parents knew they had an unusual child." How unusual the world would soon see as he emerged from the nation's capital to record a number one hit in New York and headline the Las Vegas strip.

Paul Anka returned home to Ottawa on June 9, 2005 to receive the prestigious Order of Canada medal. In a separate ceremony held in Toronto, his star was added to Canada's Walk of Fame. Since he left Ottawa in 1957 to record *Diana*, his first number one hit, he had not often returned to his hometown, living much of the time in Las Vegas. In fact, his relationship with hometown audiences had been somewhat of a love/hate relationship. Panned by local rock critics and labeled a "lounge lizard" by some writers, he had chosen to perform almost anywhere else. "I've always had great reviews," he says in his own defense. "And when I came here I realized, 'Wait a minute, everybody gets what I'm doing all over the world why is it so different here?' And I thought, 'Why do I want to put myself in harm's way? Why do I want to come back here?'"

For the record, Anka became one of the biggest teen idols of the 1950s, right up there with Elvis Presley, Buddy Holly, Frankie Avalon, and Bobby Darin. He was the first North American pop star to perform behind the Iron Curtain. He set attendance records at the Olympia in Paris, and his *Put Your Head On My Shoulder* was played on radio more often than just about any other song in history. Anka transcended the teen idol label to become an international star, performing in the entertainment capitals of the world. He has written more than 900 songs, including songs for Frank Sinatra, Tom Jones, Sammy Davis Jr., Donny Osmond, Englebert Humperdinck, and Barbra Streisand. He composed the music for Johnny Carson's *Tonight Show* that ran every week night for more years than any other talk show in TV history. Paul Anka is, in a word, a star.

Anka's previous attempts to reconnect with his roots, such as becoming a partner in the new Ottawa Senators NHL franchise, led to further controversy. In 2003, he finally healed all previous wounds by performing a show at a fundraiser for liver and kidney research. Performing for a dinner audience in a ballroom was far more conducive to his talents than playing the local hockey arena. At fundraisers he could ply his audiences with the smooth shtick he learned from Sinatra and perfected during four decades in Las Vegas and Atlantic City casinos. The charity was close to his heart. His mother had died suddenly of liver failure due to diabetes in 1961, while driving her car near the new home Paul had purchased for his parents in New Jersey. Her tragic death came at the height of his teen idol career and hit him hard. "She was my ally," he explains. "She made the difference. My father was straight. He wanted me in a legitimate business, and, back then, show business wasn't legitimate."

Paul Anka was a child prodigy and a shining example for kids like Rene Simard, Celine Dion, and fellow Ottawa-born Alanis Morissette, who followed in his footsteps. At a young age, he had a passion for music and a belief that he would become a big star even though he was a stocky, overweight preteen. He wasn't even the best teenage vocalist at his school, but he had begun to write his own songs and that skill would become his biggest asset.

| I don't care just what they say | |
| 'Cause forever I will pray | |

"I had a knack for writing," Anka later explained to John Rogers, "and my dad always wanted me to be a journalist, but I got kicked out of shorthand class. No way did I want to do those little squiggles." He found it much easier to make sense out of the treble and bass clefts, sharp and flat notes that baffle most journalists.

Born in Ottawa on July 30, 1941, Paul Anka began life in a downtown apartment on Slater Street. As his parents' situation improved, Anka, his younger brother Andy Jr., and sister Miriam eventually settled in west Ottawa on Patricia Street. Their friends were mostly members of the Lebanese Canadian community who frequented his father's Locanda Restaurant, which opened for business in 1951 and rapidly became a gathering place for local celebrities. As soon as he was old enough, Paul began to hang out at the restaurant, peeling potatoes in the kitchen to help his father out and making his presence known to diners. He was a clever, talented kid and a bit of a hustler, always promoting himself. He performed at every opportunity that came his way, making occasional forays into the venues that dotted the nearby communities of the Gatineau region, just across the Ottawa River in Quebec.

> You and I will be as free
> As the birds up in the trees
> Oh, please, stay by me, Diana

In the summer of 1954, a Toronto vocal group that called themselves the Crewcuts hit the top of the *Billboard* and *Cash Box* pop charts with *Sh-Boom*, which hung around at number one for nine straight weeks. Paul Anka formed a vocal group of his own with classmates Gerry Barbeau and Ray Carriere. As the Bobbysoxers, they performed at community centers and the local YMCA auditorium. They auditioned for a local TV show. However, he likely never saw himself as part of a group when it came to making it as a pop star. He was highly competitive and frequently bragged to his peers and sometimes to his audiences that he would be a big star someday. Talent contests where he could compete against others fascinated him.

Gord Atkinson, host of a local '50s TV show, recalls that "Paul was just a ball of fire. You knew this young man was going to go somewhere. Paul had a lot of chutzpah. He wanted to get somewhere. Some people in town, as is the case in any hometown, thought he was pushy. As a young kid he did have that ability to make his presence known. Paul worked this town. He would borrow his mother's car without her permission and without a license and drive to Hull and Aylmer to enter amateur nights at the big nightclubs. The winner would get 20 bucks."

"The turning point," Anka recalls, "came when I started winning those contests, realizing there was something different about me. I wasn't talking about the same things as the kids I grew up with. I was talking about singing, being in show business, leaving Ottawa going to the ballpark where the action was."

"Paul had a huge ego and had his own agenda," a classmate would later tell *The Ottawa Citizen*. "He knew where he was going and he certainly thought he knew how to get there."

"I was like a junkie," Anka admitted to the same reporter. "From a very young age, to be a singer and songwriter is all I wanted. And everyone thought I was crazy." The staff that put together his 1955 school yearbook had it right when they called him "the little guy with the big voice." He was still overweight and his voice an untrained resource, but he had a tenacity that could not be denied. Even though he was underage, he snuck into local theaters when R&B stars like Fats Domino and Clyde McPhatter came to town, and had his first encounter with his future manager, Irvin Feld. The promoter ignored Anka's declaration that Feld would soon be booking him, and kicked him out of the backstage area.

| Thrills I get when you hold me close |
| Oh, my darling, you're the most |
| I love you but do you love me |
| Oh, Diana, can't you see |

By the summer of 1956, Paul was in LA pestering his uncle to become involved in his career. Canadian groups like the Rover Boys and the Diamonds had been signed up by U.S. labels and the Crewcuts were a fixture on the radio with a string of top 10 *Billboard* hits that included the memorable *Earth Angel* and *Ko Ko Mo (I Love You So)*. Fifteen-year-old Paul Anka was hungry to taste similar success. His uncle told him he'd have to get serious or forget about becoming a star, and put him on a crash program to lose weight and get in shape. Working with a personal trainer, he trimmed down from 170 pounds to 135, which better suited his five-foot-five height. A visit to a plastic surgeon shortened his nose, but his pompadour and ducktail took years of constant combing and plenty of Brylcreem to perfect.

He collaborated with his uncle on new songs and he phoned every record company in the LA yellow pages but received no immediate encouragement. Like Elvis, he spent a lot of time in record store listening booths learning the lyrics to the latest hit records so he could imitate the stars when he got a chance to perform. All the time he was scheming as to how to get a song recorded. LA was, after all, a breeding ground for new doo-wop groups. One afternoon, listening to *Stranded in the Jungle* by the Cadets in a soundproof booth in Wallack's Music City, he noticed the address of Modern Records on the label. It was in nearby Culver City. He hitchhiked to the studio, where he met the proprietors, the Bihari brothers, Saul, Jules and Joe. The Bihari brothers were sleazy operators but they put out a lot of records. Jerry Leiber and Mike Stoller had used their Modern Records and RPM Records labels as a springboard to get artists like the Cadets, the Flairs and the Robins, and Big Mama Thornton to record their songs. Leiber and Stoller and the Coasters, who recorded their comedic R&B songs, all came out of that melting pot. Listening to the Cadets that afternoon Anka could sense the excitement.

"I walked into this garage," he recalls, "and the brothers were there. I said I was from Canada and they looked and me strangely and said, 'Sing your song.' I did it, and they said they were going to record it and told me to come back in two weeks." They also hooked him up with their A&R guy, Ernie Freeman, who had a combo that could be expanded to orchestra size. Freeman was a good arranger. "The back-up singers on the record were the Cadets," Anka confides. "I could not believe what was happening to me. The song did so-so in Canada and sold a few copies in Buffalo and then it went right into the toilet. My life had ended, I thought. I was a failure at 15 and I was going to kill myself."

> I love you with all my heart
> And I hope we will never part
> Oh, please stay with me, Diana

Returning to Ottawa and high school, Anka plotted ways to persuade his parents to let him make a second trip to the U.S., and fell head over heels in love with an older girl. It was a classic case of a teenage crush. Still, Anka managed to salvage something from the immediate angst and imagined pain. He wrote a song about the object of his affections, Diana Ayoub.

"Paul was 16 going on 17, I was 18 going on 20," Ayoub later told reporters. "We were worlds apart. Paul used to entertain at church functions and he became friends with my friend and me. We started hanging around together and he would call me." The strong-willed Anka wasn't easily put off and his persistent phone calls irritated Diana's father. When Diana and her girlfriend learned that Anka had penned a song about her, they asked him to sing it for them, and he rapidly lost his confidence. "It was the only time I saw him blush," Ayoub recalls. The songs that Paul wrote that winter were head and shoulders above his previous efforts and he pushed for an opportunity to try his luck with record labels in New York City. This time, his father, who had financed the trip to California, and, some have alleged, the recording session, was not eager to foot the bill. Ever resourceful, the 15-year-old Anka improvised and entered a win-a-trip-to-New York City contest. "I entered this contest for IGA food stores," he recalls. "Whoever collected the most soup wrappers won the trip. I took a job at IGA, collected the most soup wrappers, won the contest, went down to New York."

He had befriended the Rover Boys: two Canadians, a Brit, and a native New Yorker, who had been signed by ABC Paramount Records A&R man, Don Costa. Their cover of the Four Freshmen's *Graduation Day* was a Top 20 hit for the label, and it didn't take much to convince Costa to listen to another aspiring Canadian act.

The Rover Boys were named after a series of Horatio Alger style boys' books, written by Arthur M. Winfield (a.k.a. Edward Stratemeyer). With Anka crashing in the group's New York hotel room bathtub, what came next was a real life Horatio Alger story. "He saw something in this raw kid," Anka declares proudly. "I've really believed that along with hard work and dedication, there's some luck involved."

No doubt Don Costa, a veteran arranger and producer, was impressed with the number of complete original songs that Anka presented him that afternoon. They were not all as good as *Diana*, the one that Costa picked for the first recording session, but the songs were good melodically and they all showed intense insight into the teen dilemma, perhaps as much insight as Chuck Berry's teen lyrics. The kid was good looking and he could sing well enough that a few sessions with a voice coach could whip him into shape. Costa became Anka's mentor. "He was able to teach me and tell me where to go and where not to go in terms of the music," Anka notes. "Because the framework and the base of those arrangements is half the battle Nelson Riddle and

Sinatra, same scenario." Andy Anka was called and made the trip to New York to sign a contract for his son.

> Oh, my darlin', oh, my lover
> Tell me that there is no other
> I love you with my heart

During the weeks leading up to the session, Paul took time out to write a letter to Diana Ayoub, proudly telling her that the song she inspired had been chosen by his new record label. The orchestral arrangement that Costa drew up featured wailing saxophones that echoed Anka's plaintive vocals. The beat was a cha-lypso, a cha-cha/calypso combination that was the latest dance craze, and Costa's orchestra tore into it as Paul sang the ballad. It was a winning combination, and Paul soon found himself in demand, performing on *The Ed Sullivan Show, The Perry Como Show,* and *American Bandstand*, where he had to learn to lip synch.

"My life as a teenager ended at 16," he notes. "I went into another sphere." Mobbed by teenage girls wherever he went, Paul toured Europe, Australia and Hawaii with Buddy Holly & the Crickets. Back in Ottawa, Diana Ayoub experienced a similar loss of privacy which, to her, was an unwelcome consequence of having a hit song written about you. She was no longer bothered by Anka though, who soon transferred his affections to a cute Mouseketeer, Annette Funicello, the only member of the cast of *The Mickey Mouse Club* TV show to be personally selected by Walt Disney. Annette's crush on Paul produced her first hit, *Tall Paul*. Annette blossomed into a buxom Mouseketeer who would soon "fill a bikini" in surf movies with Frankie Avalon.

Irvin Feld now recognized the Ottawa teenager's star potential and signed Anka to perform on his fall tour. The arrangement, with *Diana* rocketing to number one as the tour kicked off in September '57, soon became a management deal with the legendary promoter of circuses and rock 'n' roll reviews. "Many nights we sat down together," Feld confided during *Lonely Boy*, a 1962 National Film Board documentary interview, "and I told him, 'Paul, you no longer belong to yourself. You belong to the world. God gave you something that I don't think he's given anyone in the past 500 years, but He's given it to you to make other people happy throughout the world.'" Feld may have believed his own hype that Anka would become the biggest pop star of all time, but more likely this was just the sort of pat on the back and keep-your-artist-in-line advice that Colonel Parker used to keep a young and headstrong Elvis Presley in line. It worked.

| Oh-oh, oh-oh, oh-oh |
| Only you can take my heart |
| Only you can tear it apart |

The Costa-Anka team continued to hit on the radio in 1958 with *You Are My Destiny* (number 7) and *Crazy Love* (number 15). In early 1959, they had a novelty hit when Paul was teamed up with the label's other teen idols, George Hamilton IV and Johnny Nash, for *The Teen Commandments*. Anka continued to tour with Buddy Holly and wrote Holly's last chart hit, *It Doesn't Matter Anymore,* before the tragic plane crash that took Buddy's life along with the lives of Richie Valens and the Big Bopper. Feld claims that he held his young protege back from climbing on that fateful flight because Andy Anka had made him promise to keep Paul with him on the bus.

Paul's relationship with Annette produced another hit song. "You're locked in a bus and you're a teenager," he recalls. "I really hit it off with her and we had a little romance going there. It got pretty serious, and she wanted to get married, and, of course, I was too young to entertain anything like that. Disney was very nervous, as you can certainly imagine. They kept telling her, 'Annette, don't get married, it's puppy love, it's puppy love.'" He composed *Puppy Love* on the spot and Annette recorded her album Annette Sings Anka soon after. Paul's *Put Your Head On My Shoulder* was his last record with Don Costa, who moved on to another record label, a number two smash for three weeks in the fall of 1959. His debut album, PAUL ANKA SINGS HIS BIG 15, was released that same year.

Paul soon met his bride-to-be, Anne Zogheb, a European teen fashion model and daughter of a Lebanese diplomat, in the Caribbean. Paul and Anne were married in Paris in 1964 and enjoyed a long and happy marriage while raising their five daughters.

When you hold me in your loving arms
I can feel you giving all your charms
Hold me, darling, ho-ho hold me tight
Squeeze me baby with-a all your might

Anka's final Top 10 hits of this era were *It's Time To Cry, Puppy Love, My Home Town,* and *Dance On Little Girl.* Both Anka and his pal, Bobby Darin, who had changed the fortunes of teen idols with his jazzy recording of Kurt Weill's *Mack The Knife,* were movin' on. As Anka recalls, "in the '50s, pop music was in the infancy stage. I was on a tour with early rock & rollers like Bobby Darin, the Diamonds, and Frankie Lymon, traveling in buses and playing arenas. On the bus, I'd sleep in the luggage rack above the seats. We'd get there, I'd do two songs, and we'd go on to the next place. It was a grind. My best friend was Bobby Darin and our idols were the Rat Pack Sinatra, Dean Martin, Sammy Davis Jr., and Joey Bishop. Bobby and I realized that this pop music thing wasn't going to last forever and we wanted to get into the club circuit." He would never regret this career choice, which led to his association with Johnny Carson, Frank Sinatra, and Tom Jones, pals to whom he handed the biggest hit songs of their sizeable careers.

"My first show in Vegas was at the Sahara," Anka reminisces. "I opened for Sophie Tucker. I was under age and not allowed in the casino, so they brought me in the back door. The place was filled with waiters, gamblers, and cigarette smoke. The audiences dressed up in suits and ties and cocktail clothes and jewelry. People came as families because the kids knew who I was. The girls were screaming. I was still doing my rock shows. And while I wasn't scared in front of my kid audiences, once we got into clubs, there was no benchmark, no consistency. Here I was, dressing up in a tux, singing for adults. In Vegas, I was totally out of my environment. I was always a very confident kid. I just tried to be cool, but for those first five years, I shook inside. It was a great training ground. After that first show, Sophie told me in that really deep voice of hers, that she couldn't follow me with all that commotion. So, from then on, I closed the show. I was a headliner from the start. I had special material written to bridge the kids and their parents. Then I'd do my hits. I charmed the kids and the adults right into the woodwork."

Oh, please stay with me, Diana	
Oh, please, Diana	
Oh, please, Diana	
Oh, please, Diana	

Johnny's Theme, written for Carson's *Tonight Show*, is said to be the longest running TV theme song of all time. Several years spent in Italy, where Anka enjoyed the Mediterranean sunshine and recorded in Italian, French, Spanish and German, led to him adapting French songwriter Gilbert Francois' *Comme d'Habitude*, providing new English lyrics that became Sinatra's signature tune, *My Way*. In 1971, Tom Jones scored a hit with Anka's *She's A Woman*. In 1974, Anka topped the charts for three weeks with the controversial *You're Having My Baby*. He followed up with a string of Top 10 hits that included two duets with his protege, Odia Coates, *One Man Woman, One Woman Man* and *(I Believe) There's Nothing Stronger Than Our Love*. He scored solo hits with *I Don't Like To Sleep Alone*, which he co-wrote with fellow Canuck David Foster, and *Times Of Your Life*. Later, Anka and Foster collaborated again on a debut album for Vancouver vocalist Michael Bublé. He has helped many other young songwriters get a foothold in the music business over the years, including Steve Goodman and John Prine.

Billboard magazine has named Paul Anka the 21st most successful artist of the modern era. At the Liberal Party Convention in November 2003, he came up with a whole new set of lyrics for *My Way* in praise of his friend, Prime Minister Jean Chretien.

Tan and fit at 64 for his Order of Canada ceremony, Anka took advantage of the media attention to release his 124th album, Rock SWINGS. "I've taken a bunch of classics by Bon Jovi, Van Halen, Nirvana, the Pet Shop Boys, Eric Clapton and others, rearranged them with a jazz beat, added a big band sound, and made them swing," he told reporters. There was no doubt that he was still young at heart.

Throughout the years he has opened and closed his shows with *Diana*, which at one time ran neck and neck with Bing Crosby's *White Christmas* as the number one record of all time, selling more than nine million copies and propelling his overall album sales over the 40 million mark. That's an Order of Canada song for sure.

Four Strong Winds

Words & Music by Ian Tyson

© 1963, 1991, Slick Fork Music, WB Music Corporation

Four strong winds that blow lonely,
Seven seas that run high,
All these things that don't change, come what may.

Despite three and a half decades of not performing together since they divorced, Ian & Sylvia reunited at the 50th anniversary of the Mariposa Folk Festival in the summer of 2010 to sing their signature song, *Four Strong Winds*. It seemed a fairy tale ending as the teary-eyed crowd sang along. Sylvia even kissed her ex-husband on the cheek for those who still hoped they would reunite. Backstage, Sylvia quipped, "I'm just glad it's over." Ian groused about the poor sound mix. Little had changed between them.

As festival headliner Gordon Lightfoot prepared to take the stage, everybody realized that their brief, unrehearsed reunion was very likely their final bow as Ian and Sylvia. The voice of the 76-year-old Longview, Alberta rancher and recording artist had taken a beating over the years, and his 69-year-old ex-wife was busier than most senior citizens on her own as a recording artist, a member of Quartette, and a narrator of film and television productions. They had better things to do than merely relive the good old days for the diminishing number of baby boomer fans who still remembered the times when they were the darlings of the Greenwich Village traditional folk music revival scene in New York City. But there was no doubt in their minds as to what song they would sing together to accommodate the hoots and hollers of "Sing *Four Strong Winds* with Sylvia" that inevitably assailed their ears after Tyson finished his set and the audience began to clamor for an encore.

Ironically, if Ian Tyson had not been goaded into writing the song by a young, wannabe-Woody Guthrie from Hibbing, Minnesota, he might not have ever become one of the top cowboy songwriters of all time. In fact, Ian & Sylvia had been signed by New York impresario

Albert Grossman and Vanguard Records solely on the basis of their eclectic, well-researched, traditional folk music repertoire of well-aged songs, not the brash, new knock-offs that Bobby Zimmerman was dashing off here, there, and everywhere around the East Village. Before this moment in the spring of '62, neither the retired rodeo rider nor his singing partner, Sylvia Fricker, had ever even contemplated writing a song of their own since they had begun performing together in Toronto.

Four Strong Winds always turns up at the top or near the top of every list of best Canadian songs. CBC Radio talk show host Peter Gzowski called it Canada's "unofficial anthem."

> But our good times are all gone,
> And I'm bound for moving on.
> I'll look for you if I'm ever back this way.

The song had a strange genesis. It was written one afternoon in the spring of '62 in response to Bob Dylan's performance of *Blowin' in the Wind*. "I saw this raggedy-ass kid up on stage," Tyson told one interviewer, "and I thought, 'boy, if that guy can write a song like that so can I.'" His gut reaction would prove to be prophetic. Ian & Sylvia's single hit number 2 on the Canadian pop chart, and Bobby Bare's cover version became a number 3 hit on the *Billboard* country chart. More hits followed but slowly. As Ian recognized, he was not a prolific songwriter. "I could never match Dylan's output. For every good song I wrote, he wrote eight." With money earned from *Four Strong Winds*, Ian bought a ranch north of Toronto.

Many music history books will tell you that Ian & Sylvia were signed by Albert Grossman after he signed Robert Zimmerman a.k.a. Bob Dylan, but that is not so. As Sylvia recalls, "We actually signed with Albert Grossman before Bobby had. And we were at least partly responsible for him signing Bobby. Not because we said 'sign him,' but because we said, 'hey, this guy's really great.'" Their recommendation to Grossman was seconded by Odetta and Peter, Paul & Mary (Peter Yarrow, Noel Stookey, and Mary Travers), who were already in his stable. Eventually, a rave *New York Times* review of a Gerde's Folk City performance sealed the deal and Grossman signed Dylan.

While Tyson admired his creativity, he appears to have had mixed feelings about the kid who was soon to become the poet laureate of American popular music. Ian and Sylvia hung out with 20-year-old Bob and his teenage girlfriend, New York artist Suze Rotolo, at her tiny Fourth Street apartment. During the days before Dylan became more successful than any previous singer-songwriter in the history of popular music, the handsome, mature, nearly 30-year-old Tyson was not only respected for his perfect pitch, professional flat-picking, and spontaneous sense of humor in his repartee with his audiences, he was widely regarded as the sexiest single ladies man in the village. He was also a far more authentic cowboy and ex-rodeo rider than show business cowpokes like Ramblin' Jack Elliott and his following of young wannabes, like Dylan, who told stories about being rodeo riders that rodeo veterans like Tyson seriously doubted.

It was Tyson, Rotolo has revealed, who turned Dylan on to marijuana, and Tyson, others have confided, who influenced many of the male folk singers of the day to wear western boots with their jeans *not* rolled up as was the fashion of pop idols. But it was definitely Dylan who had enough nerve and cockiness to defy folk purists and the East Village establishment and write his own songs, rather than merely performing and recording traditional material.

Dylan has subsequently chosen not to acknowledge Tyson's influence in his memoirs, and Ian has been downright rude in his references to Bob, beginning by calling him "an obnoxious little jerk" in his biography *I Never Sold My Saddle*. In John Einarson's recent book, *Four Strong Winds: Ian & Sylvia*, Tyson calls Dylan a "lying son of a bitch" and "a phony," but nevertheless acknowledges his gifted songwriting and admits that he loved BLONDE ON BLONDE at the time it came out in 1966. All of which is par for the course for Tyson, who has always been somewhat crusty when it comes to making comments to journalists about anything at all.

Think I'll go out to Alberta,
Weather's good there in the fall.
Got some friends that I can go to working for,

"I've told so many fuckin' lies about *Four Strong Winds*," he admitted to Einarson, "that I don't know what the truth is anymore." Sifting through some of those statements, several facts do seem to emerge. Dylan did spontaneously play and sing Tyson his latest creation, *Blowin' in the Wind*, one afternoon in the spring of '62, triggering a reaction that got Ian's creative juices flowing. After that, it only took the Canadian half an hour to come up with the melody and most of the lyrics. Sylvia has admitted that she helped out with a couple of lines in the chorus. To put things in perspective, while Ian's best song has done very well in Canada, Dylan's song has done well globally beginning with Peter, Paul & Mary's version, which hit number 2 on the *Billboard* Hot 100 and lodged at number one on the adult contemporary chart for five weeks. It was also widely performed during the civil rights protest movement along with Pete Seeger's *This Land Is Your Land* and the traditional *We Shall Overcome*. *Blowin' in the Wind* has been recorded by hundreds of recording artists, including Chet Atkins, Stan Getz, Odetta, Judy Collins, Joan Baez, Dolly Parton, the Kingston Trio, Sam Cooke, Etta James, Duke Ellington, Neil Young, Marlene Dietrich, Bobby Darin, Elvis, Stevie Wonder, and John Fogerty. *Rolling Stone* magazine has named it their Number 14 Song of All Time on their Top 500 Songs list. It has been translated into numerous foreign languages, including German, Italian, Romanian, and Bengali, and is widely acknowledged to be one of the most recognizable anthems of the American civil rights movement led by Martin Luther King in the 1960s.

Ian & Sylvia's arrival in Greenwich Village coincided with the arrival of hundreds of hungry singers, songwriters, banjo players, and guitar pickers who were drawn to the Mecca of the burgeoning folk music revival. All of these eager young musicians wanted to rub shoulders with Pete Seeger (the blacklisted lead singer of the Weavers), his brother Mike Seeger (leader of the New Lost City Ramblers bluegrass band), the legendary Woody Guthrie (who was actually lying on his deathbed in a New Jersey hospital), Ramblin' Jack Elliott, Tom Paxton, Tim Hardin, and the musical "Mayor of MacDougall Street," Dave Van Ronk. Some of the newcomers might have even heard of a young minstrel from Minnesota who went by the name of Bob Dylan and had been crashing at Van Ronk's West 15th Street apartment and Suze

Rotolo's pad on Fourth Street. Dylan's biographer Robert Shelton has described Van Ronk as "Bob's first NY guru" and a "walking museum of the blues." Van Ronk later became one of the first American folk artists to record Joni Mitchell's *Both Sides Now*, providing her song an alternate title, *Clouds*.

The beat generation lifestyle that flourished in the East Village in the late '40s and throughout the '50s had been highly romanticized in Allen Ginsberg's long poem *Howl* and Jack Kerouac's unpunctuated, stream of consciousness novel, *On The Road*. The opportunity to perform at Gerde's Folk City, the Kettle of Fish, the Washington Square, Cafe Remo, the Night Owl, or any one of the clubs that lined MacDougall Street, like the Bitter End, the Gaslight and Cafe Wha? held the additional lure of being venues where you might be discovered and signed to a record deal by someone as legendary as John Hammond, who soon signed Dylan to his first contract with Columbia Records. As Ian has recalled, "Everybody on the scene hung out at Gerde's, the Gaslight, or the Kettle of Fish. The Kettle of Fish was as much as or more of a hangout as Gerde's. Bob Dylan, Dave Van Ronk, the Greenbriar Boys, Simon & Garfunkel, Peter Yarrow, Mary Travers; everybody hung out together, and the music we played informally, which we did all the time, was predominantly bluegrass or old time music."

Opportunities were abundant within this compact melting pot to meet and compare experiences with Odetta, Carolyn Hester, Richard Farina, Judy Collins, Joan Baez, Eric Anderson, Phil Ochs, and the musicians that recorded with them. However, the Canadian duo was not as star-struck as some of the other young aspirants must have been. Ian & Sylvia had already become celebrities on their own turf, head-liners at the best Yorkville clubs in Toronto and at the inaugural Mariposa Folk Festival in Orillia, Ontario. Tyson, who still held down a day job as a commercial artist at that time, had designed the festival's orange sun logo.

Their decision to visit the Big Apple had been triggered by Pete Seeger's visit to Toronto in the spring of '61. Ed Cowan, the assistant to the promoter who booked Seeger for his 1961 Massey Hall show, introduced the young duo to the veteran folkie the afternoon before the concert. Pete was so impressed with Ian & Sylvia's awareness of authentic folk material that he invited them on stage during his show to perform.

Seeger had previously been an inspiration for both the formation of the Canadian folk group, the Travellers, who "Canadianized" his song *This Land Is Your Land* on record, and the planned establishment of a festival at Camp Nivelt near Orillia. Before leaving Canada, Seeger also provided Tyson and Fricker with some New York contact numbers.

One Sunday night in early 1962, they completed their set at a Toronto club, drove down to the Big Apple in Toronto journalist Joe Taylor's Pontiac, and met up with Cowan, who had flown down on the Monday afternoon. They were determined to find a New York manager and secure a record deal, but had limited funds and reckoned they'd better get it done before they had to be back in Toronto for their Thursday night gig. That same afternoon, they visited Harold Rosenthal, Seeger's manager, who was also the head of Folkways Records. Rosenthal liked their live audition and their six-song demonstration record or *acetate*, which had been recorded at a CBC studio in Toronto, but suggested that Odetta's manager, Albert Grossman, might be a better fit for them. Grossman had been putting together a concept group, soon to be known as Peter, Paul & Mary. Perhaps, he might take them under his wing as well. Moving on to Grossman's temporary quarters in impresario Ed Wein's apartment and office complex at 50 Central Park West, they pitched their act to Grossman, the folk music manager Dylan later described as looking "like Sydney Greenstreet in *The Maltese Falcon*."

Grossman was just getting established in New York after being run out of Chicago by some Windy City wise guys. Grossman and Wein, who were also the co-founders and co-producers of the Newport Folk Festival, liked Ian & Sylvia enough to invite the Canadians to dinner and get them a slot at one of the most influential off-Broadway folk clubs in New York, Gerde's Folk City. Albert had a reserved front row table there, and enough pull with the management that he could have his clients added to the Monday night hootenanny list at the last minute.

"Sylvia went up and did a great blues song," Cowan told *Before The Goldrush* author Nicholas Jennings. "Then Ian & Sylvia did several songs together and blew everybody away." Memories of that night are obviously heady and intoxicating for Cowan, who was, after all, merely a fan who was trying to do his best to help the young performers out and not a professional journalist who took notes. His account of events changed somewhat by the time he spoke to John Einarson. "That night

Ian & Sylvia were sensational," Cowan told Einarson, "exuding confidence and energy with a presence that was both fresh and interesting; however, it was when Sylvia tore into a big blues number that they brought the house down." Grossman was duly impressed and promised to sign them the very next day.

Loyal fans like Ed Cowan and potential managers like Albert Grossman were not the only people impressed by their Big Apple debut. "They only did three songs," Tom Paxton told John Einarson, "that's all you did in those days for a guest set, but they made an instant impact on me and everyone." Before they left the tiny folk club that Monday night, Grossman introduced the Canadians to a number of the regulars, including Bob Dylan, "one of New York's most promising young poets . . ."

Still I wish you'd change your mind
If I asked you one more time,
But we've been through that a hundred times or more.

On Tuesday afternoon, Grossman also offered to sign the young Canadians to Warner Brother Records, but the minstrels from Yorkville had something else in mind. They wanted to be signed to Vanguard Records, which, Grossman argued, had no promotion and poor distribution. "Albert tried very hard to talk us out of it," Sylvia recalls, "but we were adamant. We thought Vanguard was the label of honesty and integrity." Their intuition to choose the less commercial label may have cost them considerable airplay and record sales because Vanguard didn't promote their singles to radio or the trade magazines, but it would be a big factor in the wide acceptance Ian & Sylvia received when their album was released. They joined Joan Baez, the Weavers and Odetta on the Vanguard label and accumulated tons of credibility.

"Ian and I started out doing traditional music," Sylvia notes. "It was me who did most of the research on the traditional stuff. It's amazing material. I sort of think of it as distilled music. You know, it's been through so many hands that all of the fat is cut off it, because of having gone through so many hands in the oral tradition people just forgot the boring bits and kept the good stuff." She also stresses that they worked very diligently on their set material. As she told Richie Unterberger, "We were aware that we probably put a lot more time into arrangements. I think that the norm at that point was not really to rehearse a lot. Once you got down the chords, you just sort of played it. And we were very much aware of arrangements, and of double lead lines and things like that."

The Canadians would also be praised for their minimal accompaniment, which was mostly veteran vocalist Odetta, bass player Bill Lee, plus a second guitar track on some cuts and occasionally a mandolin or specialty instrument. "John Herald played on our albums," Sylvia recalls, citing their mainstay second guitarist. "Eric Weissberg played on a couple of things." Multi-instrumentalist Weissberg, added only a touch of mandolin here and perhaps a dash of banjo there. Their approach was never to overproduce their albums. They didn't want to turn their folk music into the kind of folk pop espoused by the Kingston Trio that influenced groups like the Brothers Four and Peter, Paul & Mary. In fact, Sylvia's comments have not been overly kind when it comes to Yarrow, Stookey and Travers, their main competition. "Peter, Paul & Mary was a manufactured group," Sylvia recently told Unterberger. "I mean, those people never had sung together before Albert Grossman and Milt Okun put them together. Although Milt certainly did a great job with their arrangements, and they were deservedly very popular. The next step on that thing of doing the contemporary songwriters of that day would be some group that did it with perhaps a little more abandon."

Having stuck to traditional material in their shows and in their sessions for their debut album, Ian & Sylvia struck a chord of approval with folk purists. These were the very people who would at first endorse Bob Dylan's early work and then become "folk Nazis," as Sylvia has referred to them, and blacklist him when he added electric guitar to his album cuts and shows. Authenticity in the folk revival era was a precious commodity that is difficult to comprehend more than 50 years after the fact. However, audiences, critics, and record reviewers were all struck with the simplicity and purity of Ian & Sylvia's live performances and studio records. Ian's guitar playing has always been tasteful and their wistful harmonizing was a treasure to be heard in those days. "I couldn't sing harmony," Ian has admitted, "and on the occasion that I tried I was out of tune. Right to the end, she was singing harmony to my lead, and whenever we tried it the other way around it didn't work."

This convenient arrangement continued through 13 amazing albums and a decade and a half performing together. The words and melodies of their American blues and European, Canadian, and Appalachian folk songs, many of which they reintroduced into the mainstream, were unique among their peers. In fact, they were the only working malefemale duo to record a body of work during the folk revival era. The release of their debut album IAN & SYLVIA in September 1962 made them highly popular on the college and festival concert circuits. Critics praised both the traditional ditty *Un Canadien Errant* and Canadian folk singer Jim McCarthy's *Pride of Petrovar*, which *sounded* traditional.

Ian Tyson was born in Victoria, British Columbia on September 25, 1933. His father was a professional cowboy, and Ian grew up devouring books about authentic American cowboys by illustrator and author Will James. He listened to records by Wilf Carter, a Nova Scotia born, yodeling, cowboy singer who had become famous in Calgary on the radio and on CPR sponsored Brewster family Banff National Park trail rides. He later became more famous on the radio in New York City as "Montana Slim." Tyson soon headed to Calgary himself. He wanted nothing more in life than to follow in his father's footsteps, and became a calf roper and bronc rider before his 20th birthday. Three years into a career as a professional rodeo competitor, which he supplemented with seasonal work in logging camps, he had a career-ending accident at a rodeo in Alberta, and turned to music while recovering in a Calgary hospital. Borrowing a guitar from a fellow patient, he learned how to play chords and then how to flat pick from listening to Johnny Cash's hit record *I Walk The Line*.

While studying graphic design at the Vancouver School of Art, Ian tried his hand at entertaining for the first time in local clubs. He sang for his supper in the Heidelberg Cafe and the Kubla Khan dinner club and played some rockabilly in the skid row joints along the Hastings Street strip. Upon graduation he hitchhiked eastward through the States with a copy of Kerouac's *On The Road* in his hip pocket. He eventually ended up in Toronto, where he secured employment in an advertising agency and continued his career working at night as a guitarist. Hanging out at the First Floor Club in Yorkville, he hobnobbed with jazz musicians like guitarist Ed Bickert, bassist Don Thompson, vocalist Don Francks, drummer Archie Alleyne, and beat poets who often read their poetry in between sets by the musicians. When the Kingston Trio hit on the radio with *Tom Dooley*, Toronto club managers began hiring folk acts, and Tyson teamed up with jazz singer Francks to do some shows.

Sylvia Fricker was born in the small town of Chatham, Ontario on September 19, 1940. Like her future husband, she was bitten by the folk music bug while visiting Toronto as a teenager. Her training as a singer came from her choirmaster and church organist mother, and her isolation from the mainstream of the entertainment business dictated that she learned a lot of her early music from song books and from hearing R&B music on a Detroit radio station. "I came to folk music through a very different process than most people who were part of the folk era," she explains. "I was from a small southern Ontario town and there were no records, there was nobody I could listen to. So I got all of my songs from books. I didn't have any preconceived notion about how they should be performed." Sylvia would find several of the songs she would later record with Ian Tyson in Canadian musicologist Edith Fouke's book *Canada in Song*, notably *Mary Anne*, a song written by a trapper, and the French-Canadian ballad, *Un Canadien Errant*.

During her first self-financed "field trip" to Toronto, Sylvia got in touch with Ian Tyson through a friend who worked at the same ad agency. She sang Ian a song over the telephone and the two met and were mutually attracted. "I was wearing brown Bermuda shorts and one of those Yugoslavian blouses that I had pinched from the costumes of the Chatham Little Theatre," she recalls. "Although that doesn't seem so peculiar today, Ian told me, years later, that it really blew his mind."

Sylvia returned to Chatham and her job in a jewelry store but resolved that she would move to Toronto as soon as she could afford to do so. By the time she made the move, Ian had gone off to Alberta to perform at rodeo events and drive Brewster Transport tour buses for Banff tourist industry pioneer Bud Brewster. Sylvia took up performing solo, securing gigs at the Clef Club and then at the Bohemian Embassy.

The Embassy featured poetry readings by the leading Canadian poets of the day, including a young Margaret Atwood, and the dean of Canadian poetry, Earle Birney. "I was the comic relief for all those terribly serious poets," Sylvia smiled during her interview with Nicholas Jennings.

Ian and Sylvia's first performance together was prompted by a CBC TV producer who wanted to include her in some footage he was shooting at the First Floor Club. At the last minute, she learned that because she was not yet a member of the musicians union she would be unable to play her guitar. Undaunted, she invited Tyson to come up out of the audience and accompany her, and he accepted the challenge. "It wasn't the breakthrough either of them hoped for," Jennings wrote. "But even then there were signs of the magic that was to follow something about the way Fricker's voice blended with Tyson's to produce a sound that was warm and gentle yet strangely unsettling, like a Chinook in the dead of winter."

Joining forces they worked up an act together as Ian & Sylvia in the smaller Yorkville clubs until they found themselves headlining shows at the biggest club, the Purple Onion. Ian was blessed (or cursed) with perfect pitch and was an intimidating performer to work with as a sideman unless you were a topnotch picker. Rather than deal with Sylvia's far less accomplished guitar playing, he bought her an autoharp, and she took to it right away, although, even with its push button system, tuning the instrument's many strings was always a headache. With their unique harmonies, Ian's strong guitar work, and Sylvia's rhythmic accompaniment on autoharp, they presented an appealing young couple with plenty of sex appeal on stage.

"People used to flock to hear them night after night," club manager Sam Gutmacher told Jennings. "Nobody ever seemed to get bored with them. People liked the idea of a couple performing, they found it very romantic." Even though the handsome Tyson and the hauntingly beautiful Fricker projected a romantic image during their shows, when they were off stage they preferred to keep the relationship a professional one. It was not until well after they had taken up residence in New York City that they did become an item, eventually marrying in '64, after which Sylvia gave birth to their son, Clay Tyson. Over the years it has come out that Tyson, who already had a reputation as something of a skirt-chaser before he met his singing partner, likely continued to have more than merely a roving eye when it came to romancing young girls he met just about here, there and everywhere.

| If I get there before the snow flies, |
| And if things are going good, |
| You could meet me if I send you down the fare. |

After hearing Bob Dylan sing *Blowin' in the Wind* on that fateful afternoon in '62, Ian Tyson wasted no time writing a folk revival song of his own. He sat there in Albert Grossman's office, where he and Sylvia often spent their afternoons when they were in town, and wrote *Four Strong Winds*, reaching back to his own vagabond roots for inspiration. He would later reveal in the liner notes for their second album that the bittersweet romance he was chronicling in his song *Four Strong Winds* took place among migrant workers in his home stomping grounds. "Canada has many seasonal workers," he noted, "and when the weather turns harsh they must move on and find a different type of work. Many of these people cross the country every year from the tobacco harvest in Ontario to the wheat harvest on the Prairies to the apple picking in British Columbia. With the advent of fall, they move on, perhaps to return again."

Even though he wasn't known for writing songs, Tyson soon revealed that *Four Strong Winds* was not the very first song he had written. Many years before this, while "playing rockabilly in the Chop Suey bars of Vancouver," he had written his first, which was a flat out 'three-chords-and-the-truth' country song. "I couldn't play very well as I only knew A and D and E," he recalls, speaking of those days in the mid-50s when he was enrolled at the Vancouver School of Art. "That's when I wrote *Summer Wages*." It was a roughhewn gem that he eventually polished up in New York and added to their repertoire, although they didn't record the song until a few years down the road. Judy Collins would popularize *Summer Wages* for the masses.

Soon after, Sylvia wrote *You Were On My Mind*. Becoming songwriters reenergized both of them. "Once we started to write," Sylvia has said, "we always liked to do the material of other writers. It gave us a bit more variety in what we were doing. Plus, we really liked the songs, too."

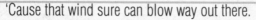

But if you wait until it's winter,
It will be no good
'Cause that wind sure can blow way out there.

Columbia released Dylan's debut album a few months before Vanguard released Ian & Sylvia's debut. "This little sucker is going to change everything," Ian predicted when he marched into the Village Corner Club in Yorkville, waving Dylan's self-titled disc in David Wiffen's face. Exposure to Dylan singing *Song To Woody* and *Talking New York Blues* in his nasal twang was a shocker for most folk music fans. However, within weeks after the release there was a demand for original folk songs.

Ian & Sylvia's second album, released in early 1963, was titled FOUR STRONG WINDS and included both Ian's new song and Dylan's *Tomorrow Is A Long Time*. "I think we recorded Dylan's songs before anybody else really was doing them," Sylvia asserts. "He was certainly well known in New York, and was just getting to be known outside of the New York area at that point." Joan Baez soon became the quintessential Dylan interpreter, and, that summer, Peter, Paul & Mary took his *Blowin' in the Wind* to the top of the *Billboard* pop charts. The trio was signed to Warner Brothers, as Grossman had argued Ian & Sylvia should have been, and the trio's records were selling millions of copies. Ian & Sylvia were now making at least $400 dollars an engagement on the tour circuit, but their record sales and air play were minuscule compared to the trio Grossman had put together, Monkees style, merely so he would have a folk pop act to book on the circuit. *Four Strong Winds* wasn't an immediate hit," Sylvia admits. "It was a slow build. Vanguard wasn't into putting out singles. We sold a lot of albums, our second album (Four Strong Winds) even charted, which surprised everybody. Joan Baez charted, but other than that Vanguard records didn't chart. Their big idea for promotion was to put an ad in *Evergreen Review*. So, we weren't exactly putting out singles."

Bobby Bare's cover of *Four Strong Winds* failed to click on the pop charts, unlike his previous releases *Detroit City* and *500 Miles From Home* had, but the record went all the way to number 3 on the country charts. Then in the summer of '65, the San Francisco based folk rock group, We Five, released Sylvia's *You Were On My Mind* and it bound-ed to the top of the *Billboard* adult contemporary chart and stayed there for five weeks, while rising to number 3 on the *Billboard* pop chart, and number one on the *Cashbox* pop chart. Because this electrified pop success had come from a cover version of Sylvia's song, Ian & Sylvia could still cling to their folk purity, but it wouldn't be long before they made a move toward folk rock production themselves. Meanwhile, they had introduced the world to the songs of fellow Canadian, Gordon Lightfoot, recording his *Early Morning Rain* and *For Loving You*. Peter, Paul & Mary would follow suit, thus guaranteeing Lightfoot's entry into the American recording scene as a solo artist in his own right.

By doing things their own way, Ian & Sylvia had become one of the most respected and influential acts of the folk revival. They had helped their fellow Canadian songwriters by recording songs by Gordon Lightfoot and then Joni Mitchell, and they went on to pioneer a country rock sound with their GREAT SPECKLED BIRD album and band, recording in Nashville, as Dylan had begun to do, where the best pickers lived. They returned to Canada in the '70s, where Ian hosted a series of TV shows, and each sought separate careers as solo artists. They divorced in '75, but reunited again in 1980 to videotape *Four Strong Winds* for *Heart Of Gold*, a CBC TV history of Canadian popular music put together by journalist Martin Melhuish. Six years later they again appeared in front of TV cameras and this time a live audience for a CTV Special produced by Sylvia's manager Alan Kates and network producer Sandra Faire.

By this time, Ian had begun issuing his ongoing series of cowboy and campfire songs on albums like OLD CORRALS & SAGEBRUSH, IAN TYSON, COWBOYOGRAPHY, I OUTGREW THE WAGON, AND STOOD THERE AMAZED, and EIGHTEEN INCHES OF RAIN, which were far more acoustic in nature than the current new country productions coming out of Nashville, but nevertheless won the veteran an armload of Canadian Country Music Association awards and a Juno Award as best male country singer.

COWBOYOGRAPHY (1986) is the gem of the decade-long series, sporting the award-winning *Navajo Rug*, which Ian co-wrote with Tom Russell, a new version of *Summer Wages*, and a wagonload of new songs that sparkled with Tyson's trademark harmony arrangements and some nifty picking and playing from the Chinook Arch Riders and producer/keyboard player Adrian Chornowol. The album was released on Stony Plain Records in Canada and Vanguard in the States and eventually sold more than 130,000 copies in Canada alone. Tyson's bands during the '80s and '90s, first featuring Great Western Orchestra members Nathan Tinkham, Cindy Church, and David Wilkie, then the Chinook Arch Riders featuring Thom Moon, John Cronin, Randy Chernier, and Myron Schott, were renowned for their precise ensemble playing and tight harmonies. As a solo artist, Sylvia also scored with Canadian country hits, including *River Road*, which was covered by Crystal Gayle for the American market in 1980, and then as a member of the all female vocal group, Quartette.

Ian returned to his ranching roots, first in Ontario, and later in Alberta, where he married his second wife, Twylla Biblow, and fathered a daughter, Adelita. When Neil Young covered *Four Strong Winds* during the Band's Fillmore show that was filmed for the album THE LAST WALTZ, and then for his million-selling 1978 album COMES A TIME, with Nicolette Larsen harmonizing on the track, Tyson received considerable royalties. He was able to purchase a 160-acre spread at Longview, Alberta, where he writes songs and breeds cutting horses to this day. In 1990, during the height of the new country explosion, when Suzy Bogguss' version of *Someday Soon* hit number 16 on the *Billboard* country chart, he received more royalties. What has most likely contributed most to Tyson's longevity is entertaining regularly at Ranchman's, the largest and most prestigious of the half dozen or so large, Texas-style nightclubs on Macleod Trail South in Calgary since the early 80s. He has remained very active touring throughout western Canada and down into the northwestern United States, becoming a fixture at the annual cowboy poetry events in Elko, Nevada.

"Elko saved me," Tyson confessed to John Einarson recently. "None of those buckaroos down in Nevada knew who Ian & Sylvia were and couldn't have cared less but they loved those cowboy songs. I had a great band and we blew the place apart. It was a rebirth for me. Hal Cannon says that I changed country music. I really didn't discover who I was until COWBOYOGRAPHY."

When CMT commissioned Martin Melhuish to put together an eight-part television documentary celebrating Canada's singer-song-writers, he chose to call his series "*Four Strong Winds*." Melhuish told interviewers that the wide-open spaces, which Tyson mentions so often in his songs, are a common denominator in many of the best Canadian songs of all time. "There's only 30 million of us living in this huge country," Melhuish noted, "and [space] seems to play into every song or certainly has some influence on every songwriter."

The Canadian map may still show a lot of space between towns and cities, but Tyson has learned firsthand that the wide-open spaces of his youth have become an endangered species. "The West was always a big empty place," Tyson recently told Tyler Tafford. "It's not anymore; there's just too many people and they all want 20 acres and a trailer and a big hat. This country was all zoned for quarter sections. That's gone. It means nothing." Still, he prefers to live in Alberta — the "weather's good there in the fall" — and there are still some musicians he can play music with and some cutting horse competitions to enter, if all else fails, come what may.

Ian & Sylvia were inducted into the Canadian Music Hall of Fame in 1992 during the annual televised Juno Awards Show. Two years later they were made members of the Order Of Canada, and two years after that they were inducted into the Mariposa Folk Festival Hall of Fame. Dozens of artists have covered Ian's signature song *Four Strong Winds,* including Hank Snow, the Travellers, the Carter Family, Marianne Faithful, John Denver, Judy Collins, Flatt & Scruggs, Tony Rice, and Stu Phillips. Dylan recorded it with the Band in their Big Pink house in Woodstock as part of THE BASEMENT TAPES album. Tyson recorded it again himself for his 1989 album I OUTGREW THE WAGON. Neil Young and the Band's version recently became available as a bonus track outtake on a CD titled THE COMPLETE LAST WALTZ. *Four Strong Winds* has proven to be ultimately durable, a standard in many folk and country artists' repertoires for many years and the number one Canadian track of all time according to the Essential 50 Tracks CBC Poll conducted in 2005.

On May 25, 2005 in Commonwealth Stadium in Edmonton during Queen Elizabeth II's visit to Alberta as part of the province's centennial celebrations, Ian Tyson performed his song despite supremely challenging weather conditions in the outdoor home of the Edmonton Eskimos CFL Team. The weather was so cold and rainy that afternoon that many of the acts booked for the event were canceled. However, old 'Eon made a brief appearance leading a chorus comprised of actor Paul

Gross (*Men With Brooms, Due South*) and singer-songwriters Carolyn Dawn Johnson, Corb Lund, and Bill Bourne. He invited the thousands of people who stuck it out through the harsh, unseasonal weather to sing along.

> Think I'll go out to Alberta,
> Weather's good there in the fall.
> Got some friends that I can go to working for,
> Still I wish you'd change your mind
> If I asked you one more time,
> But we've been through that a hundred times or more.

The following afternoon, an ensemble of Calgary Stampede singers and dancers performed *Four Strong Winds* at an indoor event staged for the monarch's visit at the Pengrowth Saddledome in Calgary, where they were not blowing in the wind as the song's author had been a day earlier. Ian Tyson has never been as prolific as the minstrel who inspired him to compose his masterpiece; however, the lyrics and melody he wrote that afternoon in Albert Grossman's office in the spring of 1962 have become a folk anthem that many, many Canadians embrace as their own. "There's Dylan and then there's the rest of us," Tyson recently noted during an interview with Larry LeBlanc, "but *Four Strong Winds, Someday Soon,* and *Summer Wages* have been very good to me."

> Four strong winds that blow lonely,
> Seven seas that run high,
> All these things that don't change, come what may.
> But our good times are all gone,
> And I'm bound for moving on.
> I'll look for you if I'm ever back this way.

Suzanne

Words & Music by Leonard Cohen

© 1967, Stranger Music Inc., Sony/ATV Music Publishing

Suzanne takes you down to her place near the river
You can hear the boats go by
You can spend the night beside her

The first time I met Leonard Cohen was in February 1967 at the University of British Columbia Festival of Contemporary Arts. As a member of the entertainment committee, I had been involved in booking Cohen, Canada's most popular poet. His Montreal poet pal, Seymour Mayne, offered to introduce Cohen at the noon-hour event. Days before the concert it was moved from a small amphitheater in the arts building to a 400-seat theater. The rumor had got out that he would be singing his new songs, including *Suzanne*, which Judy Collins had recorded in '66. By the time we arrived, the venue was packed.

Backstage, Cohen was nervously puffing on a cigarette and tuning his nylon string guitar. He went on amid a thunderous applause from the mostly female audience and began to weave his hypnotic spell, moving his bar chords up and down the fret board and delivering his *noire* lyrics in a deadpan nasal drone that we all found captivating.

And you know that she's half crazy
But that's why you want to be there

Leonard Cohen wasn't much of a guitar player. He only seemed to know three chords and had difficulty moving his capo between songs. But there was no denying his ability to focus and hold an audience's attention. After 30 minutes or so of this, he put his guitar down and began to read his poems. Many of the students in the audience had never been to a poetry reading and they were disappointed. "Sing," someone encouraged. "I have already sung all of the songs that I know on guitar," he said. "Sing them again," someone else cried out, and he did to thunderous applause.

Two years before this, Cohen had discovered that writing books of poetry and even novels were not going to provide him with the lifestyle he had been accustomed to while growing up in the exclusive Westmount district of Montreal, and decided on the spot to become a singer-songwriter. Now, at age 33, he was on the brink of recording his debut album in New York with legendary producer John Hammond. I had really liked Judy Collins' highly polished version of *Suzanne*, but I had to admit that Cohen possessed a mysterious charisma and a rough-hewn charm that totally overshadowed his limited vocal abilities.

And she feeds you tea and oranges
That come all the way from China

After the show Cohen was mobbed by teenage girls waving copies of his books at him and demanding autographs. Seymour and I hung around backstage until he tore himself free. We walked across the campus to the bohemian cafe in the basement of the Theatre Department building and shared a small lunch. The two Montreal poets chatted on about their mentors and friends Irving Layton, Louis Dudek, and Frank Scott and the current gossip that Jewish Canadian poets from Quebec shared in those days. Then I drove Cohen to his downtown hotel. Along the way, I gave him a copy of my first book of poems, *The Circus in the Boy's Eye*, making a belated apology that it was just something that Seymour and I and a couple of other local poets were putting out from our own small press, Very Stone House. I was surprised when Cohen told me that he'd done the same thing with his first book, *Let Us Compare Mythologies*. "But it was published by the McGill Poetry Series," I said. "That was me," he laughed.

Later that night there was a party for Cohen at Seymour Mayne's house in the university district, and he showed up, made the rounds, and spent a few minutes speaking with me about my little chapbook. He had obviously read my poems and encouraged me to keep writing. Then on the stroke of midnight, a svelte young blonde dressed in a white minidress and disco boots rang the front door bell and took him away from us into the night. Some of us followed them out onto the porch and watched them climb into a white limousine. We were impressed. We had heard that Leonard had a reputation as a ladies man, but we hadn't expected him to be plucked from our midst by the most stunning beauty we had seen all night. In fact, many of the women at the party had come there solely to flirt with him. It was just like his poem *A Kite Is A Victim You Are Sure Of*. Most poetry readers had never thought of a kite as a victim. That was the way he surprised you, by showing you at least one way of looking at things that you had never before considered.

| And just when you mean to tell her |
| That you have no love to give her |
| Then she gets you on her wavelength |
| And she lets the river answer |
| That you've always been her lover |

A spin off benefit of Cohen's visit was the founding of Vancouver's first underground newspaper. The embryo of *The Georgia Straight* was hatched at the party for Cohen by some of the counterculture writers and thinkers who were inspired by his presence to start a "peace paper." Poet Dan MacLeod, who had edited the TISH poetry newsletter since 1964, became the publisher of this weekly, which remains a vital publication to this day. I experienced a similar revelation and soon founded Talonbooks, a spin off from the poetry magazine I was editing at that time. I published Ken Belford's *Fireweed* and my own *If There Are Any Noahs* under the Talonbooks imprint before the year was out. Cohen had touched our perfect minds with his gracious presence.

His songs were equally mysterious and strangely soothing. I became fond of his melancholy moods and his minimalist melodies, especially *So Long Marianne* and *Hey, That's No Way To Say Goodbye*. Then there were the quick-developing surreal action scenes of *One Of Us Cannot Be Wrong*, a song about a relationship between a masochist and a possessive woman. He begins by singing, "I lit a thin green candle, to make you jealous of me. / But the room just filled up with mosquitoes, / they heard that my body was free." After confessing that he "tortured the dress that you wore," he finishes up with a flourish of consistently Canadian yet bizarre imagery that includes a shivering Eskimo and the final lines: "But you stand there so nice, / in your blizzard of ice, / oh, please let me come into the storm."

Leonard Cohen's self-titled debut album turned out to be a map of things to come, complete with merciful angels, saints, self-inflicted pain, guilt, sex, death, and redemption in the form of impossible and impractical yet necessary love. Like Bob Dylan had in the early '60s, Cohen captured the spirit of the times at the end of the decade. I didn't know that he had started out with a country & western band called the Buckskin Boys in the '50s, or that he would soon be recording his second album in Nashville. But as the fabulous '60s came to an end, I couldn't get the haunting melody and lyrics of *Suzanne* out of my head.

And you want to travel with her
And you want to travel blind
And you know that she will trust you
For you've touched her perfect body with your mind.

Leonard Cohen was born on September 21, 1934 in Montreal, educated at McGill, and spent most of the early '60s living in a house be bought for $1500 on the tiny Greek Island of Hydra. "I would come back to Canada and do some journalism or sell a short story and put together the thousand dollars I needed to live for a year in Greece," he later told the BBC. With the release of *The Spice Box Of Earth* in 1961, he became the heir apparent to Irving Layton as Canada's best-selling poet. The publication of *Flowers for Hitler* in 1964 solidified his reputation. However, neither of his novels, *The Favourite Game* and *Beautiful Losers*, sold well, although he would discover that the latter had been widely read by many writers, painters, and songwriters, including Lou Reed and Kris Kristofferson. Wrestling with the rewrites demanded by his publisher had almost done him in. As he confided to *The Village Voice*, "I wrote *Beautiful Losers* on Hydra when I'd thought of myself as a loser, financially, morally, as a lover and as a man. I was wiped out; I didn't like my life. I vowed I would just fill the pages with black or kill myself. After the book was over, I fasted for ten days and flipped out completely. I hallucinated for a week. They took me to a hospital on Hydra. One afternoon the whole sky was black with storks. They alighted on all the churches and left in the morning, and I was better. I decided to go to Nashville and become a songwriter."

Back in Montreal, he told friends he was going to become the "Canadian Bob Dylan." But the folk era had already run its course, and

Dylan had strapped on a Fender Stratocaster and was touring with the Band. Undaunted, Cohen moved to Manhattan and hung out at the Chelsea Hotel, following in the footsteps of many other aspiring young musicians who had lived there before him. His sexual exploits and a relationship with a freethinking and stunningly beautiful Norwegian model named Marianne had already given him legendary status before he left Greece. Cohen may have felt at home in the redbrick Chelsea because he knew that writers like Mark Twain, Henry Miller, and Thomas Wolfe had lived there. More likely, he found it a link to the heyday of the folk revival days when Bob Dylan and Joan Baez made it their temporary home. Since then Jim Morrison, Patti Smith, and Janis Joplin also bedded down there.

Cohen first met Joplin soon after he checked in, and as he later recalled during a song introduction at the Montreux Jazz Festival, "A long time ago, I met a beautiful young woman in an elevator in New York City. I used to bump into her at about three in the morning, every night. After a while I gathered up my courage and I said to her, 'Are you looking for something?' And she said, 'Yes, I'm looking for something.' I knew by the tone of her voice that she wasn't trying to realize some unfulfilled potential of her inner nature but she was actually looking for something. I said, 'Who or what are you looking for?' She said, 'Kris Kristofferson.' I said, 'I am Kris Kristofferson.' And I deceived her for many nights." The lyrics he wrote for *Chelsea Hotel* were bluntly explicit: "I remember you well in the Chelsea Hotel, / You were talking so brave and so free. / Giving me head on the unmade bed / While the limousines wait in the street."

Like all of his writings, Cohen took his time finishing the song. As he told another concert audience, "I wrote this for an American singer who died a while ago. She used to stay at the Chelsea, too. I began it at a bar in a Polynesian restaurant in Miami in 1971 and finished it in Asmara, Ethiopia just before the throne was overturned." A meeting with Andy Warhol protege Nico, a model and vocalist with the Velvet Underground, resulted in Cohen momentarily lusting after someone who wouldn't give him the time of day. When Marianne and her son, Axel, joined him in New York, he set them up in an apartment, but retained his rooms at the hotel. The writing was already on the wall. It wouldn't be long before he wrote *So Long Marianne*.

Leonard Cohen had always begun his songs by discovering his melody and a lyric fragment before beginning "that long process of uncovering the lyric and fitting it to the melody." He had begun *Suzanne* in this same manner, coming up with a melody and the idea of a song about an ideal, illusive woman before he had any specifics. As he told a BBC interviewer, "The song was begun, and the chord pattern was developed, before a woman's name entered the song. And I knew it was a song about Montreal. It seemed to come out of that landscape that I loved very much in Montreal, which was the harbour, and the waterfront, and the sailors' church there, called Notre Dame de Bon Secour, which stood out over the river, and I knew that there are ships going by. I knew that there was a harbour, I knew that there was Our Lady of the Harbour, which was the virgin on the church which stretched out her arms towards the seamen, and you can climb up to the tower and look out over the river. So the song came from that vision, from that view of the river."

And Jesus was a sailor
When he walked upon the water
And he spent a long time watching
From his lonely wooden tower
And when he knew for certain
Only drowning men could see him
He said 'All men will be sailors then
Until the sea shall free them'

Several commentators have confused Suzanne Elrod, who later met Cohen in an elevator at the Plaza Hotel during a scientology convention, with the Suzanne in his song. Elrod was a 19-year old Jewish beauty from Miami who had a sugar daddy who kept her in a posh Plaza apartment. Cohen could not resist her charms, and she could not resist his advances. She chose his humbler rooms in the Chelsea, gave birth to his two children, Adam and Lorca, and, unlike the independent and easygoing Marianne, made many demands of his time and money.

Smitten and captivated for much of the next 10 years, Cohen once said, "God, whenever I see her ass I forget every pain that's gone between us." He has also credited her with being able to make him laugh. However, Collins had recorded *Suzanne* before he met Elrod.

During a 1994 BBC interview, he set the record straight. "At a certain point," he explained, "I bumped into Suzanne Vaillancourt, who was the wife of a friend of mine. They were a stunning couple around Montreal at the time, physically stunning, both of them, a handsome man and woman, every man was in love with Suzanne Vaillancourt, and every woman was in love with Armand Vaillancourt."

Cohen was fascinated by Suzanne Verdal Vailancourt and would compose a poem about her that was published in his 1966 collection *Parasites Of Heaven*. She was a dancer and her husband a sculptor, and they often attended the same soirees as Cohen. "I bumped into her one evening," he recalls, "and she invited me down to her place near the river. She had a loft, a space in a warehouse, and she invited me down, and I went with her, and she served me Constant Comment tea, which has little bits of oranges in it. And the boats were going by, and I touched her perfect body with my mind, because there was no other opportunity. There was no other way that you could touch her perfect body under those circumstances. So she provided the name in the song."

Suzanne Verdal later described the 'beat' scene in Montreal during the late '50s and early '60s during a BBC interview. "It was live jazz and we were just dancing our hearts out for hours on end, happy on very little," she recalled. "I mean we were living, most of us, on a shoestring. Yet, there was always so much to go around. There was so much energy and sharing and inspiration and pure moments and quality times together on very little or no money." She also recalled the first time she and Cohen met. "It was maybe several months into my relationship with Armand, which was mostly based on being dancing partners together. And he would watch us dancing, of course. And then I was introduced to Leonard at Le Vieux Moulin. But we didn't really strike a note together until maybe three or four years later."

| But he himself was broken |
| Long before the sky would open |
| Forsaken, almost human |
| He sank beneath your wisdom like a stone |

Verdal's account of their relationship differs somewhat from Cohen's. As she told Kate Saunders in 1998, "He got such a kick out of seeing me emerge as a young schoolgirl, I suppose, and a young artist, into becoming Armand's lover and then wife. So, he was more or less chronicling the times and seemingly got a kick out of it." She maintains that it was not until she was separated from her husband that she and Cohen connected. "Leonard heard about this place I was living, with crooked floors and a poetic view of the river, and he came to visit me many times." However, Suzanne Verdal does agree totally with Leonard that their relationship was special and spiritual in nature. "He was 'drinking me in' more than I even recognized," she told the BBC. "I took all that moment for granted. I just would speak and I would move and I would encourage and he would just kind of, like, sit back and grin while soaking it all up, and I wouldn't always get feedback, but I felt his presence really being with me. We'd walk down the street, for instance, and the click of our shoes, his boots and my shoes, would be, like, in synchronicity. It's hard to describe. We'd almost hear each other thinking. It was very unique, very, very unique."

Leonard Cohen's quest to secure a record deal was aided by Mary Martin, who also had a hand in hooking Dylan up with the Hawks and Emmylou Harris with Brian Ahern. Martin's first introduction, though, to an arranger who duped Cohen into signing away his royalties to *Suzanne* and two other songs, was disastrous. He would not recover the rights to his signature song until he confronted the villain 20 years down the road.

A second introduction to Judy Collins would click. As Collins recalls, "I listened to his songs in my living room. He sang *Suzanne* and *Dress Rehearsal Rag* that night, sitting on the couch, holding the guitar on his knee. There was something very ethereal and at the same time earthy about his voice. When Leonard sang, I was entranced. We would have tea together and walk around Greenwich Village. I recorded *Suzanne* and *Dress Rehearsal Rag* on IN MY LIFE in 1966, and it went gold in 1967."

Cohen's association with the beautiful, blue-eyed Collins, who was really hitting her stride with her clear unblemished vocals and lushly orchestrated folk-pop albums, appears to have been every bit as platonic as his relationship with Verdal. Judy also got him through his first bout of stage fright. As she recalls, "He was terribly shy. I knew once he got over his fear, he would be powerful on stage. I was going to appear at a concert for Sane against the Vietnam War at Town Hall. I asked Leonard if he would sing *Suzanne* there." He told her he couldn't do it, he would "die from embarrassment." In retrospect, his reticence is surprising. He'd been in a country band and had performed his poetry with jazz groups in the '50s. He had been featured in a NFB film *Ladies and Gentlemen: Mr. Leonard Cohen* and recited his poetry and sung his songs before sizeable audiences in the '60s in Canada. Nevertheless, Collins had to coax him, and even then he was exceedingly nervous. As Judy recalls, "I introduced him, he walked onto the stage hesitantly, his guitar slung across his hips, and from the wings I could see his legs shaking inside his trousers." Cohen began to play and sing *Suzanne* but faltered and left the stage. The audience had liked what they heard and they called out for him to return. "I can't do it," he told Judy, "I can't go back." He hung his head on her shoulder. "But you will," she told him, and "he shook himself and drew his body up and put his shoulders back and walked onto the stage. He finished *Suzanne* and the audience went wild."

And you want to travel with him
And you want to travel blind
And you think maybe you'll trust him
For he's touched your perfect body with his mind.

Columbia Records' A&R man John Hammond invited Cohen to lunch to size him up before they went up to his rooms in the Chelsea for an audition. Hammond quickly came to respect Cohen's poetic talents but also realized that he was out of his element in the music business. As he told the BBC, "*Suzanne*, of course, was his great tune. Judy loved him, but Joan Baez loved him, too. Women all feel very protective about him because he's a very dark, gloomy looking man, you know, and they all want to protect him." The two men soon discovered a mutual passion for playing pinball. "So, I listened to this guy and he's got a hypnotic effect," Hammond recalls. "He was enchanting. He was not like anything I've ever heard before. They all looked at me at Columbia and said, 'What, are you kidding? A 40-year-old Canadian poet? How are we going to sell him?' I said, 'Listen to him,' and lo and behold

Columbia signed him." When Cohen became distracted by the musicians during their first session, Hammond sent them home and hired a professor from the Yale music department, bass player and French horn player, Willie Huff. When Cohen asked if they could find a mirror so he could see himself while he sang, Hammond sent out for a mirror. He was very accommodating. "That was in Studio E," Hammond explains. "It was a small studio we had at 49 East 52nd Street. He was alone in the studio and it used to be lit with incense and candles and we had no lights on in the studio, and it had a very exotic effect. He had a hypnotizing effect on everybody, and he felt comfortable with the mirror, and I thought, 'Well, here's a true original.'"

"The support that Willie Ruff brought to those sessions was crucial," Cohen recalls. "I couldn't have laid down those tracks without him. He supported the guitar playing so well. He could always anticipate my next move." The only problems that arose took place after Hammond was hospitalized and another producer added backing vocals and instrumental arrangements that were not to Cohen's liking. His solution was to mix them back behind his lead vocals, which further contributed to the eerie overall sound of the finished album. John Hammond would later tell the BBC that Cohen "knew about three chords, and I think he still knows about three chords, and it didn't matter. The only thing I could do was to stay out of his way, and give him whatever reassurance he needed, and I could do that pretty well."

When Leonard Cohen met Joni Mitchell at the Newport Folk Festival in 1967, they felt an instantaneous mutual chemistry, which sparked a romance and a long-lasting friendship. His appearance at Newport created a buzz and he never looked back. Cohen moved to Tennessee soon after to record his second album SONGS FROM A ROOM, which included his slow motion rock anthem, *Bird On A Wire*. Kris Krisofferson liked it so much he told Cohen that the first three lines "Like a bird on a wire / A drunk in a midnight choir / I have tried in my way to be free" would be his epitaph. He lived there for two years with Suzanne Elrod in the Nashville suburb of Franklin, launching his first tours from there and using Nashville musicians to back him up. *Bird On A Wire* and *Suzanne* have remained concert favorites ever since.

Now Suzanne takes your hand
And she leads you to the river
She is wearing rags and feathers
From Salvation Army counters
And the sun pours down like honey
On our lady of the harbour

The second time I met Leonard Cohen, he had come to Kitsilano on a sunny afternoon in 1972 with Joni Mitchell to pick up some supplies. We bumped into each other outside Lifestream Natural Foods on Fourth Avenue. He and Joni were hanging out together at her house in Half Moon Bay on the Sunshine Coast, he told me, and they had drunk up all her red wine. While Joni went off to compare notes on dulcimers with my roommate, I invited Cohen to join me for a drink. "It's a bit early for that," he said. "Follow me," I said, and led him inside the natural food store to the back where there was a restaurant and a juice bar. While we sat sipping at tall glasses of freshly pressed juice, he told me that he was planning on returning to the Zen monastery in California where he had been practicing Zazen. Coincidentally, I had spent the much of the past two years also meditating morning and night in the Zen posture. So there were things to talk about, and then he and Joni were gone in their Land Rover.

I carried Cohen's *The Energy Of Slaves* and Shenryu Suzuki's *Zen Mind, Beginner's Mind* around with me on my travels for the next few years but didn't get back into Cohen's songs much until Jennifer Warnes' 1987 album FAMOUS BLUE RAINCOAT was released. Her rendition of *First We Take Manhattan* was something else, Cohen's map of his campaign to gain worldwide recognition laid out like a military strategy. His *Tower Of Song*, from his 1988 album I'M YOUR MAN, would make it all clear to me. He might have told people that he was going to become "the Canadian Bob Dylan," but his primary heroes had always been Federico Garcia Lorca and Hank Williams. Leonard Cohen's songs would find their way onto numerous movie soundtracks. More than 1,000 cover versions have been recorded, 140 of *Suzanne* alone. His reputation as a songwriter was fostered by covers of his songs by Joan Baez, Harry Belafonte, Neil Diamond, the Flying Lizards, Peter Gabriel, Suzanne Vega, Johnny Cash, Willie Nelson, Trisha Yearwood, k.d. lang, the Indigo Girls, and many others. My favorite Cohen covers can be found on Tom Northcott's 1997 CD, THE JOYFUL SONGS OF LEONARD COHEN.

Cohen's popularity in the United States has never been as large as it is in Canada and Europe. He has long enjoyed a cult status in France and Germany. In 1991, when he was inducted into the Canadian Music Hall of Fame at the Juno Awards, he read the lyrics of *Tower Of Song* as his acceptance speech, and declared that "at 56, I'm just hitting my stride." He owned the early '90s and his golden years have truly been golden.

"I didn't know much about Leonard's stature," Anjani Thomas admits, "until he asked me to sing backup and play keyboards for his Various Positions Tour in '85. It is no understatement to say his fans worship him. In Poland I was assigned a bodyguard (the same one who protected the Pope). I thought this an excessive gesture until the concert in Warsaw." That concert was delayed for hours while police "filtered out 3,000 people with counterfeit tickets. Distraught fans rocked our tour bus, begging to be let in, crying for a glimpse of Leonard through the dusty windows." In Switzerland, Anjani asked Cohen why they were playing the Montreux Jazz Festival when he was a folk act. After their set and a five-minute standing ovation he told her, "Darling, I am the original jazzer."

Since 1971, Cohen has pursued his quest for spiritual discipline with Zen master Joshu Sasaki, living much of his life in a simple hut at the Mount Baldy Zen Center in the San Gabriel Mountains. He also maintains a home and office in LA, and residences in Montreal and Greece. One pilgrim, who sought him out on the mount bearing a CD he had recorded of Cohen's songs, told me that Leonard's pursuit of a spiritual life has not meant that he has given up his pursuit of stunningly beautiful young women.

Some of these liaisons, such as his relationships with Parisian fashion photographer Dominique Issermann and film star Rebecca de Mornay, have been well documented. His 20-year musical and spiritual friendship with the beautiful and gifted Anjani Thomas has blossomed along with his longstanding co-writing partnership with Susan Robinson. Cohen took three months off when his son Adam was critically injured to be by his side, and has seen Adam come back with albums of his own.

| And she shows you where to look |
| Among the garbage and the flowers |
| There are heroes in the seaweed |
| There are children in the morning |
| They are leaning out for love |
| And they will lean that way forever |
| While Suzanne holds the mirror |

In 1993, when Cohen was once again acknowledged at the Juno Awards he said, "My cup runneth over. It's only in a country like this that I could get the Male Vocalist of the Year award." Leonard has been showered with many acknowledgements of his contributions to our culture. He has been inducted into the Rock & Roll Hall of Fame, initiated into the Buddhist faith as a full-fledged Rinzai monk, and accepted the prestigious Order of Canada medal from Governor General Adrienne Clarkson.

In October 2004, one month after Cohen's 70th birthday, Columbia issued his 11th studio album, DEAR HEATHER, which he co-wrote and co-produced with Anjani Thomas and Susan Robinson. He has lived a full and rewarding life and is still a vital force on the music scene, although there might be one more detail he still needs to take care of. During her 1998 BBC interview, Suzanne Verdal revealed that she, too, lives in Los Angeles and teaches dance lessons, not that far from where Cohen lives. Her only regret was that Leonard had never looked her up since those bohemian days they enjoyed together in old Montreal.

| And you want to travel with her |
| And you want to travel blind |
| And you know that you can trust her |
| For she's touched your perfect body with her mind. |

The Weight

The Band

Words & Music by J.R. Robertson

© 1970, Dwarf Music.

I pulled into Nazareth, was feelin' about half past dead;
I just need some place where I can lay my head.
"Hey, mister, can you tell me where a man might find a bed?"
He just grinned and shook my hand, and "no" was all he said.

When the Band took the stage at Winterland on April 19, 1969 for their very first gig as Capitol recording artists, their guitarist and chief songwriter, Robbie Robertson, was in a trance. He had come down with a fever after flying up to San Francisco from LA where the group was recording their second album. "The whole time going up there," Robbie told *Bill Graham Presents* author Robert Greenfield, "this person was, like, hacking and coughing and wheezing and it was horrible. I felt like I had the worst case of stomach flu in the world. These doctors came over and gave me some shots. The rest of the guys were rehearsing." Another doctor arrived and administered more medication, but Robbie's condition did not improve. He had a temperature of 104. "I was just getting weaker all the time with all these drugs in me," he recalls. Manager Albert Grossman and promoter Bill Graham put their heads together and a hypnotist was brought in. Robertson had worked himself to the point of exhaustion in the weeks prior to boarding the flight north, so maybe it was all in his head.

"He was a French hypnotist," Robbie recalls, "with silver hair in a black suit, white shirt, and black tie. He looked like he had come to deal with the dead." The hypnotist shooed everybody out of the hotel room and got down to business, eventually managing to get the guitarist into a deep trance. "A bunch of us were just hanging out and waiting in the lobby area of the Seal Rock Inn by the pool," Graham related to Greenfield. "Albert came out and I said, 'How's it going?' He said that the guy was working on Robbie with a faceted crystal ball on a string. 'I think he's got it out of his legs. Now it's on top.'"

If the Band had been a typical rock band, and Robertson a posing, prancing front man, he would not have been able to summon the effort required to perform. However, the Band featured ensemble playing with little or no "showmanship" and vocals from piano player Richard Manuel, bass player Rick Danko, and drummer Levon Helm. Their three-part harmonies were a wonderful thing to behold.

> Take a load off Fanny, take a load for free;
> Take a load off Fanny, and (and) (and)
> You can put the load right on me.

The Band had come together backing Ronnie Hawkins in Toronto and met Bob Dylan through backing John Hammond in a New York studio. Touring with Dylan had led to a record deal with Capitol, and their debut, MUSIC FROM BIG PINK. Bass player Rick Danko was seriously injured in a motor vehicle accident and that kept them from touring in support of the album. Bill Graham sought them out in the Catskills and signed them to a lucrative $25,000 contract for three nights. He didn't want anything to spoil their concert debut, which he had promoted to the hilt. The public was eager to see the Band, which they had only heard on the radio performing their debut single, *The Weight*, with a lead vocal by Arkansas-born drummer Levon Helm.

Robbie Robertson performed that first night at Winterland seated on a chair, his hypnotist seated nearby. Robbie was a team player and the Band was a team like rock & roll had never seen. As Robbie later told Kevin Ransom, "See, with Ronnie, I played a solo in every song and then when we hooked up with Bob Dylan for the 1965 and '66 tours, I played even more solos. Bob had never played with a band before, not as far as I could tell, and we were like this newfound musical toy for him. He'd sing a couple of verses, look over at me, and I'd solo; he'd sing another verse, look over at me, and I'd solo; then, after the final verse, he'd look over at me again, and I'd solo to end the song. So by the time of the Band's first album, I was soloed out, and I'd gotten to a place where, for me, it was about finding the right emotion, and I figured my role was to support that emotion. I got so I just wanted to play parts and grooves instead of solos."

> I picked up my bag, I went lookin' for a place to hide;
> When I saw Carmen and the Devil walkin' side by side.
> I said, "Hey, Carmen, come on, let's go downtown."
> She said, "I gotta go, but m'friend can stick around."

"Chemistry," Levon Helm told Ruth Spencer, was the key element to the group's unique sound, "the chemistry of the people who were in the Band. Collectively, five people can add up to more than five. That's what helped us. We'd been back to back for a long time. We were birds of a feather; there was a common denominator. We all had an appreciation of music, art and human nature. When it finally got down to the simple proposition of making music, then you have five heads, which are better than one or two. When it got that simple, our chemistry was pretty well cultivated, tried and tested under fire. We had played everywhere and done everything two or three times."

The fact that they could also pick up fiddles, mandolins, and accordions and add their own special ambience to the mix made them unique. "Robbie played the set sitting down," Bill Graham told Greenfield. "His voice was good, it just did not have the physicalness in it. The Band kicked *ass*. Two or three times during the show, Robbie would look over there and the guy would hold up the little crystal ball." The hypnotist had told Robertson to look over and he would say the word, "grow," and Robbie would feel replenished. As Robertson recalls, "I could hear it over the crowd and the music. I could hear it so clearly that it reverberated through my body and I began to feel okay again."

Robbie Robertson was born on July 5, 1943 in Toronto. According to *Before The Gold Rush* author Nicholas Jennings, he was "a street kid who kept his eyes and ears open. Born to a Jewish gambler and a Mohican woman, he spent his youth in the twin worlds of downtown Toronto and the Six Nations Reserve near Brantford, Ontario." While learning how to play a Telecaster, Robbie formed the Suedes and soon found his band opening for his idols, Ronnie Hawkins & the Hawks. The Hawks "played the fastest, most violent rock 'n' roll I'd ever heard," he told Jennings. "It was exciting, and exploding with dynamics. The solos would get really loud. Ronnie would come in and growl and it would get quiet, then fast and loud again. It was these cool looking guys doing this primitive music faster and more violent than anybody, with overwhelming power." Before turning 16, Robbie wrote tunes that Hawkins recorded, but they didn't repeat the success of his early hits, *Forty Days* and *Mary Lou*, or his signature song, *Who Do You Love*.

Robertson was first hired to play bass. He borrowed a bass and pawned his Telecaster to purchase a bus ticket so that he could join the Hawks in Arkansas. As Nicholas Jennings chronicles, "Stepping off a Greyhound bus, Robertson stood by the banks of the Mississippi River and breathed in his surroundings. Here he was, a 16-year-old Canadian boy in a strange new world, and his senses were working overtime. 'There wasn't anything in Toronto like it,' he recalled. 'It smelled different and moved different. The people talked and dressed different. And the air was filled with thick and funky music.'"

Robbie quickly moved up from bass to rhythm guitar and finally to lead. In order to bend and pull his guitar strings with maximum effect, he substituted two banjo strings, after seeing how Fred Carter Jr. had done this before leaving the group. One by one Hawkins' American sidemen fell by the wayside to be replaced with Canadians. Garth Hudson was the last to join the Hawks. A classically trained pianist who preferred jazz to the rockabilly that was Hawkins' bread and butter, Hudson was lured into the fold by an offer of extra pay for tutoring Robertson, Danko, and Manuel. Hudson's contributions on sax and organ would help define the group's distinctive sound; his knowledge of music theory would enrich their arrangements and harmonies. As Richard Manuel recalls, "Garth taught us all that. He taught us all the proper voicings for chords, and for different effects. He is totally musically educated."

Levon Helm hung in there with the young Canadians. "I went from Arkansas up to Canada and ran into them up there," he told Spencer. "The fella I went up to Canada with, Ronnie Hawkins, fell in love with it, the same as I did. But he fell in love with a Canadian girl, too. So he married and stayed up there and raised a family." By the time the group left their mentor and began billing themselves as Levon & the Hawks, they had a unique sound.

Robbie and Levon had bonded during Robbie's first tour of duty in the South. He lived with Levon's family and the impressions he formed would later inform many of his best songs. "I'd hear something at night," he recalls, "and not know whether it was an animal, a harmonica, or a train. But it sounded like music to me."

> Go down, Miss Moses, there's nothin' you can say
> It's just ol' Luke, and Luke's waitin' on the Judgement Day.
> "Well, Luke, my friend, what about young Anna Lee?"
> He said, "Do me a favor, son, woncha stay an' keep Anna Lee company?"

Robbie Robertson and Levon Helm backed Bob Dylan at Forest Hills, and convinced him to hire the Hawks to accompany him on his world tour. Dylan joined them in Toronto, where they had two weeks remaining on a previous booking and rehearsed with them in the club. On the road with Dylan, they faced hostile audiences comprised of irate folk purists. Helm left the tour. "I don't think Levon could handle people booing every night," Robbie recalls. "To me it was like `Yeah, but the experience equals this music in the making. We will find the music.'"

First Edition drummer Mickey Jones replaced Helm and they soldiered on. "In the beginning, it was a little bit too much bashing," Robbie admits. "By the time we did the Australia and Europe tours, we had discovered whatever this thing was. It was not light, it was not folky it was very dynamic, very explosive and very violent." Their final show was at the Royal Albert Hall. After that, Dylan retired to Woodstock, New York, an artist colony, to work on editing film footage that had been shot on the tour. Robertson used his time off to write songs. He credits Dylan for his improved songwriting.

"That's the door that he opened," Robbie recalls, "but at the same time I was just as influenced by Luis Buñuel or John Ford or Kurosawa. I got this hunger for education and knowledge because I hadn't gone to school. I started with Ronnie Hawkins when I was 16. So I decided to read a whole lot and I started to see these kinds of films. I got into all kinds of mythologies. It influenced me in a style of storytelling."

After Dylan was injured in a motorcycle accident in July '66, Danko, Manuel, and Hudson rented a big, pink house off Stoll Road, in West Saugerties, and Robertson a house nearby. They were available to fulfil their contract with Dylan, but they were determined to make a record of their own. "From 1960 to 1965 the band played every night in night-clubs," Rick Danko explains. "We didn't really know any better and that's all we knew to do. And then Bob put us on some kind of retainer, and that allowed us some freedom to figure out what an artist really is."

During his convalescence, Dylan showed up nearly every morning at the band house. The informal sessions were taped and some of the cuts were unofficially released on the GREAT WHITE WONDER bootleg and more of them on Capitol's THE BASEMENT TAPES a few years down the road. These sessions in the basement of the big, pink house would become the inspiration for many country rock pioneers. The Byrds immediately recorded the easygoing *You Ain't Goin' Nowhere* on their SWEETHEART OF THE RODEO album. "Back when people were stacking up Marshall amps and blowing out their eardrums," Danko notes, "the Band was down in the basement at Big Pink trying to get a balance. It wasn't about one person trying to blow the others away, it was about trying to play together and find economical common ground."

Eric Clapton, who was winding up his final tour with Cream, got hold of an advance copy of the Band's album. As Eric recalls, "I used to put it on as soon as I checked into my hotel room, do the gig and be utterly miserable, then rush back and put the tape on. And go to sleep fairly contented until I woke up the next morning and remembered who I was and what I was doing. It was that potent!"

Bob Dylan seldom collaborates with anybody. The situation at Big Pink, however, was so casual and so relaxed that he made some exceptions. As Richard Manuel recalls, "He came down to the basement with a piece of typewritten paper and he just said 'Have you got any music for this?' I had a couple of musical movements that seemed to fit, so I just elaborated a little bit, because I wasn't sure what the lyrics meant. I couldn't run upstairs and say, 'What's this mean, Bob?'" Dylan sang *Tears Of Rage* in the basement, but Manuel would sing it in his high falsetto on the Band's Music From Big Pink. Dylan handed the rough lyrics to *This Wheel's On Fire* to Rick Danko. "At the time," Danko recalls, "I was teaching myself to play the piano. Some music I'd written on the piano the day before just seemed to fit with Bob's lyrics. I worked on the phrasing and melody, and then Bob and I wrote the chorus together."

"Maybe 150 songs were recorded in a seven or eight month period," he recalls. "Bob would come and bang the songs out on his typewriter and we'd go down into the basement and make some music up for them. The tapes were part of Bob's rehabilitation; he was getting stronger and feeling better. And from that we started getting our writing chops together a little bit." Many of the songs Dylan composed at Big Pink did not surface until years later. He chose a whole new slate of songs to record in Nashville for his sparse JOHN WESLEY HARDING album and followed that up with the rollicking country rock of NASHVILLE SKYLINE. However, three Dylan songs recorded in the basement would form the core of the Band's MUSIC FROM BIG PINK, framing its centerpiece, *The Weight*.

"We were just up there living," Robbie recalls. "There was nothing that we had to do, no obligations. But Bob had been wanting us to record for a long time." Levon Helm didn't need very much encouragement to be persuaded to rejoin his mates. As he recalls, "I was certainly lonesome for the band. I guess I believed at some point that we would get back together. I didn't figure that they would give up their dreams just to be Bob's backup band."

Crazy Chester followed me, and he caught me in the fog.	
He said, "I will fix your rack, if you'll take Jack, my dog."	
I said, "Wait a minute, Chester, you know I'm a peaceful man."	
He said, "That's okay, boy, won't you feed him when you can."	

Robbie Robertson wrote *The Weight* in a single session. "I just wrote it," he recalls. "It's just one of those things. I thought of a couple of words that led to a couple more, and the next thing I knew I wrote the song. It had a kind of American mythology I was reinventing using my connection to the universal language." This new American mythology made reference to the birth of Martin Guitars factory in 1838 when Christian Frederick Martin moved his one-man guitar building business to Nazareth, Pennsylvania. Martin and Gibson acoustic guitars were the instruments upon which the bulk of American string-based music was composed. And in that special sense they were sacred. But Robbie's reference is not heavy handed, he drops it as casually as he does the nicknames of former band mates like "Luke" and local characters like "Crazy Chester," and in much the same way that poets Walt Whitman and William Carlos Williams and had written a purely

American poetry. "The song was full of our favorite characters," Levon Helm told Spencer. 'Luke' was Jimmy Ray Paulman. 'Young Anna Lee' was Anna Lee Williams from Turkey Scratch. 'Crazy Chester' was a guy we all knew from Fayetteville who came into town on Saturdays wearing a full set of cap guns on his hips he was like Hopalong Cassidy and a friend of The Hawk's."

Many years later in the liner notes to a boxed set Robbie revealed that surrealist filmmaker Luis Buñuel had been his primary influence. "Buñuel did so many films on the impossibility of sainthood," he explained. "People trying to be good in *Viridiana* and *Nazarin*, people trying to do their thing. In *The Weight* it's the same thing. Someone says, 'Listen, would you do me this favor? When you get there will you say 'hello' to somebody or will you give somebody this or will you pick up one of these for me? Oh? You're going to Nazareth, that's where the Martin guitar factory is. Do me a favor when you're there.' This is what it's all about. So the guy goes and one thing leads to another and it's like 'Holy Shit, what's this turned into? I've only come here to say 'hello' for somebody and I've got myself in this incredible predicament.' It was very Buñuelish to me at the time."

Legions of fans have imagined their own movies based on *The Weight*, usually starring *Gunsmoke* characters and an historical Jesus. Leonard Cohen has written numerous somber, brooding songs, poems and even a novel about the impossibility of sainthood, but in Robbie's song things just keep getting worse and worse. The song barely made the cut during their sessions. As Robbie recalls, "That song was the only song on Music From Big Pink that we never did rehearse. We just figured that it was a simple song, and when it came up we gave it a try and recorded it three or four times. We said that's fine maybe we'll use it. We didn't even know if we were going to use it."

> Catch a cannon ball now, t'take me down the line
> My bag is sinkin' low and I do believe it's time.
> To get back to Miss Fanny, you know she's the only one.
> Who sent me here with her regards for everyone.

Contrary to popular misconception, MUSIC FROM BIG PINK was not recorded in the basement of the pink band house; the album was begun in New York and completed in LA. Teamed with producer John Simon, the Band quickly recorded *Tears Of Rage, Chest Fever, We Can Talk, This Wheel's On Fire,* and *The Weight* during the New York sessions. "He was technically light years ahead of us," Robertson told interviewers. "He had all the expertise in the studio and we had none."

Choosing to open the album with a ballad was the Band's first declaration that they were going against the grain. Rock albums never opened with ballads. Richard Manuel's mournful delivery of parental heartbreak in *Tears Of Rage* set the tone this was not to be a good times party album. An eerie cover of a Lefty Frizzell standard, *Long Black Veil,* was equally enigmatic. "It was a great song, lyric-wise," Robertson notes, "in the tradition that I wanted to begin writing in." A primitive Bob Dylan painting was chosen for the front cover art, a photo of Big Pink for the back, and rumors spread quickly that Dylan must be somehow involved in the tracks. He was, of course, as a songwriter, but the allure of their association with Dylan definitely added to the mystery surrounding the group with the generic name.

The Weight was featured on the soundtrack of *Easy Rider.* Many people merely thought that Levon Helm was singing the lead vocal throughout, but Rick Danko contributed the fourth verse and Richard Manuel contributed the high moans in the choruses. Levon and Rick sang the final verse together. Richard Manuel closed the album with Dylan's *I Shall Be Released* and many listeners were, after his final falsetto strains had come to an end. The Band's photo looked like it had been taken during the Civil War and the "Next of Kin" portrait featured four generations of the group's relatives. Contrary to a frequent rock & roll ethic, they were definitely not "parent haters."

Capitol Records released *The Weight* on a 45 that was mailed to radio stations in advance of the album's release. Because they were still deciding whether to call themselves the Crackers or the Honkies, and hadn't yet hit on the name they would become known by, *The Weight* was credited to all five musicians, which added an initial mystery to the release.

MUSIC FROM BIG PINK seeped into the mainstream. It was never an overwhelming bestseller, but people who embraced it sometimes judged new neighbors by whether or not they had the album in their collections. Chances were, if you did, you were mellow folks. The

Band's traditional approach to contemporary music was timeless, and a pleasant relief from an overabundance of rebellious bands and their stacked Marshall Amps. The Band's roots approach has remained influential down through the decades. "We were rebelling against the rebellion," Robertson told interviewers, "whatever was happening. If everybody was going east, then we were going west and we never once discussed it. There was this kind of ingrained thing from us all along."

Take a load off Fanny, take a load for free;
Take a load off Fanny, and (and) (and)
You can put the load right on me.

The second and third nights at Winterland in '69 were in Bill Graham's words "awesome," and the Band was hired immediately to play the Fillmore East in New York. "They were even better than they were in San Francisco," Graham reported. "People were just blown out because the music on the stage was better than on the album 'Big Pink'. They just stood and played and sang. They didn't jump around. No one had seen anything like them before. They were really one of a kind."

With the release of MUSIC FROM BIG PINK and their unique stage presence, the Band had given birth to Americana. "It was intense and it was serious to us," Robertson recalls. "And it wasn't a party. It *wasn't* a party. It was a joyous experience and we were never going to be smiling at nothing. That was not allowed in this church. We didn't smile for nothing; we only smiled for *something*. And Bill adapted to this thing. He got it just like *that*. He treated it as if this was the way it should be. He put emphasis in places and then they figured out the lighting to make it a little more dramatic instead of flashy."

In 1969, Aretha Franklin's cover of *The Weight*, featuring Duane Allman on slide guitar, rose into the *Billboard* Top 20. That same year, the Band scored a number 25 hit with *Up On Cripple Creek*, but their considerable influence on the music of their time was not driven by hit singles. People liked their music because it was alive and they could feel its roots as they listened along. The Band teamed up with Bob Dylan again in 1974 for the triumphant Before The Flood Tour. And in '76, the Band returned to Winterland with filmmaker Martin Scorsese to film *The Last Waltz*. Bill Graham borrowed props from the San Francisco Opera and fed 5,000 guests Thanksgiving dinner before the show, which featured special guests Paul Butterfield, Eric Clapton, Neil Diamond, Bob Dylan, Emmylou Harris, Ronnie Hawkins, Dr. John, Joni Mitchell, Van Morrison, Ringo Starr, Muddy Waters, Ronnie Wood, Bobby Charles and Neil Young. *The Last Waltz* has been called the best live concert film ever. The Band re-formed in 1983 without Robertson on board and was inducted into the Canadian Music Hall of Fame in 1990 and the Rock & Roll Hall of Fame four years later. In 1992, while introducing the Band at the Bob Dylan Tribute Concert in New York, Eric Clapton said, "Back in 1968, I heard a record called MUSIC FROM BIG PINK that changed my life, and it changed the course of American music."

Both Sides, Now
Words & Music by Joni Mitchell

Rows and flows of angel hair
And ice cream castles in the air
And feather canyons ev'rywhere
I've looked at clouds that way.

Joni Mitchell's first success as a songwriter was *Urge For Going*, a number 7 country hit for former teen idol George Hamilton IV in 1967. At the time, she didn't see herself as an aspiring country artist or as a serious songwriter, for that matter. "I picked up music more for fun," she confessed to *Goldmine*. "I had no ambition to make a career of it at all. Of course, when I began to write my own songs I was slightly ambitious for them." One of those songs was the *The Circle Game*, also recorded in 1967 by Canadian artists Ian & Sylvia. Another was *Both Sides, Now*, which rose to number 8 on the Billboard pop charts when recorded by Judy Collins.

By 1967, Joni Mitchell had begun to perform on the folk circuit in the American Midwest, covering artists like Judy Collins, and soon gained a reputation as a talented folk song writer. Later in her career she dabbled in rock and studied jazz, eventually creating a sound that is best described as "Joni Mitchell Music," which has often irritated critics and confused her fans. She defies easy categorization, much as her Canadian colleague Neil Young does. There is something unique about their sound, as Joni explained in an article in *MacLean's* magazine. "There's a lot of prairie in our songs … I think both of us have a striding quality to our music which is like long steps across flat land."

Mitchell's and Young's careers have much in common. They left their prairie homes to join the folk scene in the Yorkville district of Toronto and found fame and fortune on the Sunset Strip in Los Angeles. "When I went to Toronto to the Mariposa Folk Festival to actually see Buffy Sainte-Marie," Joni recalls, "I still didn't have an image of myself as a musician. I found I couldn't work, and I didn't have enough money to get into the union. So I worked in women's wear in a department store. I could barely make ends meet. And then I finally found a scab club in Toronto that allowed me to play. I played for a couple of months. Then I married Chuck Mitchell."

The newlyweds moved to Detroit near the campus of Wayne State University, where they shared an apartment that became home to wayward folk artists. It was these overnight guests who performed her songs and hawked them to record company A&R scouts. Tom Rush recalls that when he first met Chuck and Joni they were industriously scraping paint off the doors and doorframes in their apartment and restoring the natural wood. "We had a big apartment, Chuck and I," Joni explains, "and we billeted a lot of artists. Eric Andersen stayed there, and Tom Rush stayed there. The rent was really cheap and we had three or four bedrooms in this old place. So, artists stayed with us frequently, and Tom, I think, carried off *Urge For Going*. So, he played that around and the next time he came to play The Chess Mate he said, 'You got anything else?'" Mitchell played him *The Circle Game*. Dave Van Ronk carried away *Both Sides, Now* and referred to it as *Clouds*. Buffy Sainte-Marie recorded *The Circle Game* and *Song To A Seagull*. With her memorable cover of *Both Sides, Now*, Judy Collins, the artist Joni had started out covering in Calgary folk clubs, put the young Canadian into the pop charts.

Joni later told *L.A. Times* critic Robert Hilburn that she wrote *Both Sides, Now* during an early tour. "I was reading Saul Bellows' *Henderson and the Rain King* on a plane," she told Hilburn, "and early in the book Henderson is also up in a plane. He's on his way to Africa, and he looks down and sees these clouds. I put the book down, looked out the window, and saw clouds, too, and immediately began writing the song. I had no idea that the song would become as popular as it did."

But now they only block the sun
They rain and snow on ev'ryone
So many things I would have done
But clouds got in my way.

Chuck and Joni Mitchell toured together throughout their short, turbulent marriage, but they did not exactly become the next Ian &

Sylvia. In fact, they often performed separate sets during their book-ings. Some nights they were not even on the same page. "We are both strong-minded people," Chuck admitted in one interview. For Joni, the fit was less than perfect, and Chuck did not endear himself to his wife when he responded to *Both Sides, Now* with a disparaging remark. "When I wrote *Both Sides Now*," Joni recalls, "Chuck Mitchell said to me, 'Oh, what do you know about life, you're only 21.' But I knew a lot about life. I'd gone through a lot of disease and personal pain. Even as a child. I'd had three bouts with death. I was not unaware of my mortality." "It was not a marriage made in Heaven," she told another interviewer. "He was relatively well educated and in contempt of my lack of education. I was developing as an original unschooled thinker but he ridiculed me in the same way that Pierre Trudeau ridiculed his wife Margaret when she wrote her book. He (Trudeau) said, 'My wife is the only writer I know who has written more books than she has read.' So there was this educated pride against the uneducated, and the mar-riage didn't last very long."

Joni Mitchell was born Roberta Joan Anderson on November 7, 1943 in Fort MacLeod, Alberta, and raised in rural Saskatchewan near Saskatoon, not far from Buffy Sainte-Marie's birthplace in the Qu'Appelle Valley. Her father, Walter, was a grocer; her mother, Myrtle, a schoolteacher. She credits her grandmothers, both of whom were frustrated musicians who survived the tough and challenging conditions of the pioneer homesteading era, as inspirations for her own strong will and character. Growing up in the late '40s and early '50s, she was not subject to the same arduous struggle for survival that her grandmothers had been, but there would be plenty of challenges along the way.

"I would have been an athlete," she told Steve Matteo, "but I had a lot of childhood illnesses that developed a solitude and fostered 'artis-ticness'. I had polio when I was nine, and I remember that there was a boy in the bed next to mine in the polio ward who was really depressed. He didn't even have polio as bad as I did, but he wasn't fighting it. He wasn't fighting to go on with what he had left. Polio is the disease that eats muscles. If it eats the muscle of your heart, it kills you; if it eats the muscles that control the flexing of your lungs, you end up in an iron lung; if it eats the muscle of your leg, it withers, or of your arm, it withers. In my case it ate muscles in my back. The same thing happened with Neil Young. I had to learn to stand, and then to walk." The very solitude and struggle that challenged the preteen contributed to an active imagination that would stand her in good stead when she began to write her own songs. She would also make strides as a visual artist, an avenue of expression she would explore at art school in Calgary. "Through all of this," she told Matteo, "I drew like crazy and sang Christmas carols. I think that the creative process was an urgency then, that it was a survival instinct, and I left that ward long before that boy, who had a mild case of polio in one leg. He lay with his back to the wall, sulking. When the spirit of child's play enters into the creative process, it's a wonderful force and something to be nurtured."

I've looked at clouds from both sides now
From up and down and still somehow
It's cloud's illusions I recall
I really don't know clouds at all

Singing in her hospital ward inspired other patients to sing along. Her enthusiasm for her drawings and poems inspired her schoolteachers to nurture her raw talent. She would spend only one year at art school in Calgary before heading east to Toronto to become a folksinger, but the fairy tale characters she chronicled in her early songs would always benefit from her visual memories of the Western Canadian mountains, towns and vast expanses of prairie. "I was writing a mythology," she later told a Philadelphia deejay.

Moons and Junes and Ferris wheels
The dizzy dancing way you feel
As every fairy tale comes real
I've looked at love that way

The loves of Joni's life have been many she and Leonard Cohen bonded almost immediately upon meeting at the Newport Jazz Festival. However, they kept their tryst from the press as long as they could and by the time that their liaison leaked out they had loved and moved on.

David Crosby has said that, "Joni is not a person that you stay in a relationship with. It always goes awry, no matter who you are. It's an inevitable thing." A short-lived 1964 liaison with Calgary college student Brad McMath resulted in an unwanted pregnancy, but it did not deter the resolute 20-year-old Mitchell from climbing on a train and heading to the Mariposa Folk Festival. The lengthy railway journey led to Joni's first memorable original song, *Day After Day*. However, after the excitement of the festival she found herself broke, pregnant and unable to perform in most of the Toronto clubs because she couldn't raise the $160 necessary to join the Toronto local of the musicians union.

> But now it's just another show
> You leave 'em laughing when you go
> And if you care, don't let them know
> Don't give yourself away.

Doggedly, she worked as a sales clerk and auditioned at non-union clubs. Meeting Detroit folkie Chuck Mitchell at this low point in her brief career as an entertainer, she was appreciative of the hope and help he offered. Her daughter, Kelly Anderson, was born in February 1965, but Joni would opt for adoption a month later. News of the birth was successfully kept from the press for many years. "I had had a child," she confessed in *Vogue* magazine in 1994, "and I was broke, literally penniless. And I met Chuck Mitchell, and he said he would take us on. I was kind of railroaded . . . we were never suitable. I went down the aisle saying, 'I can get out of this.'" She would be reunited with her daughter in 1997 but it would be a long and winding road that led to that mother and daughter reunion.

> I've looked at love from both sides now
> From give and take and still somehow
> It's love's illusions I recall
> I really don't know love at all

As a teenager Joni had endured piano lessons but lacked the diligence to make much headway with the Toronto Conservatory classical music-training regimen employed by all licensed piano teachers in those days. "I wanted to play piano," she told Stewart Brand in a 1976 interview, "but I didn't want to take lessons. I wanted to do what I do now, which is to lay my hand on it and to memorize what comes off it and to create with it. But my music teacher told me I played by ear, which was a sin." She turned to bass ukulele and eventually to guitar, teaching herself to play from a Pete Seeger method book. She had to purchase it herself with money made from modeling because her mother had forbidden her to play the instrument. Fiercely independent, she would always have a fashion sense that provided her with a unique "look" while other performers wore the hippie garb of the day. In order to compensate for the muscle damage she had sustained from her bout with polio, she soon found herself exploring open tunings.

"In the beginning, I built the repertoire of the open major tunings that the old black blues guys came up with," she explains. "It was only three or four, the simplest one is D modal. Neil Young uses that a lot. And then open G with the sixth string removed, which is all Keith Richards plays in. And open D, and then going between them, I began to get more modern chords." Eric Andersen taught her some tricks of the trade. "Eric started teaching me open tunings," she explains, "an open G, a drop D. For some reason, once I got the open tunings to get the harmonic sophistication that my musical foundation inside me was excited by, my writing began to come. But I was still pretty much a good time Charlie."

Musical friendships and an ongoing exchange of information among her peers would enrich Joni's music and help her make rapid strides toward the stardom she has always said she never wanted. When she met Neil Young, he played her his song *Sugar Mountain*, and she spontaneously wrote *The Circle Game* as an answer song. Many of these musical friendships sprang from her passion for innovative open tunings that led her to discover her unique melodies. She would also receive tips and exchange tunings with Tom Rush. After recording *Day By Day* for Rush's manager Arthur Gorson's Wild Indigo label as a demo, she and Chuck formed their own separate publishing companies. Siquomb Publishing was derived from an anagram for her Queen in her mysterious song mythology of small people and imaginary places. Rush tried unsuccessfully to pitch her early songs to some labels and artists like Judy Collins, and recorded *The Circle Game*, which was released as the title song for his influential 1968 album that also introduced the songs of singer-songwriters Jackson Browne and James Taylor. Meanwhile, Joni recorded some sides with the classically trained Siegel-Schwall Blues Band and bided her time.

Dissatisfied with her marriage, she eventually packed her belongings into a rental van and headed for New York City where she rented a small apartment in the Chelsea district. It was not an opportune moment to enter the Greenwich Village scene. As she recalls, "I came in late. Basically, clubs were folding and bands were the new thing." She was resolute that she would not sign with a folk label like Vanguard, which put little effort or money into production and had no budget at all for promotion. "Record companies offered me terrible slave labor deals in the beginning," she has said, "and I turned them down." The smaller folk labels all wanted to sign her up, however, major label executives thought she sounded too much like Judy Collins or Joan Baez. So she continued to gig and to write songs. *Chelsea Morning* portrayed the lively energy of life in Manhattan. *I Had A King* chronicled her failed marriage. Wary of managers but aware of the need to employ someone to help out with her bookings and her quest for a record deal, she eventually settled on Elliot Roberts because he didn't want a piece of her publishing and was a kindred spirit. Roberts and his pal, David Geffen, would go on to play major roles in her early career, but a chance meeting with David Crosby after a set in the Gaslight South club in Florida would result in a sudden change of fortune.

Tears and fears and feeling proud
To say "I love you" right out loud
Dreams and schemes and circus crowds
I've looked at life that way.

David Crosby's time with the Byrds had ended on a sour note and he had come to Florida to seek a new beginning. He was thinking of buying a boat, not falling in love with a chick singer from Canada. "I went looking for a sailboat to live on," he told Wally Breese. "I wanted to do something else. Find another way to be. I was pretty disillusioned. I walked into a coffeehouse and was just completely smitten. She was standing there singing all those songs . . . *Michael from the Mountains, Both Sides Now,* and I was just floored. I couldn't believe that there was anybody that good. I was extremely fascinated with the quality of the music and the quality of the girl. She was such an unusual, passionate and powerful woman. I was fascinated by her tunings because I had started working in [open] tunings, and I was writing things like *Guinevere.* So things like that made me very, very attracted to her."

The feelings were mutual, as Joni chronicled in *The Dawntreader*: "Like a promise to be free / Dolphins playing in the sea / All his sea dreams come to me." When Joni returned to Canada for her second appearance at the Mariposa Folk festival in the summer of 1967, three years after she had gone there as a fan to hear Buffy Sainte-Marie, she was no longer an unknown folksinger. As Nicholas Jennings recalls in *Before the Goldrush*, "Joni Mitchell faced a much more receptive crowd that summer. In fact, Mitchell returned to the festival as one of its most popular attractions, joining a lineup that included Lightfoot, Doc Watson and the New Lost City Ramblers. Dressed in Paisley and accompanied by guitarist David Rea, Mitchell captivated her audiences at both her evening and afternoon performances. This time, she brought a suitcase full of new songs, including *Both Sides Now* and *Night in the City*, which, she told her audience, was inspired by her time spent in Yorkville. 'Music comes spilling,' she sang, 'colors go flashing in time.'"

With David Crosby on board as producer, the major labels were suddenly interested in Joni Mitchell as a recording artist, and she was signed to Reprise before the end of the year. Her time in her apartment on West 16th Street in Manhattan had come to an end. She accompanied Crosby to Los Angeles and lived with him in his West Hollywood house while her own house was being readied for occupancy. Crosby facilitated her rapid rise to fame by inviting influential guests and fellow musicians over to hear her sing her songs. Three nights at the Troubadour, performing before packed audiences, spread the word, too. Crosby had agreed to produce her album but the set of songs they agreed on to record did not contain any of her most well known numbers from her live performances. Notably missing were *Chelsea Morning, The Circle Game,* and *Both Sides Now*. Of course, these were the very songs that other artists had fixed on to record. Both Tom Rush and Dave Van Ronk changed the title of *Both Sides Now* to *Clouds* for their albums. Judy Collins dropped the comma that Joni had been using after the second word in her title. Collins credits Rush with pitching *Both Sides, Now* to her over the telephone. She recalls the incident vividly in her 1987 biography *Trust Your Heart*: "The first time I heard *Both Sides Now* was on a phone in 1967 in the middle of the night. I got a call from Tom Rush, who was very excited. Tom, a great fan of Joni's, had earlier introduced me to her fine song *The Circle Game.* 'Joni has a new song and I want you to hear it. I think you'll love it.' He put Joni on the phone and she sang *Both Sides Now*. I immediately fell in love with the song and knew it was a classic."

Rush does not remember the incident. In fact, he disagrees with Judy one hundred percent. As he revealed to Wally Breese, "She (Joni) told me once, 'You know when I wrote *Clouds*, I really thought it would suit you, Tom.' But she sent it to Judy Collins." Rush denies that he pitched it to Collins, saying, "Judy's memory is flawed. I don't think that's true because I remember being mildly miffed that Judy got the song before I did! Now I did, early on, send Judy some Joni Mitchell songs. Maybe that's what she is remembering."

Judy Collins recorded *Both Sides Now* on September 28, 1967 at Columbia Studios in New York. Her producer Joshua Rifkin conducted the orchestra and played the familiar harpsichord part that will forever be associated with Joni's best-known song. Before Joni packed up and headed west, Judy visited her at her flat on West 16th Street, and the two bonded. "Joni and I had dinner together," Judy wrote in her biography, "and talked about triumph and disaster. Joni's apartment was filled with candles and crystal and velvet tapestries, a long way from log cabins and mountain winds. She prepared chicken and salad, and we ate our meal sitting at a low table."

The romance between Crosby and Mitchell was challenged soon enough when Joni went on tour and met the Hollies' Graham Nash during an engagement at a club in Ottawa. When the Hollies hit LA, a road weary Nash visited Crosby and collapsed. Joni "played Florence Nightingale," and then took Nash home with her to her new house in Laurel Canyon. She was open to simultaneous relationships with both musicians, but Crosby soon returned to his former girlfriend. "It only stopped being fun when I started producing her first record," Crosby later told Wally Breese. "We were starting to have friction and at the same time I was starting to produce her record and I didn't really know how."

Despite making some technical errors involving microphones and tape hiss, which he and Joni solved by erasing some of the overdubs and thus making the album even sparser than they had intended, Joni's debut album was a splendid acoustic beginning. However, it was a surprise for Reprise executives who had expected a rollicking folk-rock production.

> Oh but now old friends they're acting strange
> They shake their heads, they say I've changed
> Well something's lost, but something's gained
> In living every day.

Judy Collins' *Both Sides Now* was released as a single in the fall of 1968 and rose to number 8 on the *Billboard* chart by the end of the year. Collins' version of *Chelsea Morning* inspired Bill and Hilary Clinton to name their daughter Chelsea. Joni Mitchell's happy days with Graham Nash were chronicled in his song *Our House* before she moved on to a romance with James Taylor. Her own version of *Both Sides Now* was included on CLOUDS, a second album that sold much better than her enigmatic debut had sold.

As the demand for Joni's presence at festivals and concerts grew, she surprised journalists by telling them that "I liked playing in small clubs the best, still do. I never liked the roar of a big crowd. I could never adjust to the sound of people gasping at the mere mention on my name. David Geffen used to tell me that I was the only star that he knew that wanted to be ordinary."

Despite her reticence to play before large audiences, Joni Mitchell eventually played the Royal Albert Hall in London and Carnegie Hall in Manhattan. She was a big hit at Newport in '67, but nearly missed the event altogether. As she recalls, "Judy stood me up, and she was my hero. It was kind of heartbreaking. I waited and waited and waited, and she never did come to pick me up to take me to Newport." Joni went there alone and recalls that "When I played there, I got that large roar and it made me incredibly nervous."

Joni Mitchell retired from performing soon after composing *Woodstock*, which became an anthem for a generation of rock & roll fans when it was recorded by Mathew's Southern Comfort and Crosby, Stills, Nash & Young. She came back with a unique album, BLUE, two years later.

By 1970, *Both Sides Now* had been covered by many instrumentalists, including Chet Atkins, Floyd Cramer, Percy Faith, Stan Getz, Dizzy Gillespie, Mantovani, Boots Randolph, and the best-selling piano duo of Ferrante & Teicher. Frank Sinatra, Bing Crosby, Robert Goulet, Dion, Andy Williams, Glen Campbell, and Nana Mouskouri also recorded it. Since then, more than 802 cover versions of *Both Sides Now* have been issued, and many of the great vocalists of the 20th century, such as Anne Murray, Cleo Laine, Neil Diamond, and Willie Nelson, have made their own records of Joni Mitchell's classic song.

Ironically, in 1998, after more than 30 years in the music business and nearly as many albums, Joni told Austin deejay Jody Denburg that "I'm a painter first, and a musician second." Most of her fans were well aware of at least some of her paintings, even if they'd never been to an exhibition in an art gallery. Some of us have developed a sincere affection for those paintings, like the self portrait that Joni painted for the cover of her February 2000 release of her BOTH SIDES NOW album, which combines her songs with a selection of standards to explore the dynamics of human relationships. Accompanied by a classy orchestra conducted by Vince Mendoza at Air Studios in London, Joni delivered yet another cover version of her signature song.

Joni Mitchell has written some of the most memorable lyrics of the 20th century, including one of my all-time favorite lines: "I wish I had a river I could skate away on . . ." But the haunting, beautiful melody and simple, no frills language of *Both Sides, Now* have become ingrained in the mind of an entire generation of baby boomers who are not likely to forget them in this lifetime.

I've looked at life from both sides now
From up and down, and still somehow
It's life's illusions I recall
I really don't know life at all

Born to Be Wild

Steppenwolf
Words and Music by Mars Bonfire

Get your motor runnin'
Head out on the highway . . .

Both the early heavy metal band Steppenwolf and the counterculture movie *Easy Rider* had their origins in Toronto. It was there, in the hippie ghetto of Yorkville in 1964, where vocalist, guitarist, and harmonica player John Kay joined the Sparrows, a Canadian group modeled on British Invasion bands. The Sparrows would migrate first to New York City and eventually to Los Angeles, where they signed a record deal with ABC Dunhill, changed their name to Steppenwolf, and recorded their debut album in December 1967.

That same year, Peter Fonda attended a film exhibitor's convention in Toronto to promote his latest AMI film, *The Trip*, in which he co-starred with Bruce Dern and Dennis Hopper. After giving a short speech at the convention, Fonda retired to his room in the Lakeshore Motel and began signing the hundreds of 8 x 10 glossies that were to be handed out to autograph seekers. While he was scribbling away, the idea for a new film popped into his head. As he recalls, "I was a little bit loaded, and I looked at a photograph from *The Wild Angels* of me and Bruce Dern on a chopper. Suddenly, I thought, 'That's it! That's the modern western; two cats just riding across the country . . . And they make a big score, see, so they have a lot of money. And they're gonna cross the country and go retire to Florida . . . when a couple of duck poachers in a truck rip 'em off because they don't like the way they look.'"

Lookin' for adventure
And whatever comes our way . . .

A call to Dennis Hopper set the wheels in motion for the filming of *Easy Rider*. Terry Southern was called in to flesh out Fonda's treatment into a full shooting script. Bruce Dern was considered to play the role of the hitchhiker who gets killed en route, but eventually Jack Nicholson, who had written the script of *The Trip*, was chosen to play the part instead. Filming began in March 1968 during the annual New Orleans' Mardi Gras festival.

John Kay was born in East Germany in 1944, and brought to the West when his mother escaped a few years later. Immigrating to Canada when he was a teenager, he lived in Toronto for five years, before his family moved to Buffalo, and then to California. By late 1964, he had returned to Yorkville, where he worked in a nightclub and slept on the floor of a friend's apartment. The invitation to join the Sparrows came when the band kicked out their lead singer, Jack London, because he had been ripping off the rest of them. The Sparrows lineup consisted of brothers Dennis and Jerry Edmonton on guitar and drums, Nick St. Nicholas on vocals and bass, and Goldy McJohn on keyboards. The band dug John's ability to sing and play, but an image makeover was needed immediately. "He looked like James Dean," Jerry would later say, "black hair, greasy and combed back. He was a bit pudgy and was wearing white Levis, which I thought was a bit odd. I took him down to Cy Mann for some decent clothes and we washed his hair."

Yeah darlin' go make it happen
Take the world in a love embrace . . .

With John Kay on board, the group had the lineup they needed to seek a record contract. They rehearsed and gigged relentlessly. Not long after this, John and Nick began double-dating two German waitresses who had begun circulating in the Yorkville scene. It was the beginning of a life-long relationship for John Kay and Jutta Maue, who eventually married. Kay remembers this time spent in Yorkville as one of the best interludes of his life. "It was one of those rare situations where your private and professional lives totally merged," he told *After The Gold Rush* author Nicholas Jennings. "During the week, Yorkville was this isolated oasis of lifestyle and attitude. The Sparrows' gear was set up at El Patio or Chez Monique where we would rehearse in the day and play at night. And the village was our home. We ate at the Mont Blanc restaurant. And when we got the munchies, we'd go to the Grab Bag, which was sort of a hip 7-11. People lived above stores, it was a real community, and musically you could check out what everyone else was doing because it was all right there."

Moving to New York City, the Sparrows secured a gig at Arthur's, where they played for the jet set and were discovered by Columbia Records producer, David Kapralik. Signed to Columbia, they changed their name to The Sparrow and recorded and released *Tomorrow's Ship b/w Isn't It Strange*. Since leaving Toronto, the band had stretched out some and become much more focused and intense. As *Toronto Star* reporter Stan Fischler noted in his review of their show at Arthur's, their new sound was "Musical LSD a modern tonal thunderstorm."

Fire all your guns at once
And explode into space . . .

The band lived in the Hotel Albert, a Greenwich Village location where the Lovin' Spoonful had rehearsed before signing with Kama Sutra. "Their song *Summer In The City* was a hit when we arrived at the Albert," John Kay recalls. "The lobby had dozens of framed 8 x 10's of everyone famous who had stayed there. During our stay a rotating cast of characters including sundry jazz musicians, the Butterfield Blues Band, the Blues Magoos, John Lee Hooker, John Hammond Jr., David Crosby and Michael Clarke of the Byrds, all checked in at various times. We took a suite on the 7th floor and stayed there most of the summer, except when we played out on Long Island."

Driving across the continent to California, The Sparrow hooked up with Toronto pals Neil Young and Bruce Palmer, former members of the Mynah Birds, who were now playing in Buffalo Springfield. Once again, they stayed at a musicians' haunt, Sandy Koufax's Tropicana Motel near their gig at the new Sunset Strip teen nightclub, It's Boss. Nick St. Nicholas recalls, "We went down there in the afternoon, set up our equipment, then went back to the Tropicana. When we returned that evening, there were no amplifiers. So, we contacted Bruce and Neil and went down to their management office, and they leant us some Fender Twin Reverb amps."

John Kay was struck by the changes that had gone down in the year since he had last been on the Strip. "When I had gone to Ciro's the previous year," he recalls, "the crowd was chiefly folkies and rockers. But now as It's Boss, the place had turned into a psychedelic day glow dungeon. By this time the Whisky had become *the* important club, the place where musicians and record company people congregated. We did a week there opening for the Sir Douglas Quintet, and again we went down well."

The Sparrow fled the area during the riots, when many of the clubs shut down temporarily, and ended up in San Francisco in December 1966. "The Haight-Ashbury scene was already blossoming, though fairly cool and localized long hair, hippie clothes, incense, love beads, and a lot of psychedelics," John recalls. "It reminded me of Yorkville in some ways, the Victorian homes turned into head shops and boutiques with colorful drapes and tie-dyes in the windows. Everywhere you went smelt of incense and marijuana. We moved over to the Cable Hotel on Lombard Street to get our bearings. Bill Graham's original Fillmore Ballroom had started up along with the Avalon and the Matrix, a folk club started by Marty Balin before he formed Jefferson Airplane."

The band's migration had alienated their Toronto backer, but they were able to locate a new mentor who helped them set up in a vacant house in Mill Valley. "When not gigging," Kay reported, "we set up our gear in the living room and rehearsed. Things looked promising." When he finally broke into the national spotlight a year later, John's eternal sunglasses and leather pants would encourage the media to typecast him as a biker musician. Little did some of them know that he was legally blind, a physical handicap that had kept him from being drafted when he was classified 4-F. There were times, though, that his poor eyesight provided a little more excitement than he had bargained for.

As Nick recalls, "John can't see very well. I remember once at the house in Mill Valley he saw everybody taking turns with a BB gun firing at a tethered ball on a pole in the backyard. So he figured, 'Shit, my eyes aren't that bad,' and he picked up the BB gun and aimed it and fired. What he couldn't see was that there was a window. The sliding glass door was shut so he shot a hole through the window. Goldy was on acid at the time, so John blamed him for it, and Goldy apologized."

It was during the band's stints at the Ark and the Matrix that they got to kick out all the blocks that had held them back playing in clubs where they were expected to play covers. Hoyt Axton's *The Pusher* became a show number at this time. As Jerry Edmonton recalls, "We had freedom in San Francisco to go long if we wanted to. We did *The Pusher* every night and the intro part, before John would get around to singing, just kind of evolved as a time for us to do whatever we wanted. One night, Nick came out of the kitchen banging on a pot and pan making weird sounds. He started putting on echo machines and it just went on its own. People started talking about the band after that. *The Pusher* got people saying 'there's this band from Canada and they're way out there.'"

A Columbia Records executive showed up and one more attempt to record for Columbia was made; however, during this same time immigration officials pressured the four Canadian boys, which was unsettling. Dennis Edmonton announced his intention to quit the group after they had completed their engagement at the Galaxy in Los Angeles. It was there that the group met 16-year-old Michael Monarch. "I was really impressed with them," Monarch recalls. "At that time, John was playing rhythm guitar and singing some of the vocals, and Nick was doing some of the vocals, so it wasn't John up front as the leader as it became in Steppenwolf. What really impressed me with the band was that Jerry was just a kick-ass drummer. Also Goldy was great on that old Lowry organ that he had beefed up."

On the last night in the Galaxy the band ended up bickering and broke up. Nick headed off to form a new band with Michael Monarch. Dennis focused on his songwriting, securing a contract with a publisher, and John, Jerry, and Goldy were momentarily left out in the cold. John soon turned to writing songs. By this time Jutta had secured a work visa and joined him in California, but the conditions of her immigration depended on them marrying within ten days of her arrival in LA.

Racin' with the wind
And feelin' that I'm under . . .

With none of his songwriting efforts leading to anything and a baby on the way, John and Jutta hung in there, living in a tiny apartment above a garage. Then one of their neighbors came to the rescue, a young ABC Dunhill Records producer by the name of Gabriel Mekler. Gabriel listened attentively to some of The Sparrow tapes and some of the new songs that John had been writing, and encouraged him to get as many members of the old group back together as he could. Gabriel also told John he would pay for the band to cut some demos and also suggested a new band name *Steppenwolf*, the title of the Herman Hesse novel he was reading at the time. John, Jerry and Goldy hired Michael Monarch to play guitar and Rushton Moreve to play bass.

"I was really young," Monarch notes, "but I think they needed that, somebody with a rawness and energy. I thought the coolest thing to do was to turn my amp up a little louder than everyone wanted it. And I think that's part of what helped that band get started, a kind of raunchiness for the *Born To Be Wild* lyrics and for the image of the band." Drummer Jerry Edmonton recalls that "Rushton came down to the garage and he looked like a pirate. He walked in and he had this velvet Renaissance hat and the same little moustache I had. He looked just right, he was stoned, and it was casual. We started playing and it was like 'boom'! Like we had been playing together for years."

John Kay notes that he had pawned his Fender amp and Telecaster and was playing a loaner that was a hybrid "Mosrite body with a Vox neck." Goldy was still playing his same old Lowry organ through a Leslie speaker cabinet "that was so overdriven that it gave it a highly compressed sound. With Michael's buzz-saw guitar sound and Goldy's unique organ style, Steppenwolf had a much wider, fuller, nastier sound."

Everything came together when Dennis Edmonton, now calling himself Mars Bonfire, handed them a demo tape of his new song *Born To Be Wild*. "The demo tape that Steppenwolf originally heard of *Born To Be Wild*," Dennis notes, "was not from the demo sessions for my solo album that Jerry and a few others played on. It was just one guitar and one voice." On that rough demo tape Dennis had been playing around with John Hammond Jr. blues riffs. "I was fooling around with some of his riffs and guitar patterns," he recalls, "changing them around into my own thing. One of those riffs became the foundation for *Born To Be Wild*." Dennis's inspiration came to him one day when he saw an advertisement for the latest model motorbike. "I was walking down Hollywood Boulevard one day," he explains, "and saw a poster in a window saying 'Born To Be Wild' with a picture of a motorcycle erupting out of the earth like a volcano with all this fire around it. I had just purchased my first car, a little second-hand Ford Falcon. So, all of this came together lyrically, the idea of a motorcycle coming out, along with the freedom and joy I felt in having my first car and being able to drive myself around whenever I wanted."

Like a true mother's child
We were born, born to be wild . . .

At this same time, Peter Fonda and Dennis Hopper were in the midst of filming their biker movie, working title *The Loners*. However, after signing with Bert Schneider and Bob Rafelson's new BBS Films Company, Fonda's project had run afoul of Hopper's lack of experience, his tendency to lecture and pontificate rather than plan astutely, and his habit of drinking a lot and erupting into violent temper tantrums. Coupled with Hopper's capacity to consume copious quantities of amphetamines, psychedelics and whatever other drugs were around, directing his first film had made him feisty. By mid-production of the movie that would eventually become the trendsetting *Easy Rider*, he had Fonda fearing for his life, having been threatened on more than one occasion at knifepoint by his director.

As producer as well as actor, Fonda had already survived the crisis that had come up when Terry Southern had copped out on the scriptwriting and he had to finish the script himself. Now he was dealing with a mad demon of a director who was also deathly afraid of riding bikes and could barely stay on his Harley long enough to shoot the scenes where they were racing through the countryside. Hopper was always eager to get off his hog at the end of the day, plus he was rewriting the script as they went along. The day they finished shooting their choppers were stolen. They celebrated with a wrap party, and only then remembered that they hadn't filmed the campfire scene where Fonda says, "We blew it." They went back into production. And when they finally finished up, Hopper locked himself away in an editing room and began cutting the film to a hastily assembled sound track of rock & roll tunes that he had gathered while they were filming. One of those songs was *Born To Be Wild*. Another was Steppenwolf's *The Pusher*. It was Hopper's use of this raw rock music that revolutionized movie soundtracks.

Meanwhile, the studio and Fonda had commissioned Crosby, Stills & Nash to write them a nice little soundtrack that would sound something like CSN's debut album. Their director was not on the same page. First Hopper managed to get CSN fired and the studio and Fonda to accept his ragged rock & roll soundtrack. Then he delivered his first rough cut, which was more than four hours long. There was some good stuff in what he had done. Emulating the jump cut style of the French New Wave filmmakers, who had not used traditional Hollywood, dissolves and fades because they couldn't afford them, gave Hopper's edit a fast-paced documentary-like style. He also favored the underground filmmaker approach of leaving in technical imperfections like lens flairs, which the major studio editors religiously cut out of their montage. But his idea that the film could be shown in two, two-hour segments, as had been done with epic productions like *Lawrence of Arabia* and *The Ten Commandments,* was totally off the mark. They didn't have a star-studded lineup or subject matter that would entice audiences to sit in theaters that long. Frustrated but cool enough to deal with the situation, Bert Schneider shipped Hopper and his girlfriend of the day off to Taos for a month-long vacation and hired his own editors who brought the film in at the traditional 90-minute length.

We can climb so high
I never want to die . . .

The new Steppenwolf lineup had experienced a similar number of stop and go moves leading up to the release of their debut album. They had set off alarms in nearby shops with their loud rehearsal volume that summoned angry cops. They arrived late for their demo session, but then nailed 11 songs onto two-track in record time. Jay Lasker, wasn't sure at first about signing them but got a thumbs up from his teenage daughter and her friends. Reb Foster & Associates agreed to manage them and advance them money to get their instruments out of hock, buy a new van, and pay off their pressing personal debts. However, their first attempt to record their album ran afoul of traditional engineers who wouldn't let them turn up their amps. When they booked more time at American Recording and hooked up with Richard Podolor, who had produced Sandy Nelson's *Teenbeat* and the Hollywood Argyles' *Alley Oop*, they had the situation they needed with engineer Bill Cooper. As John Kay recalls, "On the first day we knocked off seven songs in a row. They all sounded killer. We were ready. We knew those songs inside and out. We had our whole lives to get ready for this album; we had rehearsed the songs over and over in the garage and played them at gigs as well. Each song was done in two takes at the most, with the attitude: 'make each part count and pull its weight.'"

"The original band had that kind of chemistry together," Bill Cooper notes, "that allowed them to come in and crank something out in four days." Richard Polodor's experience came into play during the mixing phase. As Cooper relates, "During the mix-down, that's when Richard really takes over. For example, on the drum break in *Born To Be Wild*, the band thought it was just a part of the song, but Richard, who's a real excitable guy, started jumping up and down screaming that it was great and punched it up, putting echo on it. And he was right. It was an important feature of the song. Gabriel Mekler wasn't one of those straight-laced company types, but I don't think he had much to do with the Steppenwolf sound. He got the contract and he gave them their name, but he didn't mould their sound or anything."

Steppenwolf's contract stipulated two albums a year so they were back in the studio before they knew what hit them. They didn't have an arsenal of songs but came up with the marvelous *Magic Carpet Ride*, written by John to a bass pattern of Rushton Moreve's. Moreve subsequently went AWOL because he thought California was going to sink into the ocean during an earthquake. With Nick St. Nicholas back in the band, Steppenwolf was four-fifths the original Sparrows lineup. The addition of local guitarist Mike Monarch was a serious strength, and Dennis Edmonton, a.k.a. Mars Bonfire, was still helping out from the sidelines with advice and songwriting. With *Magic Carpet Ride* Steppenwolf broke new ground. The song was definitely upbeat and positive without being at all sucky: "Well, you don't know what we can find / Why don't you come with me little girl / On a magic carpet ride."

One afternoon in early '69, film company executives invited John to a screening of *Easy Rider*. The execs couldn't afford to pay the usual fees upfront because BBS Films was a fledgling company. They wanted permission to work something out. As John recalls, "Phil Spector and I arrived a little late and caught the tail end of *The Pusher* scene, and then heard *Born To Be Wild* with Fonda and Hopper riding across the screen. We thanked them for including our songs and offered to work something out for compensation. Rumor had it that Dylan wanted to write some new stuff, which he felt would be more appropriate, but they said they wanted *It's Alright Ma (I'm Only Bleeding)* because it fit perfectly. Dylan didn't agree, so on the soundtrack Roger McGuinn sang the song. We just said, 'Cool movie. Thanks for thinking of us. Send us the check.'"

Easy Rider became a film classic, one of the movies that broke the back of the old star system and made way for the director-driven films of the seventies. It also established a new convention of using rock bands for soundtracks that would be solidified when George Lucas followed up with *American Graffiti* in 1973. One of the reasons for the success of Fonda and Hopper's counterculture film seems glaringly obvious today, however, before they made it only Fonda and Hopper could see the need to do it. As Dennis Hopper recalls, "Nobody had ever seen themselves portrayed in a movie. At every love-in across the country people were smoking grass and dropping LSD, while audiences were still watching Doris Day and Rock Hudson." No doubt, the funding that came together so quickly to enable the producers of *Woodstock* to turn their festival into a major motion picture was easier to pry from the hands of investors after the immediate box office success of *Easy Rider* in the early summer of 1969.

Born to be wild
Born to be wild . . .

"What *Easy Rider* did for us," John Kay sums up, "was to spread the Steppenwolf name worldwide, paving the way for us to tour internationally, especially in Europe." With his trademark sunglasses, John Kay and Steppenwolf would become established with early heavy metal fans as the ultimate biker band with the ultimate biker anthem. Forty-five years down the road in the summer of 2012, despite persistent rumors of their retirement, they were still playing bikers' festivals.

American Woman

The Guess Who

Words & Music by Burton Cummings, Randy Bachman, Gary Peterson, Jim Kale

© 1970, Shillelagh Music Company (BMI)

American Woman, stay away from me
American Woman, mama let me be

It began as a riff, the same smouldering, rebellious Randy Bachman guitar riff that you hear on the record at a Guess Who concert in a curling rink in Kitchener, Ontario in the summer of '69. Randy started it off like that, trumpeting a message to his band mates that he had replaced his broken guitar string and finished re-tuning his guitar. It was time to get back to work. He could see two of the guys, bass player Jim Kale and drummer Garry Peterson, who had stepped down from the stage to get some refreshments while he went about his task. They had begun to make their way back to the stage, but Burton Cummings was nowhere to be seen. The kid was probably out in the parking lot behind the venue smoking a joint or chatting up one of the cute young girls that had been hanging around the stage. Bachman was not amused. The notoriety that the band had experienced with the release of *These Eyes*, their first Top 10 *Billboard* hit, had sown the seeds of dissention with their ranks. And when the media hailed the release as the beginning of a Canadian Invasion, it had swelled some heads even further.

Randy had been through this once before, back in '65 when *Shakin' All Over* had taken off up the *Billboard* charts. They were still in high school and they had dropped everything and gone to New York only to find that a promised booking on *The Ed Sullivan Show* had merely been a ruse to maneuver them into a vulnerable position. Chad Allan had been their vocalist then, and they had made the best they could of that situation, toured with the Kingsmen, the Turtles, Dion & the Belmonts, and the Crystals, and recorded in the Scepter Records studio in New

York. However, their Scepter follow-up releases to *Shakin' All Over* hadn't exactly set the world on fire, and they returned to Winnipeg. Chad Allan quit, replaced by Burton Cummings, who was 18 when he joined the band. Now he was barely 22 and full of himself, turning into a party-hardy monster at inappropriate moments. Randy was 25 and he wasn't willing to let this one slip away. He was married and converted to the Mormon faith. There was no way he was going to become sidetracked by drugs and booze and lose his focus. As a Mormon, he had strict beliefs and a work ethic that had helped him to become the great guitarist everybody said he was. He had been taught by Lenny Breau and earned the respect of topnotch guys like Neil Young. The young guitar players on the Winnipeg scene were always showing up at their gigs and copping his licks. He looked out into the curling rink audience. The crowd was restless and a little pissed off, but he had caught their attention. He closed his eyes and squeezed some more notes out of his strings. His fingers flew across the fret-board and he squeezed again, and when he heard Jim Kale's big, fat Fender Bass notes fall in beneath his riff, he began to relax.

Don't come a hangin' around my door
I don't wanna see your face no more
I got more important things to do
Than spend my time growin' old with you

"It started as a jam," Jim Kale recalls. "We were playing in Ontario after being on the road in the States, trying to solidify our hold on the American marketplace with *These Eyes*." Randy could hear Garry Peterson's drumsticks on his snare, and then the thud of his bass drum pedal. He looked up and grinned at his band mates. Man oh man, it was hot up there under the lights. He was sweating. "In order to dispel the ominous air that was hanging over the place as we raced on the stage," Kale explains, "one by one we picked up on just this simple rhythm. Cummings came up, ad-libbed some lyrics, and it worked. It was an accident completely spontaneous."

By the early '60s, the Winnipeg band scene had exploded. Burton Cummings estimates that there were nearly 200 teenage bands vying for gigs during that brief, hectic moment in time when Winnipeg became a sort of Canadian Liverpool. The great jazz guitarist, Lenny Breau, who would go on to tour with Anne Murray and swap licks with Chet Atkins, had the best gig in town. He was two years older than Bachman and the leader of the house band on CBC TV's weekly *Music Hop* show. Neil Young & the Squires were hitting the road and gigging in exotic, far away locales like Thunder Bay and Yorkville. Neil soon became a major influence on the Sunset Strip scene as a member of Buffalo Springfield. Even before they morphed into the Guess Who with a big hit on American radio stations, Chad Allan & the Reflections were acknowledged to be the best band in town. Allan Kowbel, aka Chad Allan, was the best entertainer. Randy Bachman was regarded as a guitar god. Jim Kale was the best bass player, Bob Ashley, the best piano player, and Garry Peterson, the best drummer. They were the first local band to quit playing Shadows, Ventures, and Fireballs instrumentals and turn up the heat with British Invasion sounds.

Quality Records had capitalized on their gritty new music and created a buzz by mailing out promotional copies of their latest Canadian single *Shakin' All Over* with just the song title and the words "Guess Who" on the label. There was supposed to be some sort of contest to rename the band, but deejays from coast to coast used the mystery created as an opportunity to spread rumors that the cut was by a Beatles and Stones supergroup with Eric Clapton on lead guitar.

Burton Cummings was one of the younger boys who were starting up their own bands and following in the Reflections and Squires' footsteps. His band was called the Deverons. When he was younger, Burton's mom had to force him to practice his piano lessons. After he heard Jerry Lee Lewis and Little Richard pounding their pianos and screaming *Great Balls Of Fire* and *Tutti Fruiti* on the radio, his mom no longer had to motivate him. Right from the start he had high hopes. As he recalls, "During either grade seven or eight, my friend Ed Smith got a black Silvertone electric guitar. He and I listened to the Ventures and the Fireballs with Doug and Dwight Sparks. Watching those guys play Ventures and Fireballs records in their bedrooms was the first concrete recollection that I have of thinking, "Hey, wait a minute, maybe someone from Winnipeg *could* make it from here!"

The Deverons were one of many north end bands with aspirations to take their music beyond the garage, so they built up a solid repertoire of cover songs and soon became popular at teen hops and high school dances. "Whenever our band wasn't playing," Burton recalls, "I'd check around to see where Chad Allan and the boys were playing. We always went to see them. Ed Smith and I must have seen them eight or ten times before I even got friendly with them, before I even talked to them. We'd go and stand back about a hundred feet because we were so intimidated."

In April 1965, Gerry & the Pacemakers played the Winnipeg Arena. The Deverons were invited to open for Chad Allan & the Reflections, who were opening for the Pacemakers. Already legends in their home stomping grounds, Chad Allan & the Reflections quickly evolved into Chad Allan & the Expressions, and then into the Guess Who. Their *Shakin' All Over* was awesome, a number 22 smash in the summer of '65 on the *Billboard* chart. The Rolling Stones came to town the following spring and shortly after that a plane carrying the Beatles touched down briefly to refuel. Meanwhile, all the local bands including the Deverons had big plans. With Chad and Randy on the road, and Neil Young gone off to seek fame and fortune elsewhere, there were plenty of gigs to be had. Car dealerships and department stores were hiring bands for special promotions. The Winnipeg Blue Bombers had begun to feature local bands doing half time shows at their CFL home games.

The Deverons were cool. They had let their hair grow some and worked on their stage presence, image, and wardrobe. As Burton recalls, "We had our round-collared Beatle jackets, our Rolling Stones look with jean jackets, black turtlenecks like Manfred Mann, and our Pretty Things look where we all dressed grubby."

A day after returning from a recording session in Minnesota, the Deverons lead singer got a call that put an end to their aspirations. Cummings was invited to join the Guess Who ... and he accepted. "I was primarily asked to join as a keyboard player," he explains. "They wanted me because I was a young guy making a lot of noise around town, jumping on pianos." Limited to a secondary role as vocalist, Cummings soon upstaged Chad Allan, and Allan quit the group. "I found it very difficult to be on the same stage with Cummings," Allan told John Einarson. "Our personalities were diametrically opposed." So were their musical tastes. Allan's repertoire represented the ultimate Canadian British Invasion band vocalist. Cummings represented the harder edged psychedelic sound that was coming out of southern California. Chad Allan would eventually tell interviewers that his decision to leave the band had been a little more complicated than merely his exasperation with a young, upstart vocalist. He had enjoyed the band when they had gigged on weekends, but had not enjoyed being on the road night after night. "I was just simply drained and tired and my throat was pretty much blown at the time," he confessed. "It just got to a point where I got really sick, and I was just physically and psychologically drained and was just pushing too hard. I needed a break."

At first, things didn't go at all smoothly for the new Guess Who lineup. A trip to England, where a King Records release of *His Girl* was getting some chart action, fizzled just like the trip to New York and the Scepter deal. Returning to Winnipeg broke and dispirited, the Guess Who were prepared to eat some humble pie. Rescue was at hand, however, in the form of Chad Allan who had replaced Ray St. Germaine as host of *Music Hop*, which was being revamped and renamed as the *Let's Go* show. The new theme song was a Routers' instrumental hit that had been covered by the Ventures. They could handle that, no problem. Chad hired them as his house band. It was a cherry gig that paid union scale. *Let's Go* was broadcast from coast to coast, and it wasn't long before they got a phone call from Toronto.

Someone had heard the original songs that they were playing on TV and wanted more of the same for an album that would be sponsored by *Coca-Cola*. The Guess Who was to be featured on one side and the Ottawa band the Staccatos were to be featured on the flip. As Randy Bachman recalls, "*Coca-Cola* put out this album, which you bought with ten *Coca-Cola* caps and a dollar. And it sold over 50,000 copies. It would have been the first Canadian 'gold' album, except that it wasn't sold retail for $3.98. So, we couldn't get it certified. But it was really a great album, and it was mixed by Phil Ramone. Phil came to Toronto. Jack Richardson produced that album. He was the staff producer for McCann-Erickson, the big advertising firm, and did all the Coke commercials."

Jack Richardson liked their music so much he mortgaged his house and started Nimbus 9 Records. "Cummings and I went and wrote 15 or 16 songs," Bachman told me in 1995. "Ben McPeak, who was a great arranger, and did a lot of things with the Toronto Symphony, wrote charts for *These Eyes*; the strings and cellos and whatever else. He picked three or four songs. We didn't want every song to be covered in strings; we were a rock band. But *These Eyes* was a very special song. We knew it. And we had done it live around Winnipeg for a year or so, and we had done it live on the TV show. We went to New York and recorded *These Eyes* at Phil Ramone's A&R Studios and did the rest of WHEATFIELD SOUL. That was the beginning! When it came out, it had a special sound on the radio. And it still sounds good today."

Jack Richardson didn't even blink when Canadian deejays refused to play *These Eyes* because it was by a Canadian band that had pretended to be a British Invasion band. He promoted it in four key American radio markets, and when it took off up the *Billboard* chart, Canuck deejays were forced to play it. His diligence was rewarded by a deal with RCA and sales of more than one million copies, the Guess Who's first gold record. *These Eyes* peaked at number 6 on the *Billboard* Hot 100. *Laughing* stalled at number 10. And in January 1970 *No Time*, the lead single from AMERICAN WOMAN, began its rise to number 5. They were on a roll.

American Woman, get away from me
American Woman, mama let me be
Don't come a knockin' around my door
Don't wanna see your shadow no more
Colored lights can hypnotize
Sparkle someone else's eyes
Now Woman, I said get away
American Woman, listen what I say-ay-ay-ay

Burton Cummings dashed back into the Kitchener curling rink and scrambled up onto the stage, but he couldn't recognize the song his mates were playing. "We're jamming in E," Randy yelled, "play something." He sat at his piano and took a solo, picked up his harmonica and soloed, and reached for his flute. He was soloing his ass off and the band just kept cooking as if there was no end in sight. "Sing something," Bachman ordered. Cummings looked out over the throng of groovy Canadian chicks that kept pressing themselves closer and closer to the stage. After some of the weird stuff that had gone down on their tour through the American South, these girls looked real fine. He had already been up close and personal with a couple of real cuties during the break. To hell with American women, he thought, to hell with the war and the draft and the riot police, he was back in Canada and Bachman and the boys were cooking! He stepped to the microphone and belted out the first words that came into his head. "American woman . . . stay away from me . . ." The line sounded perfect. He sang it again, four times in all, before Bachman brought the jam to a crashing finale. Over the next few nights, Cummings added more lyrics, piling image upon image, stuff that was currently going down in urban ghettos and Southeast Asian jungles. "We thought it would make a great record," Bachman quipped during one interview. "I was up there alone, tuning up my E and B strings on an old Les Paul," he recalled during another. "I started playing that riff and in the audience, heads started turning. The band got up and I said, 'keep playing this, I don't want to forget it.' Out of the blue Burton just screamed, 'American Woman, stay away from me!' That was the song — the riff and Burton yelling that line over and over. Later, he added other lines like, "I don't need your war machine, your ghetto scenes." When the Guess Who played the song at the Seattle Pop Festival, the crowd of 150,000 fans, who were all hearing *American Woman* for the first time, went nuts.

American Woman, said get away
American Woman, listen what I say
Don't come a hangin' around my door
Don't wanna see your face no more
I don't need your war machines
I don't need your ghetto scenes

Most Canadians thought it was an anti-war anthem. Ironically, many Americans thought it praised their women. Some American women, like the President's daughter, Tricia Nixon, just loved it. In fact, Tricia Nixon loved their song so much that she lobbied her father to invite the Guess Who to play at the White House. They were scheduled to perform there during Prince Phillip's visit but told they'd better not play "that anti-war song." Whichever way people looked at it, *American Woman* was controversial, blatantly sexist if you interpreted every single word literally. On the other hand, it was rock & roll and it was at the same time celebratory. In my case, I was dating an American woman at the time it came out, and we both dug it a lot. The debate raged on in both the media and people's everyday lives.

Coloured lights can hypnotize
Sparkle someone else's eyes
Now Woman, get away from me
American Woman, mama let me be

Jim Kale's "take" on the song makes ultimate sense. "The popular misconception was that it was a chauvinistic tune, which was anything but the case," he maintains. "The fact was, we came from a very straitlaced, conservative, laid-back country, and all of a sudden there we were in Chicago, Detroit, New York all these horrendously large places with their big city problems. After that one particularly grinding tour, it was just a real treat to go home and see the girls we had grown up with. Also, the war was going on, and that was terribly unpopular. We didn't have a draft system in Canada, and we were grateful for that. A lot of people called it anti-American, but it wasn't really. We weren't anti-anything. John Lennon once said that the meanings of all songs come after they are recorded. Someone else has to interpret them."

American Woman entered the *Billboard* Top 40 in late March 1970. By early May it was resting at the top of the chart where it hung around for two more weeks, providing the Guess Who with their third gold record and Canadian artists with their very first *Billboard* number one. Randy Bachman left the band a week later, citing health concerns and lifestyle differences as his reasons for leaving. The Guess Who soldiered on, but the breakup of Canada's first great rock & roll songwriting team severely cramped their style.

Lyrics	Notation
Go, gotta get away, gotta get away now go, go, go	
I'm gonna leave you woman	
Gonna leave you woman	
Bye-bye . . . Bye-bye . . . Bye-bye . . . Bye-bye	
You're no good for me	
I'm no good for you	
Gonna look you right in the eye	
Tell you what I'm gonna do	
You know I'm gonna leave	
You know I'm gonna go	
You know I'm gonna leave	

As Burton Cummings later admitted, their collaborations had been marvelous. "It was chemistry," Cummings told interviewers. "I learned a lot from him because I was only 18 when I joined the band in December 1965." Randy Bachman went on to form Brave Belt with Chad Allan and then BTO with Fred Turner and his own younger brothers. Burton Cummings' solo career took off in 1976 with the release of a self-titled album and the Top 10 *Billboard* hit *Stand Tall*. He continued to score Top 40 hits in Canada with *I'm Scared* and the infectious, driving *My Own Way To Rock*. For many years the bad feelings between Randy and Burton remained unresolved. Then in 1983 at the request of Manitoba Premier Gary Filmon, they buried the hatchet and shared a stage for the first Guess Who reunion as part of the province's centennial celebrations. A short tour ensued and a live album was released. Then as the millennium came to a close, Lenny Kravitz covered *American Woman* and all of a sudden there was renewed interest in the Guess Who. You began hearing *American Woman* in Nike commercials, Tommy Hilfiger jeans commercials, and Castrol Oil advertisements, and on August 8th 1999 the original Guess Who played four songs during the closing ceremonies of the Pan Am Games. They performed *No Time, These Eyes, Undun,* and *American Woman* and were paid $200,000. A combined live and television audience of nearly one million witnessed the event, and the stage was set for their long anticipated reunion tour, which is said to have grossed nearly five million dollars. Lenny Kravitz' version of their song appeared on the soundtrack of Mike Meyers'

Austin Powers II: The Spy Who Shagged Me. And in September 2000 at the MuchMusic Video Awards in Toronto, where the Guess Who were handed Lifetime Achievement awards, Kravitz joined them on stage during their performance of the song that had made the Guess Who a household name, *American Woman*. Randy and Burton have continued to tour with their Bachman-Cummings Band throughout the new millennium and *American Woman* continues to be the highlight of their shows.

You know I'm gonna go-o, woman
I'm gonna leave you woman
Goodbye American woman
Goodbye American chick

THE STORY BEHIND

Snowbird

Anne Murray   Words & Music by Gene MacLellan

© 1970, EMI Blackwood Music Inc.

Beneath this snowy mantle cold and clean
The unborn grass lies waiting for its coat to turn to green
The snowbird sings a song he always sings
And speaks to me of flowers that will bloom again in spring

It is spring 1970 and Capitol Records executives in New York, Nashville, and Hollywood are scratching their heads as they try to figure out how to market a barefoot Canadian singing gym teacher. Their Toronto subsidiary has just handed them a made-in-Canada album titled THIS WAY IS MY WAY by Anne Murray. Murray is cute as a button. She can sing like a thrush. In addition, she's at home in front of a television camera after being featured on a national TV show produced in Halifax.

The Capitol execs consider releasing Anne's cover of *Snowbird*, written by singer-songwriter Gene MacLellan, but decide instead to promote MacLellan's *Bidin' My Time* to radio deejays. Despite Capitol Canada's Paul White's protests, records are pressed on both sides of the border, with *Bidin' My Time* on the A-side and *Snowbird* on the B-side.

Things don't always work out exactly as planned, Paul White recalls. "A guy named Happy Wilson worked his butt off, and went around to every radio station in the country, pushing *Bidin' My Time*. It began to show up on the tip sheets but radio stations began listening to the flip. Then stations in Canada followed. It went on to become a million seller." The B-side became one of the most popular songs in Canadian recording history and the title of Anne Murray's debut album for the American market. *Snowbird* and Anne Murray became synonymous, leaving Gene MacLelland in obscurity. There would be many more best-selling albums for Anne, a shelf load of Grammy Awards in America, and more Juno Awards than any other Canadian artist. She became "our Anne," no less endearing than that other famous Maritimer, Anne of Green Gables, though she was not a product of the imagination.

Anne Murray was born in Springhill, Nova Scotia on June 20, 1945. Her father was a doctor, her mother, a registered nurse. From an early age, she demonstrated that she had a natural talent for singing. "As far back as I can remember, I sang," she explains. "The first time I became aware that I could sing maybe a little better than others, I was driving in a car. I was nine years old, and I was singing along to the radio. My aunt-to-be was in the front seat and she turned to my mother and said 'My, Marion, she has a beautiful voice.' I later found out that Aunt Kay was tone deaf, but I guess it doesn't mean she couldn't detect talent!" Growing up in a large family with five brothers, she was noted to be competitive, excelling in sports and getting good grades in all her school classes. She would later observe that "I often think that perhaps the reason I became a successful singer was that, as a kid, I could never do anything as well as my brothers. I wanted to do something better than they did."

When the opportunity to sing on TV arrived, Murray began performing barefoot on *Singalong Jubilee*, a summer replacement for the popular *Don Messer's Jubilee* in 1966. She continued the tradition when she was hired to sing on CBC-TV's *Let's Go* show two years later. *Singalong Jubilee* music director Brian Ahern convinced Anne to move to Toronto to launch an international career. He would produce her first ten albums. She soon followed, accompanied by producer Bill Langstroth, who had discovered her, and would eventually marry her. Leonard Rambeau, a local promoter, became her manager. Murray and her cohorts were dubbed "Barefoot Annie" and the "Maritime Mafia" by the Toronto media. As Patrick Conlon observed in *Toronto Life*, "Little Miss Snowbird is surrounded by a canny clan of downeasters who manage her the way Dalton Camp managed Bob Stanfield."

In addition to Langstroth, Ahern, and Rambeau, lawyer David Matheson and accountant Lyman McInnis were crucial in setting up and running Anne's Balmur management company. According to Murray, she coined the term "Maritime Mafia." She also claimed that she wished she had never uttered the words, which were tossed off lightly at a vulnerable moment when she was suffering from the flu while accepting a Juno Award.

Anne Murray's arrival in the financial capital of the country coincided with a coordinated effort by Canadian arts agencies to create a Canadian star system and a homegrown music industry. The likes of Paul Anka, Neil Young, and Joni Mitchell would not need to emigrate to the United States to pursue a performing career and place their records on the *Billboard* charts.

National fervor was running high in the years that followed Expo '67 centennial celebrations. Canadian Prime Minister Pierre Trudeau acted swiftly to quell a Quebec Separatist terrorist threat by calling out the troops. He also appointed Pierre Juneau to head up a CRTC commission to examine how a Canadian music industry might be created. Juneau recommended that Canadian radio stations should give thirty percent of their airtime to playing music by Canadian artists. This proposal soon became the policy known as "CanCon." Anne Murray and Gordon Lightfoot were the first Canadian superstars to taste international success *and* continue to live in Canada. Canadians would soon have their own Grammys, the Juno Awards, named in tribute to Pierre Juneau.

Brian Ahern was the first of the "Maritime Mafia" to make the move to Toronto, where he produced low budget releases for Arc Records. They produced compilations of *Singalong Jubilee* performances for $1.98 an album. Arc also produced low budget solo albums. The best of these would be Catherine MacKinnon's debut album, which sold more than 200,000 of these $1.98 LPs. Anne Murray's first album was made for Arc at Bay Street Studios.

WHAT ABOUT ME was a folk pop album that included covers of Joni Mitchell's *Both Sides, Now* and Dylan's *The Last Thing On My Mind*. It sold well enough that Ahern, Langstroth, and Murray were able to shop her talents to several major labels. As she later revealed, "We wanted a bigger company, one that was a US subsidiary. We went around to a couple of them and they said they would give us $3,000, but they wanted to be in on the production. But even at Arc, Brian had creative freedom. So we went to Capitol and told them everything we wanted and they gave it to us. We were just flabbergasted." Ahern may have been less surprised than Murray, who had reluctantly quit her job as a gym teacher in Summerside, PEI. Bill Langstroth encouraged her and a romance sparked between the married TV producer and the friendly Murray.

Murray and Langstroth hid their blossoming romance, until Langstroth secured his divorce, by sharing a Toronto mansion with one of her brothers and members of her management team. Ahern was their fearless leader. "Brian had spent so much time convincing me I was the greatest thing since sliced bread," Anne told an early interviewer. "He kept saying, 'Now listen, before we go out to talk to the record companies, you are the most talented broad in the world, and I'm the most talented producer in the world, and together we're going to do it.' I said, 'Okay, Brian,' not believing it for one minute. I got what I expected from the other record companies. But when we went in to Paul White and said, 'We want this and we want that,' and by this time I was almost convinced, he said, 'Fine.' They gave us $18,000 to do the album."

When I was young my heart was young then, too
Anything that it would tell me, that's the thing that I would do
But now I feel such emptiness within
For the thing that I want most in life
Is the thing I can't win

Brian Ahern's genius was to recognize just how unique Anne Murray's voice really was. "The quality of her singing was incredible," bass player Skip Beckwith recalls. "She was dead in tune and she had this very interesting voice." Langstroth had been both smitten and impressed when she auditioned. "I thought she was singing to me right from the start," he admitted years later. "The voice went right through me and had me pinned like a specimen to the wall. Voompf!" Unbeknownst to Murray, Langstroth, and Ahern, Capital Records' A&R director Paul White was already a fan before they walked through his office door. As he recalls, "I started watching *Singalong Jubilee*, which was a rotten show, and every now and then out would trot this little blonde without any shoes on. Every time she came out, she was refreshing. I checked her out and found that she was already on another label." When he learned that Murray was seeking a better deal than Arc could offer, he was determined to sign her. "It was the easiest afternoon I've ever spent in my life," he says. "I don't think they came up with anything we couldn't go along with."

Anne Murray's Capitol Records contract called for two albums a year. THIS WAY IS MY WAY was recorded in the fall of 1969. The sessions for the follow up album HONEY, WHEAT & LAUGHTER were recorded at Vanguard Studios in New York in early 1970. Her first American release, SNOWBIRD, made use of the best tracks from both Canadian albums. The Bay Street sessions began in high spirits with the best musicians Ahern could put together. He was no longer fettered by a limited budget. Bassist Skip Beckwith, guitarist Amos Garrett, and drummer John Pace anchored the rhythm section as Ahern recorded the bed tracks on an eight-track machine, adding his own guitar rhythms. Several keyboard players, pedal steel player Buddy Cage, and multi-instrumentalist Maurice Beaulieu also contributed tracks. Ahern created the arrangements and called the shots, working with engineer Miles Wilkinson, who engineered and mixed Anne Murray's first ten albums. Rick Wilkins' string arrangement for *Snowbird* was the most elaborate connivance employed, the icing on the cake, so to speak, of what Ahern believed to be the track with the most potential. Nevertheless, when he deferred choice of the lead single to Paul White, White picked Eric Anderson's *Thirsty Boots*, which was not picked up by very many Canadian radio stations. The b-side of her second single, her first in the States, would soar all the way to number 10 on the *Billboard* country chart and number 8 on the pop chart.

> Spread your tiny wings and fly away
> And take the snow back with you
> Where it came from on that day
> The one I love forever is untrue
> And if I could you know that I would fly away with you

Brian Ahern's most remarkable accomplishment was the song selection on the first two Canadian albums. Each song was okayed by Murray. They included James Taylor's *Fire and Rain* before it was a hit for Taylor, a superb cover of Dylan's *I'll Be Your Baby Tonight*, and a third Gene MacLellan song, *Put Your Hand In The Hand*, which had hit single written all over it. Ahern and Murray pushed for a single release for *Put Your Hand In The Hand*, but Capitol hesitated and Arc impresario Bill Gilliland brought Janice Morgan's pop quintet Ocean in to record the song. Ocean's Arc release did well in Canada and even better in the States where it was released on Kama Sutra, rising to number 3 on the *Billboard* Hot 100 and selling more than 3 million records. Ultimately, failing to capitalize on the song would not matter because *Snowbird* also spent six weeks at number one on the relatively new Adult Contemporary chart. Crossing over from country to pop on a regular basis, Anne would own the "middle of the road" MOR and AC formats in both Canada and America for the next 20 years.

When *Snowbird* took off up the charts, the CBC signed Anne Murray to headline her own annual TV Specials. By summer 1970, Hollywood was calling and Anne was signed to guest appearances on *Glen Campbell's Goodtime Hour.* When she returned to Canada to rehearse with a touring band put together by Skip Beckwith, she was a star in her own right, Canada's own songbird.

Touring with a band in America and juggling television appearances and Grammy nominations proved to be a challenge for Murray and her team. "I was a complete and total wreck," Murray confessed to one journalist. In December 1970, when Murray misfired during an engagement at the prestigious Imperial Room in the Royal York Hotel, a call was made to Leonard Rambeau. He had previously hired her for a benefit in Cape Breton and a concert at St. Mary's University, where he was employed as a federal student placement officer. He had been asked to escort her to basketball games and other functions, and he had begun to suspect that her current management was in need of some help. "I started to see things that bothered me," he told one interviewer. "Like, press releases weren't being sent out to the big Toronto machine. Nobody really knew what was happening she just went and did things."

The dine and dance crowd in the upper crust York Hotel's Imperial Room had not appreciated it one bit when she had doffed her shoes and performed barefoot while they were nibbling their salads and sipping their cocktails. The press had a field day, portraying her as if she were some sort of country bumpkin that knew no table manners. Legendary publicist, Gino Embry, remembers the incident well. "It's really true about singing in bare feet," he recalls. "Anne made her debut in the room and soon after called me for help. She wanted someone to take over managing her." The role was handed to Rambeau, who was convinced to leave his position with the federal government in the

Maritimes and take a walk on the wild side in the music business with Anne Murray. Embry never forgave himself for passing up an opportunity that could very well have been his. "I gave her my accountant's number," he says, "stupid, stupid, stupid. She signed a photo to me, 'to my first and bitchy Italian PR man.' I worked with her at the Royal Alex and at the Junos and many others."

"Annie. Our Annie," Patrick Conlon wrote in his *Toronto Life* story about the incident. "She gets up on the stage of the Royal York's Imperial Room and the first thing she does is take off her shoes, just like down home. She's a big star now, our Annie. *Snowbird* was just the beginning. She owns a big house in Forest Hill now, and she's making millions of dollars and she's from Nova Scotia. She showed 'em, that's what she did." For some readers of the magazine it was difficult to tell whose side he was on.

Leonard Rambeau's arrival on the scene brought focus to Balmur's efforts to make Anne Murray into a big star on the international stage. He and Murray are said to have never signed a personal management contract, preferring a handshake deal instead. For the next 25 years, until his untimely death in 1995, he would be fiercely protective of his client. According to Conlon, Rambeau had "an uncanny talent for timing, for announcing decisions at exactly the right time to maximize their impact. Thus, he is wary of the press and dispenses information like candy. He trusts few people and enjoys playing with rumors; he juggles them like oranges. His press releases are crisp, one-page bulletins mailed without folds in large envelopes."

Richard Flohill's *Canadian Musician* story declared that "the hidden key to Murray's success can be found in the person of Leonard Rambeau, her long-time manager, friend, and combination Barnum and Svengali. Rambeau runs her management company, Balmur Ltd., in an easy and informal style but he knows how to be tough when he has to be, and he knows how to keep the flak away from Murray herself. They never fight, and she takes part in all the decision-making." Having missed the opportunity to take her career to the next level in the US with *Put Your Hand In The Hand*, Anne Murray and her associates struggled to come up with another hit. Her association with Glen Campbell, his management company, and his booking agency had quickly soured.

"It was totally demoralizing," she told *Today* magazine. "They just kept me working. Nothing was planned. There were no career moves happening." Tying her career to Campbell's TV show and tour schedule had been a big mistake. "But a lot of the trouble was my attitude," she later confessed. "I'd get this close to the top and then backed off. I'd get hot in the States then go off to England. Maybe I was running away. But it wasn't pleasant. It was awful. Most of the time I just wanted to quit."

A big factor in the turnaround that Rambeau masterminded was the dismissal of Campbell's manager Nick Serveno and his booking agency, and the hiring of Alice Cooper's manager Shep Gordon and veteran public relations man Ron Grevatt. Shep Gordon was a resourceful guy, credited with setting up the so-called accidental Troubadour photo opportunity with Anne Murray posing with John Lennon, Harry Nilsson, Alice Cooper, and Mickey Dolenz, which appeared in so many magazines and newspapers. All of a sudden Anne Murray was hip. She was featured in articles in *Time, Newsweek, Rolling Stone, Seventeen,* and *The National Observer,* and appeared on *The Tonight Show, The Merv Griffin Show,* and *Midnight Special.* When featured on TV Specials with Chicago and Englebert Humperdinck, she resorted to performing her signature song, Gene MacLellan's *Snowbird.*

Gene MacLellan was a reclusive songwriter who suffered from depression and misfortune throughout his life. A childhood victim of polio, he had survived only to suffer a facial disfigurement as a result of a near fatal automobile accident. He wore a black eye patch that could potentially have provided him the same notoriety that a similar eye patch provided Dr. Hook & the Medicine Show's Ray Sawyer, but it didn't work that way for Gene.

MacLellan was born in Val-d'Or, Quebec in 1939, and raised in Toronto. He first surfaced on the Yorkville scene as a member of Little Caesar & the Consuls. As a singer-songwriter, he was hired to perform on *Don Messer's Jubilee* and *Singalong Jubilee,* where he met producer Bill Langstroth and vocalist Anne Murray. After the success of *Snowbird* and *Put Your Hand In The Hand,* he was in much demand, winning a Juno, playing the Riverboat, the Canadian National Exposition, and

Massey Hall, as well as appearing on CBC TV shows hosted by Tommy Hunter and Ian Tyson. Signed to Capitol, he recorded three solo albums and had modest success on the Canadian country charts with *The Call, Thorn In My Shoe,* and *Lonesome River* before retreating from the limelight to live with his family on Prince Edward Island.

One day while Gene was relaxing in his home in Pownal, PEI, he got a call from Elvis, who complimented him on writing "that pretty little love song," *Snowbird,* and asked for his permission to record it. Elvis told Gene that he was his favorite songwriter and Anne Murray was his favorite vocalist. Gene MacLellan ended his own life in 1995, the same year that Leonard Rambeau passed away.

Brian Ahern continued to produce great Anne Murray albums until he left the fold to produce and marry Emmylou Harris in Hollywood, taking Miles Wilkington along with him to man his newly construct-ed mobile Enactron Truck recording studio. Ahern found Gordon Lightfoot's *Cotton Jenny,* which got Murray back into the Top 40 and peaked at number 11 on the *Billboard* country chart. In 1973, Kenny Loggins' *Danny's Song* earned Anne her second Top 10 hit on the *Billboard* pop chart. His *Love Song* hit number 5. In 1974, Anne's cover of Lennon and McCartney's *You Won't See Me* peaked at number 8 on the pop charts. *He Thinks I Still Care,* an answer song to a George Jones' *She Thinks I Still Care,* became her first number one country hit. Anne Murray and Bill Langstroth were married in 1975. Their first child, William Stewart Langstroth, was born in August 1976. Their daughter, Dawn Joanne Langstroth, was born three years later. Anne Murray recorded a kid's album during her career hiatus.

In 1978, she began working with Nashville producer Jim Ed Norman and hit on the radio with a cover of the Everly Brothers' *Walk Right Back. You Needed Me* became her first number one hit on the *Billboard* Hot 100. Over the years she won so many Juno awards that one pundit suggested changing their name to "the Annies." Credited with selling more than 40 million albums over her long and illustri-ous career, Queen Anne has not always been gracious when criticized. When Terry Jacks argued publicly that her claim that she had been the first Canadian female to be awarded a gold record in the States was false, a public feud ensued. Jacks had a point. His wife, Susan, had been there and done that with the Poppy Family's *Which Way You*

Going Billy. But Murray deflected the thrust of his argument and cast attention instead on other issues. "For some reason he says I'm stupid for putting my money back into my company, and developing other Canadian talent," she said in her own defense. "Whereas he takes his money and salts it away. He doesn't have any people around him, and I have people around me to handle things. *Seasons in the Sun* and nine million records later, he's rich." Somehow this made sense to Murray at the time. Debate about whether or not *Snowbird* had been the first gold record awarded to a Canadian female lay forgotten on the cutting room floor. Jacks' mistake was to have attacked her signature song at all. He might have better spent his energy and time promoting his wife's song. Susan Jacks, who is a terrific person, divorced him, married an ex-football player, and moved to Nashville. She had worked just as hard as Terry on the production of his massive nine-million-seller and received no credit at all. *Seasons in the Sun* suffered mightily, losing all credibility over the years, and is often cited as the worst Canadian track of all time.

Despite periodic threats to quit the music business and live the personal life she has said her stardom has denied her, Anne Murray continues to record and entertain to this day. *Snowbird* has been translated into 27 languages and recorded by more than 100 artists. Gene MacLellan put a lot of himself and his travels into the song, perhaps to heal a broken heart, and in the process provided a healing salve for people who felt the heartache and loneliness that results from a love than cannot be. Anne Murray's version made "Snowbirds" synonymous with the Canadian tourists that flocked to the southern states in the winter, and *Snowbird* one of Canada's most treasured songs.

| The breeze along the river seems to say |
| That she'll only break my heart again should I decide to stay |
| So little snowbird take me with you when you go |
| To that land of gentle breezes where the peaceful waters flow. |

Heart of Gold

Neil Young

Words & Music by Neil Young

© 1972, Silver Fiddle Music

I want to live

I want to give

I've been a miner for a heart of gold

Neil Young's performance on September 21, 2001 at the benefit concert *America: A Tribute To Heroes* struck a harmonic that was deeply felt by many of the 89 million viewers who tuned in to this simulcast. Ten days after terrorists attacked the World Trade Center, people were still in shock, not just in New York itself, but around the globe. Seated at a piano and accompanied only by a small string section, rock & roll's most enigmatic survivor surprised everyone by singing John Lennon's *Imagine*. At a moment in history when hawks were beating war drums and doves were in retreat, evoking the spirit of the Woodstock generation's most ardent advocate of peaceful solutions was a daring move. Lennon's lyrics were heard again in a whole new light: "Imagine there's no countries / It isn't hard to do / Nothing to kill or die for / And no religion too / Imagine all the people / Living life in peace."

MacLean's magazine later declared "The Canadian from that 'town in north Ontario' has carved a jagged trail on America's frontier of rugged individualism. He's the hermit rock star. But when he steps into the light, there's a precarious honesty in his music that's uncanny. Torturing his guitar on the edge of an arena stage, he's like Lear wading into the storm. Alone at a piano, singing *Imagine* at the telethon for the victims of September 11, he created the night's most intimate moment. Call him crazy, but Neil still knows how to keep it real."

Neil Young's decision to sing Lennon's song instead of one of his own was most definitely not made due to lack of choices. Next to Bob Dylan, Neil Young remains the most vital and prolific of the '60s rock poets who rallied a generation and elevated popular music from a medium mired in silly love songs to one that could also include meaningful social commentary. The fact that *Imagine* had been "grey-listed" on September 12th as one 150 songs not deemed appropriate for current air play by America's powerful radio syndicate, Clear Channel, was never mentioned as a factor in his decision.

"Pegi, my wife," Young recalls, "got an e-mail from a friend of hers after the 11th with the words to *Imagine* on it. And it was at the same time as I was trying to figure out what to play, because we only had two-and-a-half, three days' notice to do the show. I guess it was the night before that we first practiced it. So we ran though it about 10 times, until it finally started to gel and we knew what we were doing. We used the original charts from the original record, and did everything we could to do justice to the original version. We weren't trying to do anything other than that. Just trying to make it like John Lennon, basically. It was just such a great song for the moment." The godfather of grunge also appeared playing organ with Pearl Jam's Eddy Vedder and Mike McCready, and again during the finale when he joined Willie Nelson and many others to sing *America the Beautiful*.

Neil Young was familiar with censorship of his music. However, he had the last laugh in 1988 when MTV banned the video for *This Note's For You*, which lampooned corporate sponsorship and MTV in particular, then play-listed it, and eventually awarded him their Video of the Year award. History repeated itself in the weeks following 9/11 as a web-site lampooning political figures lip-synching to *Imagine* kept the classic song in the public eye and ear. The suggested grey list would boomerang, drawing unwelcome attention to Clear Channel's vast empire of radio stations and electronic signs, all of which staunchly supported pro-war rallies that were organized to counter the mounting anti-war rallies that preceded hostilities in Iraq.

Neil Young's genre-defying body of work from his debut with Buffalo Springfield, his association with Crosby, Stills & Nash, and more than 35 solo albums (which include 1995's MIRROR BALL, recorded with Pearl Jam) has never become merely a repertoire of golden oldies. When Eddy Vedder inducted Young into the Rock & Roll Hall of Fame in January 1995, he paid Neil the ultimate compliment. "I don't know if there's been another artist that has been inducted into the Rock 'n' Roll Hall of Fame to commemorate a career that is still as vital as he is today," Vedder said. "Some of his best songs were on his last record."

After the speeches, Led Zeppelin took the stage and began to perform *When The Levee's Gonna Break*, and Neil spent the next ten minutes jamming with Jimmy Page, a televised guitar duel that had long been anticipated by fans of both guitarists. The action was so intense that Robert Plant strapped on a guitar and entered the fray. Page finally put up his hands in mock acceptance of defeat, signifying enough, already, and the two guitar-slingers hugged before leaving the stage. The jam with Page inspired Young to write the lyrics to *Downtown*, which he recorded with Pearl Jam. Later that night, when Young took the Hall of Fame stage at the Waldorf Astoria Hotel with Crazy Horse, he broke another rule of thumb and performed a new song, *The Act Of Love*. "The following night," he recalls, "I played it with Pearl Jam at the Pro-Choice Benefit Concert and that version was so powerful I decided then and there to record it with them as soon as possible."

The association with Pearl Jam has been a two-way street, with Vedder and his mates telling journalists in '93 that touring with Neil and his backup band at the time, Booker T & the MGs, had taught them a lot. On another occasion, Young had subbed for an ailing Vedder, jumping up after three songs and fitting right in during a Peal Jam concert, which had led to him filling in for some Vedder-less European shows, as well. Young's manager and best friend, Elliot Roberts, who lives on a ranch near Young's Broken Arrow Ranch in California, has testified that "the music had a consistency level that was staggering. One of the greatest tours we ever had in our lives. Neil got off every f***in' night!"

"I'd never felt, for lack of another word, as high as when I'd look over and see Neil playing lead on *Down by the River*," McCready told one interviewer. Of course, playing live on stage with the unpredictable aging hippie icon had not been without its challenges. "We get along like old neighbors when we're in the studio. It's as comfortable as can be," Vedder added. "But when you're on stage playing with Neil well, it's one thing to be at the zoo and watch an animal pace around its cage. It's another to be in the cage with him."

"Recording MIRROR BALL," Young says, "was like audio verité, just a snapshot of what's happening. Sometimes I didn't know who was playing. I was just conscious of this big smouldering mass of sound. On a purely musical level this is the first time I've been in a band with three potential lead guitarists since the Buffalo Springfield. Plus, there's Jack Irons, their drummer, who was just unbelievable."

Even though Young would soon publicly oppose the war in Iraq, he was also one of the first to respond in song to the 9/11 tragedy, writing *Let's Roll* before the dust had fully settled in the New York harbor. His inspiration was the heroic actions of passengers aboard United Flight 93 and Todd Beamer, who had uttered those fateful words before launching a counterattack at the hijackers in the air over Pennsylvania. As Young told LAUNCH, "It struck me as heroic, heroic in a legendary way, heroic in a way that was more than heroism."

When it comes to making political statements on a rock & roll record, Neil Young has been at the center of the cyclone a few times. In 1967 with Buffalo Springfield, he recorded *For What It's Worth*, which was prompted by the Sunset Strip riots and has become one of the anthems of the '60s. In 1970, when four Kent State students were gunned down by National Guard troops, he wrote *Ohio*, and recorded it and Joni Mitchell's '60s anthem *Woodstock* with CSN&Y. In 1979, he endorsed Johnny Rotten and the punk scene on RUST NEVER SLEEPS. And in the 1990s during the Gulf War, his *Rockin' in the Free World* became a politically relevant statement when he performed it in concert with Crazy Horse. Pearl Jam had begun to cover it and has performed *Rockin' in the Free World* more than 300 times. Timely performances just seem to come naturally to Young. Few who were there will forget the time that he stole everyone's thunder at the Tribute To Bob Dylan concert at Madison Square Garden in 1992, taking the stage and rocking out Jimi Hendrix style on *All Along The Watchtower*.

Neil Young's intuition as to what songs to perform or record has often surprised his audiences, ticked off music critics, and dumbfounded his record companies. For example, his decision to follow Dylan and Cohen to Nashville to record his third album was not anticipated by anybody to result in his most commercially successful album and his only number one hit, *Heart Of Gold*. Yet that is precisely what happened when Neil showed up in Tennessee on February 17, 1971 to tape a performance for Johnny Cash's last TV show, and hired a producer and musicians on the eve of the first day of the sessions.

As HARVEST producer Elliot Mazer recalls, "Neil, Linda Ronstadt, James Taylor, and Tony Joe White were in town to shoot the final Johnny Cash Show for ABC-TV. I was living in Nashville, working mostly at Quad (Quadraphonic Sound Studios), which I co-owned with David Briggs — the Nashville musician, not the David Briggs who had produced other Neil Young records — and Norbert Putnam. I decided that the studio would host a dinner for some of the guests and some of our studio friends. I called Elliot Roberts, Neil's manager then and now. I had produced Linda's SILK PURSE LP. So, I called Peter Asher, Linda's manager, and he brought Linda and James Taylor. During dinner, Elliot introduced me to Neil, and we started talking about studios and musicians. Neil had heard of our band, Area Code 615, and asked if I could get the drummer, a bass player, and a steel player into my studio the next day."

Young already had the songs for the album in his pocket when he arrived in Nashville. He had been performing *Old Man, A Man Needs A Maid, Heart Of Gold,* and *The Needle and the Damage Done* on his "Journey Into The Past" solo tour, the basis for his movie of the same name. He just hadn't found the right situation to record them until he hooked up with Mazer. "Neil came in and sang the songs and looked at the studio," Mazer recalls. "I helped him get the band. We set up the studio so that he could be right in between the members of the band. He asked if we could put him near the drums. Quad was in a two-storey Victorian era house. The control room was the porch, the playing rooms were the living room and the dining room, which were connected by sliding doors. The living room had wood panels and was lively, the dining room was padded. Neil sat between the rooms in the doorway. Kenny (Buttrey) was in the living room to his left and the rest were to his right bass, steel, piano, second guitar, banjo. The leakage gave the record character and we knew we were not going to replace anything. Each song was cut in a few takes. With Neil, you can tell from the start if a take is going to be magic. He lets that happen when he feels the band and the studio are ready. Neil sang all his parts live."

Young would keep a solo version of *The Needle and the Damage Done*, recorded at Royce Hall in LA on January 30th 1971, rather than record the stark lyrics of his reaction to Danny Whitten's increasing heroin use with any accompaniment that might detract from his brutally honest assessment. Leaving Nashville, he flew to London, England where he performed solo on February 23rd at BBC TV Studios and four days later at the Royal Festival Hall. These were gigs that his manager had arranged to complement his recording session with the London Symphony Orchestra at London's Barking Town Hall with Beatles' engineer Glyn Johns at the console. The overseas expedition had been prompted by a request that Young had made to his long-time collaborator, arranger Jack Nitzsche. "Neil and I did a record called *A Man Needs A Maid*," Nitzsche recalls, "and he wanted to do it with a symphony orchestra. So, I said, 'why don't you use the LSO.' I thought it was a joke. He said, 'Okay.' We all went to London. I did two arrangements for the HARVEST album using part of the LSO." Upon returning to the United States, Neil handed the tracks for *A Man Needs A Maid* and *There's A World* over to Elliott Mazer for mixing.

Later that year, Mazer produced sessions (featuring the same Stray Gators lineup that had recorded in Nashville) in a barn on Young's ranch near Big Sur. "*Words, Alabama,* and *Are You Ready for the Country,*" Mazer relates, "needed to be cut in a big room. We had cut a version of *Alabama* at Quadraphonic, but it was not as good as the one we cut at the ranch."

> It's these expressions I never give
> That keep me searching for a heart of gold
> And I'm getting old
> Keeps me searching for a heart of gold
> And I'm getting old

When Young first played them *Heart Of Gold*, the Tennesseans realized it was special. "Kenny Buttrey and I made eye contact while listening," Mazer recalls, "and we both raised a finger that said we knew it was going to be a number one hit. It took a few minutes for the band to learn the song and figure out how to capture the magical feel that Neil was laying down. Neil was very specific to Kenny about what not to play. Tim Drummond (bass) and Kenny (drums) played together so much that they just connected to each other. Teddy Irwin (piano) found some harmonics and rhythm chops, and Ben Keith (pedal steel) just sailed through the song. We did one or two takes. After we got the master take, we got Linda and James to add their harmonies in the control room while sitting on the couch. Two passes and it was finished. I guess it took less than two hours to record everything on *Heart Of Gold*. I don't recall why we started to use slap-back echo on Neil's voice, but that worked wonderfully. Neil really got excited when he heard the first playback. Later on, after he had gone home to California, he told me that this was the first time a tape sounded better at home than in the studio."

HARVEST would not be released until early 1972. "The mixes were complicated and they did take a long time," Mazer notes. "Trying to recapture the feeling of the original sessions was the challenge."

Neil Young was born on November 12, 1945 in Toronto, and survived the ravages of polio, diabetes, epilepsy, and the divorce of his parents, author Scott Young and "Razzy" Young, to become one of many teenagers to form bands in Winnipeg in the early 1960s. By the time that he migrated back to Toronto, he had also begun performing as a folk singer, and he has juggled these two personas rocker and folkie throughout his career. His earliest influences were cowboy singers like Frankie Laine. "I loved that stuff," he told *Rolling Stone*. "I even covered one of his songs on the OLD WAYS album, *The Wayward Wind*. It was one of his biggest hits up in Canada. See, I used to walk by a railroad track on my way to school everyday. There was even a real 'hobo's shack' there. The song and the image have always stayed with me. When I hear it, I always think of being five or six walking past that old shack and the rail-road tracks gleaming in the sun and on my way to school everyday with my little transistor radio up to my ear."

Young's tranquil rural childhood was disrupted in 1951 by the polio epidemic that swept through Canada. He barely survived. Arriving home after one "disinfectant bath, his black hair in spikes," he said, "I didn't die, did I?" Many years later his mom told biographer James McDonough that "Neil got polio and lost all his girlish curves. Damn near died. He looked like hell on the highway skin and bones. He never got fat again. We didn't know if he would ever walk . . ." No doubt, the near brush with death and agonizing recovery contributed to an introspective personality and many hours spent in a fantasy world of model railroading with his beloved Lionel electric trains.

In 1960, his parents' divorce precipitated a move with his mother from Omemee, Ontario to Winnipeg. He arrived just in time to become part of an active teenage band scene that Burton Cummings has said would soon swell to an estimated 200 bands. Young's first guitar hero was the Shadows' Hank Marvin. "My first [instrument] was this little plastic Arthur Godfrey ukulele," he told *Mojo*. "Then I seem to remember a baritone 'uke', then I had a banjo. So I had all these different sounding instruments which I played the same way. I played electric lead guitar first then I started rocking out with a Community-Club teenage band. First we were called the Esquires. Then we changed it to the Stardusters. After that we settled on being called the Squires."

"A lot of songs Neil wrote had a Shadows' twang to them," Squires' drummer Ken Smyth told *Winnipeg Sixties Rock Scene* author John Einarson. "[Al] Bates was a trained guitarist, and Neil played just by ear but he wrote a lot. We'd get together at my parents' house to practice a couple of times a week, and he'd show up each time with a new song or two, he had piles of songs!" The Squires recorded two of Young's compositions and issued a 45 of *The Sultan b/w Aurora* on their own V Records label. Hearing Dylan's first album inspired Young to become a vocalist. "That left a big impression on me," he told *Mojo*, "and later, the Byrds were great. What they did was deeply 'cool'." One night after a gig in Fort William, Ontario, Neil met Stephen Stills. It was the beginning of a lifelong friendship. During this same era, Neil also bumped into Joni Mitchell. They had a lot in common, not the least of which was that they had both nearly died during the polio epidemic of the early '50s.

"In 1965 I was up in Canada," Mitchell would later tell her audiences. "And there was a friend of mine up there who had just left a rock 'n' roll band in Winnipeg, Manitoba to become a folk singer a la Bob Dylan, who was his hero at that time. He had just newly turned 21, and that meant in Winnipeg he was no longer allowed into his favorite hangout, which is kind of a teenybopper club and once you're over 21 you couldn't get in there anymore. So he was really feeling terrible because his girlfriends and everybody that he wanted to hang out with, his band, could still go there, you know, but one of the things that drove him to become a folk singer was that he couldn't play in this club anymore. But he was over the hill, so he wrote this song that was called *Sugar Mountain*, which was a lament for his lost youth. And I thought, God, you know, if we get to 21 and there's nothing after that, that's a pretty bleak future, so I wrote a song for him, and for myself, just to give me some hope. It's called *The Circle Game*." Young has said that he wrote *Sugar Mountain* on his 19th birthday when he found himself alone in his room during an engagement at the Flamingo Hotel in Fort William. After a sojourn in Thunder Bay, Young and the Squires headed into Toronto.

Like his idol, Young had a distinctive vocal style that irritated many people. Where Dylan was hoarse and raspy, Young was in the midst of perfecting a high nasal whine that he often followed with blasts of high-energy electric guitar notes. Neil Young fans would soon learn that their hero was best appreciated at high volume. Many years later, Dylan would write lyrics for *Highland* that indicated he, too, had become a Neil Young fan: "I'm listening to Neil Young, I gotta turn up the sound / Someone's always yellin' 'Turn him down!'"

Opportunities didn't develop quickly in Toronto. As Neil recalls, "After I arrived in Toronto I tried to keep my band going and then tried to work with several others. But it just never worked out for me there. I could never get anything going in Toronto, never even got one gig with a band. I just couldn't break into that scene. So I moved instead towards acoustic music and immediately became very introspective and musically inward. That's the beginning of that whole side of my music."

An invitation from Atco Records to record an acoustic demo in New York City led to Young's first rejection. According to legend, he was told "You're a good guitar player, kid, but you'll never make it as a singer." At the time, he was still on the outside looking in. As he told *Mojo*, "The Hawks were the best band in Toronto, which is the biggest city in Canada, musically. And I'd just come from a place called Thunder Bay, which is between Winnipeg and Toronto. We'd done really well there but couldn't get a gig to save our lives in Toronto." When a second recording project, an album with Rick James and the Myna Birds, was torpedoed by James' arrest on charges he was a deserter from the U.S. Navy, it was time to move on. Neil and his bass-playing buddy, Bruce Palmer, climbed into Young's battered 1953 Pontiac hearse and headed for Hollywood, where they hoped to hook up with Stephen Stills. Neil loved the Rolling Stones' early records and he hoped to get a similar chemistry going with Stills. As he told biographer, McDonough, "What I really liked about the Rolling Stones was Brian Jones and Keith Richards playing guitar together. *Satisfaction* was a great record!"

Young and Palmer checked into a Sunset Strip motel and began to look around for Stills and Richie Furay. One afternoon in a traffic jam, Stills and Furay recognized the hearse with Canadian license plates and they pulled their vehicles into a supermarket parking lot. "It took us about ten days to find them," Neil recalls. "When we met them in February '66, the Buffalo Springfield began the same day." Within weeks they were opening for the Byrds at the Whisky A Go Go. Stills and Young soon discovered that they shared a passion for playing in D modal tuning. "We'd play in that tuning together a lot," he recalls. "This was when 'ragas' were happening and D modal made it possible to have that 'droning' sound going on all the time, that's where it started. Only I took it to the next level, which is how *The Loner* and *Cinnamon Girl* happened. You make a traditional chord shape and any finger that doesn't work you just lift it up and let the string just ring. I've used that tuning throughout my career right up to today. You can hear it on everything from *Fuckin' Up* on RAGGED GLORY to *War Of Man* and *One Of These Days* on HARVEST MOON."

The relationship between Stills and Young remained stormy both on and off stage, resulting in some brilliant guitar duels, and three terrific albums. The tension between the two, however, resulted in Neil being in and out of the band. He missed performing at the Monterey Pop Festival altogether. Neil contributed *Mr. Soul* and *Broken Arrow*. However, it was Stills' *For What It's Worth* that got the most airplay. Meanwhile, Neil was hanging out in Topanga Canyon and meeting a whole new slew of musicians, including Phil Spector protégé, Jack Nitzsche. Jack arranged Neil's *Expecting To Fly* for a Buffalo Springfield recording session. "Jack taught me a lot," Neil recalls. "He'd already worked as an arranger for Spector, and had played piano on recording sessions with the Stones. I met him in a club in Hollywood right when the Springfield first started. We just liked each other and always had a great time together. Plus, I liked hanging out with him because he got all the new records sent to him and he'd sit and listen to them. He worked as an independent arranger then. He was a very sought-after guy. When I quit the Springfield, I was living at Jack's house with him, his wife Gracia, and his son 'Little Jack'. I remember the day we got the first Jimi Hendrix Experience single this was way before the first album had been released and all of us were just awestruck at how raw the guy sounded. That first album of mine was basically just Jack and me."

Joni Mitchell's manager, Elliot Roberts, facilitated Young's move to a solo career. As Roberts confided to *Broken Arrow*, a British fanzine, "I started working with Neil when he was with Buffalo Springfield. I negotiated the break-up of that band and then started representing Neil as a solo artist. He was so prolific at that point and writing so many things that to just have Buffalo Springfield as a release for his material, so many good songs weren't getting recorded. And Neil didn't want to work in the confines of another group at that point, so he left. He has always been an individual, he's never been motivated by anything but the pure desire to play."

Reprise released his solo debut NEIL YOUNG in January 1969, but Young had already become exasperated with Nitzsche's Spector-style mode of assembling tracks, which he called "overdub city." Anxious to find his own solution, he soon conscripted guitarist Danny Whitten, bass player Billy Talbot, and drummer Ralph Molina. "We all knew each other from the Laurel Canyon days when Neil was with Buffalo Springfield," Talbot recalls. "We'd meet up and play music acoustically in each others' houses and stuff. When he was ready to do his second solo album, Neil came and sat in with us at the Whiskey A Go Go when we were known as The Rockets and then asked us to play on the album."

EVERYBODY KNOWS THIS IS NOWHERE by Neil Young & Crazy Horse, as he had renamed the Rockets, was released six months after his debut and eventually sold a million copies. Record buyers were eager to purchase the LP after they heard *Cinnamon Girl* and the extended jam versions of *Down By The River* and the even longer *Cowgirl in the Sand* on the new FM stations that were playing album cuts. That summer, after a short tour with Crazy Horse to support his solo albums, Young was invited to join Crosby, Stills & Nash on their inaugural tour.

He couldn't resist. Even though CROSBY, STILLS & NASH didn't outsell Neil's EVERYBODY KNOWS THIS IS NOWHERE, the trio's debut album had a huge impact. People loved their easygoing front porch harmonies and acoustic approach, and the timely release heralded in the era of the singer-songwriter.

"In 1969, when CSN had finished the album," Nash later told Debbie Kruger, "we knew that we would be going on the road. Stephen, as a great lead guitarist, needed someone to 'play off' to inspire him to play better. Neither David nor I were that person. We decided that we would ask Neil to come along and join the band. At first, I was a little reticent to have this happen. I thought that we had a complete band and a wonderful vocal blend. I spent one morning at breakfast with Neil on Bleeker Street in New York City and when we were finished I was completely sold on Neil joining. He was incredibly funny and very committed to music." Their second show together would be before a million fans gathered at Woodstock.

The tour that followed solidified the musical relationship. Neil Young became the most prolific rock artist on the scene at the end of the '60s. 1970 saw the release of both his After The Goldrush (with the standout tracks *Southern Man* and *When I Dance I Can Really Love*) and DEJA VU (with his marvelous *Helpless* and Young & Stills' *Everybody I Love You*). CSN&Y was also featured in the film *Woodstock* and soundtrack album. When Neil was not on tour with CSN&Y, Elliot Roberts kept him busy performing solo concerts. Early 1971 found him back in Winnipeg, this time headlining at the Centennial Concert Hall. "Obviously," he told the locals, "there was more happening for me in Winnipeg than happened in Toronto." He had hoped to run into his old band mates at a party after the concert. However, they didn't show. "I didn't see Bates or Smyth," he told John Einarson. "I was hoping to see them, though. You never realize at the time that you'll never see some people again."

Following the release of HARVEST in February 1972, Neil Young performed core songs like *Old Man, Heart Of Gold, Harvest*, and *The Needle and the Damage Done* with CSN&Y and at the Mariposa Folk Festival as a solo artist. When touring with CSN&Y came to a close and the double live LP FOUR WAY STREET was released, he put together a band of his own. His solo albums were selling well, and *Heart Of Gold*, which had topped the *Billboard* Hot 100 in March 1972, had won over many new fans. He had become so popular by this point that his influence could be heard in new bands like America, whose *A Horse With No Name* nudged *Heart Of Gold* from the number one position.

Bob Dylan told *Uncut* magazine, "I always liked Neil Young but it bothered me every time I listened to *Heart Of Gold.* I'd say, `Shit, that's me. If it sounds like me, it should as well be me.' I needed to lay back for a while, forget about things, myself included, and I'd get so far away and turn on the radio and there I am. But it's not me. It seemed to me somebody else had taken my thing and had run away with it and, you know, I never got over it." Dylan and Young would eventually meet and begin a long musical friendship by jamming with the Band at a Bay area benefit and then during the filming of THE LAST WALTZ.

The rehearsals for the 1973 tour did not go well. It was becoming obvious that Neil's lyrics to *The Needle and the Damage Done* were coming true. He had written, "I came to town / And I lost my band / I watched the needle take another man." When Danny Whitten was dismissed on the eve of the tour, he overdosed on heroin he had bought with his severance pay, triggering Neil's descent into his darkest days. The death of CSN&Y roadie Bruce Berry around this same time also brought Young down, big time, and it showed as the band with Molina, Talbot, Nitzsche, Ben Keith, and guitarist Nils Lofgren on board headed out on tour. They were still performing core songs from HARVEST, but as the weeks passed Young began to introduce more and more new songs, songs that portrayed his dark mood and his growing depression. At the same time, Young had arranged for his shows to be taped for a live album, TONIGHT'S THE NIGHT, an album that was a polar opposite from the sweet melodic approach of HARVEST and would not be released until 1975. Compounded with his grief over the loss of Whitten and Berry, Young was not having good reactions to the Top 40 success he had tasted briefly with the release of HARVEST.

"*Heart of Gold* put me in the middle of the road," he would declare in the liner notes to his first compilation, Decade. "Traveling there soon became a bore so I headed for the ditch." TONIGHT'S THE NIGHT, as ragged and edgy as it was, has become the most popular of the "ditch trilogy," which also includes TIME FADES AWAY and the even bleaker

1974 album, ON THE BEACH. With ON THE BEACH, however, Young had begun to come to grips with his inner demons and his harshest critics. As these lines from *Walk On* indicate: "I hear some people been talkin' me down / Bring up my name, pass it 'round. / They don't mention happy times. / They do their thing I'll do mine. / Ooh baby, that's hard to change / I can't tell them how to feel. / Some get stoned, some get strange / But sooner or later it all gets real. / Walk on . . ."

Many years later Young told BBC deejay Dave Ferrin that "my least favorite record is TIME FADES AWAY. I think it's the worst record I ever made but as a documentary of what was happening to me, it was a great record. I was on stage and I was playing all these songs that nobody had heard before, recording them, and I didn't have the right band. It was just an uncomfortable tour. It was supposed to be this big deal I just had Harvest out, and they booked me into 90 cities. I felt like a product, and I had this band of all-star musicians who couldn't even look at each other. It was a total joke."

I've been to Hollywood
I've been to Redwood
I crossed the ocean for a heart of gold

He would later tell *The Boston Globe* that it was a "good musical period. I'm glad I lived through it. Could have gone under a couple of times during that period, but not because I wasn't having fun." Compounding Young's situation was the birth of his first son, Zeke, by actress Carrie Snodgrass. Zeke developed a mild case of the cerebral palsy. Neil's second son, Ben, by his wife Pegi, had a more serious case. Neil and Pegi have enjoyed a long and fruitful marriage, but it has not been without its challenges.

Young began swerving into unpredictable directions again in the 1980s, prompting David Geffen to sue him for not making "Neil Young records." He would later reveal the cause to be another troubling personal event, the birth of Ben, who was so severely afflicted with cerebral palsy that he couldn't speak to express himself. Neil's solution to his problems had begun in 1976 when he reunited with Crazy Horse for the straight-ahead gem, ZUMA. He then patched up his differences with Stephen Stills long enough to record the highly enjoyable LONG MAY

YOU RUN. He found himself more comfortable with the melodic acoustic approach for COMES A TIME, which included a cover of Ian Tyson's *Four Strong Winds* and the lyrical *Lotta Love* with Nicolette Larsen.

In 1979, a compromise solution saw the issue of a set of acoustic tracks on one side of RUST NEVER SLEEPS and a total garage band rock out with Crazy Horse on the other. The tour that ensued led to the double LP LIVE RUST and both albums became million sellers. Through his long association with Crazy Horse, Neil was able to play the jazz solos he had admired most in his youth. As he told *Mojo*, "my guitar improvisations with Crazy Horse are very, very Coltrane-influenced." Frank Sampedro, who replaced Whitten in Crazy Horse, has openly acknowledged his acceptance of Young's multifaceted genius and his need to be in a constant state of change. As Frank told *The Halifax Daily News* in 1996, "I was frustrated and angry when he first took off to play with other players (the Ducks). But you've got to realize that Neil has a lot of different paths he's got to take. And there's only one band that he keeps coming back to consistently."

> I've been in my mind, it's such a fine line
> That keeps me searching for a heart of gold
> And I'm getting old.
> Keeps me searching for a heart of gold
> And I'm getting old.

Neil Young's solutions to his many personal dilemmas came to include becoming a founding director of Willie Nelson's "Farm Aid" benefit concerts and working with his wife Pegi to found the Bridge Foundation and a special school for handicapped children. "I don't really do much," he says. "I'm just a figurehead, public relations kind of guy. My wife does all the work." Over the years Neil has invited pals like Willie Nelson, Bruce Springsteen, Simon & Garfunkel, Don Henley, and Bob Dylan to perform at the Annual Bridge School Benefit concerts at the Shoreline Amphitheater in Mountain View, California. At the same time, he has had to deal with post-polio syndrome, a condition that has also afflicted Joni Mitchell in recent years. "It affected me particularly badly in the mid-'80s," he told *Mojo*, "when I couldn't even pick up my guitar. My body was starting to fall apart on me. That's when I started working out. It's proven to be my salvation. Lifting weights and exercising have completely changed everything for me, with regard to my health."

Along with his renewed health, he had come to more fully understand his unpredictable, contrary nature. His decisions to change bands and projects for no apparent reason at all was similar to the epileptic seizures of his youth. There was little he could do other than go with the flow. Resistance merely made him deeply unhappy. It was an understanding that his Crazy Horse band-mate Ralph Molina also shared. As Ralph told *Les Inrockuptibles*, "We are used to these up and downs. Neil's career is cyclic and Crazy Horse has to live with that. We don't have any choice but to be available for Neil and to live deeply the moments we are together."

"I have been living with these cycles for such a long time now that I can anticipate it," Young told Emmanuel Tellier. "I feel these things, I'm ready for these upsets, and I always try to warn the others with my projects as soon as possible. Right now, I don't know what I'll do after "Year Of The Horse." I'm thinking that doing something with Jack Nitzsche should be a great idea, but perhaps I will go in the studio with Crazy Horse. It's not me who will decide, it's the songs."

"You certainly have to live daily with Neil to feel how he lives with his music," Molina adds. "Neil doesn't give a damn about his status, his position in rock history. The only thing that matters for him is to grab his guitar, write songs, record them, with or without Crazy Horse, and then to play these songs in concerts."

Young has mellowed with age, but he hasn't slowed down. In fact, counting his activities with his son, Ben, who shares his love of model trains, he has remained rust resistant throughout the years. His initial efforts to communicate with Ben first surfaced on Trans in the mid-'80s, with Young's vocals electronically altered by a vocal synthesizer. Since that time they have developed a number of innovations for Lionel Trains, including a multi-function remote controller and improvements to the train sounds generated by Lionel. He has even become a part-owner of the company, and he and Ben have begun to introduce interactive train sets that incorporate tiny cameras that transmit views from speeding electric trains as they pass through elaborate mountainous layouts to the operator's computer monitor. Despite having a recording studio in the barn, but Neil is often found down the road at nearby club jamming with his pals. Put simply, playing music keeps him sane and healthy.

With all this family and community involvement added to his constant musical output, it must have been gratifying when some of the bands that had grown up listing to Neil Young records put together a tribute album, The Bridge: A Tribute To Neil Young. Terry Tolkin's No.6 Records donated the proceeds to Pegi's Bridge School project. And when Neil heard his songs recorded by Nick Cave, the Pixies, Sonic Youth, Soul Asylum, Dinosaur Jr., and half a dozen other aspiring young acts, he kept the CD on the bus. He liked listening to it so much that Sonic Youth soon found themselves opening for him on a tour. He hadn't known it before this but he had fathered a generation of alternative rockers, as well as his own children, Zeke, Ben, and Amber. These alt-rockers had grown up listening to Neil, and he soon learned that he fit into their scene, an acceptance that guaranteed he would not be put out to pasture in the near future. It was yet another indication of the impact his songs and records have had since his debut with Buffalo Springfield all those years ago.

When Neil Young unleashes, there seems to be no stopping how much impact it will have. Take *Rockin' in the Free World* from his 1989 album FREEDOM. When it was first released, it seemed to refer to the tearing down of the Berlin Wall. Then when the world learned of the Tiananmen Square tragedy and Young mentioned that before performing the song during his shows, it appeared to refer perfectly well to that international event. Then when Young and Crazy Horse played searing versions of it during the Gulf War, it became an anti-war song, their trademark encore. In the new millennium, when the Bush administration announced its intention to invade Iraq, the song appeared to be even more relevant. By 2004, *Rockin' in the Free World* had been used by Young in his feature length music video *Greendale* and by Michael Moore on the soundtrack to his anti-war documentary *Fahrenheit 9/11*. Neil's own movie making efforts include *Journey Through The Past* (1972), *Rust Never Sleeps* (1989), and *Greendale* (2004), all directed by Bernard Shakey, a.k.a. Neil Young. His instrumental contributions to the soundtrack of Jim Jarmusch's *Dead Men* led to Jarmusch film-ing Young & Crazy Horse for his 1997 feature film, *The Year of the Horse*. When he was asked to write a song for a title track for Jonathon Demme's *Philadelphia*, starring Tom Hanks, Neil found himself per-forming his song on the Academy Awards show along with Bruce Springsteen. Springsteen's *Streets of Philadelphia* won the Oscar, but the occasion precipitated an additional appearance by the Boss at Neil and Pegi's Bridge School benefit in Mountain View.

Over the years, Neil Young may have downplayed *Heart Of Gold* and HARVEST, maintaining a hands-off ambivalence during interviews, but he has also stated that he had his reasons. "When people start asking you to do the same thing over and over again," he told *Rolling Stone*, "that's when you know you're way too close to something that you don't want to be near. I can't hold that against HARVEST, which I did; it's certainly got the depth of the other records. But it took a while to get to that. I just didn't want to do the obvious thing, because it didn't feel right." When drafting his own epitaph, there was no doubt in his mind what song he would include: "*This man, the longest living rock 'n' roll star, died searching for a heart of gold.*"

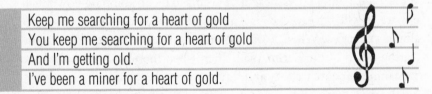

Keep me searching for a heart of gold
You keep me searching for a heart of gold
And I'm getting old.
I've been a miner for a heart of gold.

Neil Young has performed *Heart Of Gold* more than 537 times in con-cert, according to his archivist, second only to *Powderfinger*, which he has performed more than 600 times.

Takin' Care of Business

BTO
Words & Music by Randy Bachman
© 1974, Ranbach Music, Sony/ATV Songs

They get up every morning
From the alarm clock's warning
Take the 8:15 into the city . . .

Randy Bachman believes that great music comes from spontaneity. He should know. It was a fluke, slap-back echo that mysteriously appeared on the playback of *Shakin' All Over* during a 3:00 a.m. recording session on a cold January night in 1965 that led to his first *Billboard* hit. The track became an instant rock anthem, an inspiration for a generation of Canadian teenagers to join bands and make their own 45 rpm records. Featuring Randy's blistering guitar riffs, eerie whammy-bar chords, and Chad Allen's raw vocal, *Shakin' All Over* was huge in the summer of '65, and it took their band from Winnipeg to New York, where Bachman met legendary producer, Phil Ramone.

Every Canadian guitarist worth his salt learned Randy's lead guitar licks and played *Shakin' All Over* in clubs and dance halls from Vancouver Island to Newfoundland. Bachman went on to write several rock anthems, including his signature song, *Takin' Care Of Business*.

There's a whistle up above
And people push and people shove
And all the girls who try to look pretty . . .

"We recorded *Shakin' All Over* in a TV station with the announcer's mic in the middle of a big concrete room that was the *Teen Dance Party* room," Randy recalls. "All it had was a big canvas curtain that was kind of our baffle. I remember we did three or four takes of the cut. The engineer had been at it since ten in the morning. They had already done *Teen Dance Party* that afternoon. We had played our dance that night. We were all very tired. We'd all been at it for 18 to 20 hours. Because this was a mono machine with one mic and a patch bay in the studio, we had to keep unplugging the machine and re-plugging it so that we could hear the playback. And one of the times he plugged something in wrong, and we went in to hear it and there was this 'slap-back echo' on it."

The boys in the band were excited. They had chosen to record *Shakin' All Over*, a number one hit in the UK in 1960 for Johnny Kidd & the Pirates, because they wanted to get in on the new sounds of the British Invasion bands. The recording gear had mysteriously made them sound really, really British. "We said, 'Whoa, this is Elvis *Baby, Let's Play House* or *Mystery Train*,'" Randy recalls. "We loved it. That was the version we kept, even though there was a mistake or two on it. The previous version was better, as far as playing goes. But we kept the one that had that great 'slap-back echo' on it."

Chad Allen had also turned in an exceptional vocal that surpassed his previous efforts. "Chad had a sore throat from a cold," Randy told me, "and he had already sung three hours at a dance. Normally his voice is smooth, but that night he had this great raspy voice that was perfect for screaming." When Randy first joined the band they had been called Al & the Silvertones, which they changed to Chad Allen & the Expressions when Chad joined, and they had already built up a local reputation. Their game plan was to release their cut on Quality Records in Canada, which was a lease label that also distributed hit records by U.S. artists like Little Richard and Fats Domino; however, George Struth, the head of leasing at Quality, intervened. "The label said, 'This is too good to waste,'" Randy explains. "We had already had 10 or 12 singles that had each sold maybe a hundred copies in Winnipeg. There were bands all over Canada doing that, all selling a couple hundred copies of their 45s. The record label in Toronto said, 'This can sell more than a couple of hundred copies.' But they didn't want to put our name on it. They didn't want people to know we were a local Winnipeg band."

The band's first reactions were mixed. As Bachman recalls, "The first promo copies, which are very rare and selling for three or four hundred dollars now, was a white label with just a big GUESS WHO on it and the title. I remember when it came out we were not really thrilled about it. Chad Allen, especially, wasn't thrilled that suddenly his name was eradicated."

And if your train's on time	
You can get to work by nine	
And start to sleep and talk to get your pay . . .	

Subsequent pressings would read "The Guess Who or Chad Allen & the Expressions," but in the moment they were not sure they had made the right decision. "We had built up this name in Winnipeg," Randy continues, "from the early 60s to the mid-60s, and suddenly our name was gone. I remember it coming on the radio and I remember the deejay saying, 'This was done in a basement in Liverpool, and it's one of the Beatles and one of the Stones and one of the Pacemakers. And they can't put their name on it or they'll all be sued, so they put GUESS WHO on it.'" The US release on Scepter Records got it all wrong and read: "The Guess Who's." When *Shakin' All Over* began to climb the *Billboard* charts, they could no longer bite their tongues and remain silent. "It was like, number 3 in Winnipeg with a bullet," Randy recalls with a chuckle, "and I couldn't stand it. I phoned the station, telling Doc Stein the deejay, 'It's us, it's us!' And he said, 'No, no.' But finally we did get our name put on it. And then it got dropped, and we were forced to change our name to the Guess Who." These were exciting times. They had a hit record in New York and LA and Toronto but they were still playing local teen dances.

"We were still in high school. We didn't realize the scope of it," Bachman admits. "I remember going down to Kresge's department store, and they had a record bar there, a lady named Ivy ran it. She had dyed blonde hair and she played all the latest hip Little Richard and Elvis and the country stuff like Guy Mitchell and all that rockabilly stuff Jerry Lee Lewis and Carl Perkins — she played it all." Ivy also received weekly copies of *Billboard* magazine in the mail. It wasn't something you could purchase at a newsstand in Winnipeg in 1965. "I remember going down there," Bachman continues, "with Jim Kale or Garry Peterson or Chad and we'd say, 'Oh, *Shakin' All Over* is number 22 this week with a bullet!' And we'd close the *Billboard*, and say, 'Isn't that neat!' And go back to school the next week. We were still playing dances around Winnipeg." Then they got a call from New York. "Did they want to be on *The Ed Sullivan Show*?"

If you ever get annoyed
Look at me I'm self-employed
I love to work at nothing all day . . .

"Well," Randy says with a gleam in his eye, "we had seen the Beatles on *Ed Sullivan* and the Dave Clark Five and everybody else. We were gone. We cleaned out our lockers. We left school, borrowed my father's car, and drove all the way to New York." When they arrived at the theatre where *The Ed Sullivan Show* was produced, nobody knew who they were. The next day they learned they were not on Phil Spector's label, as they had been telling everyone. Sceptor Records and its sister label WAND Records were run by Florence Greenberg and A&R man Luther Dixon, and their label mates were the Shirelles, Dionne Warwick, and the Kingsmen.

The Winnipeg teenagers were mighty disappointed. However, after they got things straightened out with the guy that had made the phone call to Winnipeg, they would end up working with some pretty cool Big Apple teenagers. As Randy recalls, "Monday morning we went to Paul Kanter's office and said, 'What happened to *Ed Sullivan?*' And he said, 'We'll get it later.' We never did get it, but we did do the Kingsmen tour. That was fabulous. It had the Guess Who, the Kingsmen and Dion & the Belmonts they just sang Do-Wop all the time on the bus, which was wonderful. It had Barbara Mason (who had the hit *Are You Ready*), Eddie Hodges (who had *Gonna Knock On Your Door*), and, later on, the Turtles and Sam the Sham & the Pharaohs."

Perhaps the coolest people they met were two teenagers who had to cut classes to pitch their songs to the boys from Winnipeg. As Randy Bachman recalls, "Scepter Records wanted us to record at their studios, which was at 354 West 54th Street on the 2nd floor. They had a 4-track studio. So, we went up there. They wanted to re-cut some of our Canadian stuff. We re-cut *Stop Teasin' Me*, which was a song I wrote before we recorded *Shakin' All Over*. They liked that tune. And they began to bring in other writers, because we hadn't written enough stuff. And in those days, nobody did demos. When you wrote a song, you came in and played it on piano and everybody gathered around and learned to sing it. So, they brought in these three black kids, who happened to be Nick Ashford and Valerie Simpson and another girl. Ashford and Simpson are big today. They've written *Ain't No Mountain High Enough* and all that, but they also wrote *Hey, Ho, What You Do To Me* and some of the Guess Who's early stuff. They skipped school to come there and play and sing us the demos and they had to get home by 4:30 so their mothers wouldn't know they'd skipped. They taught us the songs. We had a great friendship with them. And we recorded in New York."

It was during these formative months spent in New York that Randy Bachman learned to become a professional musician capable of taking care of business.

And I'll be . . .
Takin' care of business (every day)
Takin' care of business (every way)
I've been takin' care of business (it's all mine)
Takin' care of business and working overtime
(Work out!)

Offered the opportunity to go on the road as a backing band for the Crystals and the Ronettes, they accepted. They knew the material, and, as Bachman notes, "The Guess Who were really, really good musicians." When they were not on the road, they absorbed as much ambience as they could. As Randy recalls, "Dionne Warwick was still recording then with Burt Bacharach and Hal David, and they were in the same office and she was being engineered by Phil Ramone. So, here we were meeting these guys. Hal David and Burt Bacharach, when they wore black leather jackets and jeans. And we cut several records there at Scepter Studios in New York." The Guess Who, with Chad Allen gone and Burton Cummings on board as lead vocalist, went on to become the first Canadian supergroup. They hit into the upper echelons of the *Billboard* chart with *These Eyes, Laughing, No Time* and *American Woman* before Bachman left to form a band that rocked a little harder. With management from Bruce Allen, he would have the push that he needed to take his music to even greater heights.

Randy's new band Brave Belt once again featured Chad Allen as lead vocalist. After two unsuccessful albums, bassist Fred Turner replaced him. During their shows, Randy sang some Neil Young and Bob Dylan songs to give Fred a break. He wasn't a great singer, but he *was* a great guitar player. His teacher had been jazz guitar great, Lenny Breau. When a 15-year-old Randy had put aside his violin and picked up his first guitar he wanted to play "like the guys who I saw on TV like Scotty Moore backing Elvis, like James Burton backing Rick Nelson." And he was impressed when he heard 17-year-old Winnipeg teenager Lenny Breau's unique finger picking style. "We fell into being buddies together," he recalls. "I didn't realize how great he was at the time. We were just kids. In that year-and-a-half I had this hunger to play the guitar and Lenny taught me everything. He taught me 15 years of guitar in a year-and-a-half. Everything that I've written, like *She's Come Undone, Blue Collar, Lookin' Out For #1,* all that thoughtful, great playing is pretty much all Lenny Breau." In the new millennium, Randy would pay tribute to Lenny Breau with a series of "Jazz Thing" albums.

Randy's recollection of the transition between Brave Belt and BTO hinges on being dropped by Reprise Records and getting picked up by RCA. "I began to send out that album, which was going to be Brave Belt III," he explains. "I sent it to 26 record labels and got 26 refusals. Finally, somebody who had refused it in late January called back in March and said they had listened to it again and were reconsidering it. But we had to change our name. And they wanted me to use my name. The name Brave Belt was so anonymous nobody knew who it was." Bachman Turner Overdrive with Fred on lead vocals and bass, Randy on guitar and vocals, and his kid brothers Tim (on guitar) and Robbie (on drums) was formed in early 1972. The overdrive part they took from a cool trucker's magazine.

As Randy recalls, "I said, 'well, there's three Bachmans and a Turner in this band, we'll just call ourselves Bachman-Turner.' They said, 'That's fine.' But that was the era of Brewer & Shipley and Seals & Crofts, and everywhere we went people thought we were two guys with acoustic guitars and we would arrive and blow the windows out of these little coffeehouses that we were being booked into. So, the label said, 'You need something to show that you play heavy music.'

Late one night in Windsor, we stopped at a truck stop after a gig, and right at the cash register when we were paying our bill we saw a trucker magazine called *Overdrive*. We opened it up and there was a centerfold and it was a guy's truck! It showed the inside of his cabin, the truck was all leopard skin, a microwave oven, a place to sleep in the back, a stereo, chrome wheels on the rig and everything. I thought this was very cool. I called the record label the next day and said, 'How about Bachman Turner Overdrive?' It was a powerful, driven name. At that point no one had used the name 'Overdrive' to talk about music. It had only been used with cars. Ferrari had overdrive gears. Lots of cars had third and fourth gears and then an overdrive gear. And the label said, 'That name is too long. It will never fly.' I said, 'How 'bout BTO?' And the label guy said, 'Fine.' They let us use both. We went and found an overdrive gear and put Bachman Turner Overdrive around it and BTO in the middle and it became a world-recognized trademark, a symbol. Now 'overdrive' is everywhere. It's on every amplifier, every foot pedal every kind of machine that's got that overdone, overdriven sound."

People see you having fun
Just a-lying in the sun
Tell them that you like it this way

"BRAVE BELT III became BTO I," Bachman summarizes. "It had all rock & roll on it except for one song, *Blue Collar*. And that was my Lenny Breau guitar influences, everything I had learned from Lenny. There was three of us cutting it — Turner on bass, myself on all guitars and Robbie on drums." Randy overdubbed several guitar tracks, using every Lenny Breau trick he had learned. "The first track was *Let It Ride*," he continues. "We had this album that was a milestone album, but it didn't really have a big hit. *Blue Collar* wasn't a big hit. *Let It Ride* rose to number 23."

They did come up with some incredible vocal and guitar sounds on the first BTO album. As Randy recalls, "What happened on *Let It Ride* is that the vocals were so intricate that we tried singing it and couldn't. And I had learned this trick back with the CBC five or six years earlier. We got Fred Turner to sing all the vocals. So, he is singing every part on *Let It Ride*, and when you double and triple your own voice there is something about the quality of it, there is this 'jet plane' phasing kind of thing. Same with the guitar, I doubled the guitar, and, in the middle of the solo with the wah-wah pedal doubled, it sounds like phasing. That's what phasing and flanging is. It is trying to double the thing with a machine and it gets so close that it kind of veers off itself. Sort of like a jet plane soaring in the sky." Randy and Fred had got their special effects the hard way. Soon after their album came out a flood of effects pedals appeared on the market, pedals that basically enabled vocalists and guitarists to phase and flange their notes electronically.

"The album sold 300,000 copies and then stopped," Bachman recalls, "but it stayed on the charts two years. And eventually became gold. But it just didn't have that hit to get it above the level of album radio. And we were very happy with it." Happy was a key word. BTO played heavy music, but it wasn't exactly heavy metal. Randy's solos were exuberant explorations not merely fancy fretwork or ego-driven virtuoso displays of dexterity for dexterity's sake. BTO was perfect for the album driven FM format. "However," Randy notes, "our label representative came to us and said, 'Look, you know how to write hit singles. Now that you've got this base of a quarter of a million fans, now it's time to double that. Do your album tracks, but give us three or four hit singles.'" What the label guys were telling them made sense. Randy immediately put his mind to writing a hit single.

It's the work that we avoid
And we're all self-employed
We love to work at nothing all day

"I was fooling around with this guitar riff," he recalls, "and out of the blue I pulled out this old song that I had written back in '67, which was a take-off on *Paperback Writer*. That old song was *White Collar Worker*. I wanted to write a song like that. And I had spent a lot of time with the Guess Who in New York at Scepter studios (in '67) and our engineer had to leave every night at eleven to get home and then in the morning he had to take the 8:15 to get back into the city. So I wrote a song about it and I called it *White Collar Worker*." On the way to their club gig that night in Vancouver, Bachman heard deejay Darryl B say, "This is Darryl B on C-Fun and we're takin' care of business," on his car stereo. He thought it was a great title for a song, but he didn't realize how soon he was going to write it. As he recalls, "Fred Turner lost his voice and said I had to sing the last set. Up 'til that point I had only sung Neil Young and Bob Dylan songs with BTO songs where you didn't need a great voice, where everybody can sort of sing along. Suddenly, I had to sing alone. I thought, 'What can I do? I can't tell them all the chords to *White Collar Worker*.' I turned around and instead of saying the chords for this song are "E, A-flat minor, C#, B and all these things... I simply said, 'C, B-flat and F! Endlessly! And when I get to the hook, help me.' And Robbie and Fred said, 'Help you what?' I said, 'I'm doin' a new song.'"

Fred and Robbie had no idea that Randy was going to create his signature song on the spot, combining the phrase he had heard Darryl B say on the radio with the verses from *White Collar Worker*, and rocking out on long, extended guitar solos, however, they were all consenting adults and they had jammed unfamiliar material hundreds of times. So what was the problem?

"I started that song as you hear it start," Bachman continues. "And I sang my old verses from *White Collar Worker*. When it got to the bridge instead of stopping and singing *White Collar Worker*, the original bridge, the rhythm just kept going. And I sang, 'We're takin' care of business' and the next time it came 'round, they knew it, and they sang 'Takin' Care Of Business' and I answered them: 'Everyday! Every way!' The song was over, but the crowd kept clapping. They knew we were jamming it. They kept clapping and started to sing it, so we picked up the tempo again and did the song again for about another ten minutes. The night was over. It was a success!"

Necessity, they say, is the mother of invention. In rock & roll, desperation often plays a part, too. Forced to improvise on the spot, he simply replaced his old song title and chorus with his new ones and used the verses he had already written. "I wrote *White Collar Worker* about commuters taking trains in New York during '69 and '70 when I was there recording with the Guess Who," Randy told me. "In Winnipeg, you drive to work. But these New York guys would take the 8:15 into the city and at night they would come back. I'd seen it in movies, the day in the life of a businessman in New York, and the girls were all trying to look pretty. So, it was written about a big city workday. But it was called *White Collar Worker*, and everyone hated it in the Guess Who. And later on in BTO we had *Blue Collar*. And then they would say, 'We can't have a song called *White Collar Worker* when we've already had a song called *Blue Collar*.' So, the title was no good. But I knew the verses were great:"

They get up every morning
From the alarm clock's warnin'
Take the 8:15 into the city
There's a whistle up above
And people push and people shove
And all the girls who try to look pretty

"Everybody loves those lyrics!" Randy says, proudly. "And that was my kind of Chuck Berry lyrics. Ralph Murphy and I wrote a song in '67 called *A Little Bit Of Rain*." That song had been a hit in England for Murphy. While Randy was working on his rewrite of *White Collar Worker*, he lifted the catchy guitar riff from Ralph's *A Little Bit Of Rain* and adapted it into his new arrangement. Years later at a British Columbia Country Music Association convention in New Westminster, I saw Randy and Ralph Murphy, who had not met for years, sitting at separate tables and reintroduced Randy to Ralph. After that, Randy and Ralph would perform *Takin' Care Of Business* together at songwriter events and refer to it as the hit that Randy got by stealing Ralph's riff. "That riff," Bachman notes, "is used in the middle of *Takin' Care Of Business* just to break the monotony because *Takin' Care Of Business* was three chords, over and over and over. It had no bridge, no hook no song format. Other than that it was *Louie, Louie* endless mind-bashing of three chords. The original version had 12 chords. That's why nobody liked it." The transition from a song with many chords that nobody really liked to the song we know today came about in the usual way that had happened in Bachman's past totally by accident. Spontaneity has always been his best friend.

A devout Mormon for many years, Randy Bachman never bought into the sex, drugs, and rock & roll cliche. For Randy, it's rock & roll and it's a business that he has a lot of fun working at. He has admitted that when he quit the Guess Who, he was pretty messed up, but he had not got messed up by drinking or drugging. Stress and overwork had ruined his health and he had become as difficult to get along with as he found his band mates to be. In the '80s, a second marriage to Denise McCann, the stunningly beautiful singer who had a hit on the radio in the early '70s with *Tattoo Man*, would bring stability. Bachman decided to quit BTO before he burned out and focus on his family life. He had enjoyed many musical incarnations. But he never forgot how blessed he had been when his signature song came together on stage at a gig in Vancouver.

The spontaneity continued when Randy, Robbie, and Fred went into Kay Smith's Seattle studio to record. The new song continued to evolve all on its own. As he recalls, "We went in to record *Takin' Care of Business* about two weeks later. I typed up the lyrics and gave them to Turner. He was the lead singer that I had specifically hired to sing in the band. But he said, 'I don't want to sing this. It's your song. It'll give me a rest on stage. Instead of singing Neil Young and Bob Dylan songs, you'll sing one of your own songs.'" Randy had offered his song to his pal, but here it was being handed back to him. There was a problem though, that he had to overcome. "I had a sore throat," he explains. "It was in January, I think, when we recorded it, and I had a kind of winter cold. I sang it on the first take. It was to be an album cut. The song sped up and slowed down. I didn't care. We had no rhythm machines in those days. No click tracks. We went in and played it. The guitar was a little out of tune. I was playing a Gretsch and as you bend strings on a Gretsch, the bridge moves. I thought, well, 'it sounds like Keith Richards, I'll leave it.' I didn't take a whole lot of care with that."

In the perfect synchronicity of the moment nine years after he and

Chad Allen had gone into a TV station in the wee hours of a January morning in 1965, Randy's winter cold virus actually helped him out. He had a raspy vocal, just like Chad's *Shakin' All Over* vocal. There was still that fluke factor, though, and it arrived as they were listening to a playback of the track they had just recorded. This time it was not slap back echo, it was a knock on the studio door. As Randy recalls, "It was two o'clock in the morning, we were hearing a playback of the track, there was a knock on the door of the studio and there was a guy standing there with two pizzas. He said, 'Did you order the pizzas?' We said, 'No, they're down the hall.' Steve Miller was recording down the hall and so was War. The guy is standing there with the pizzas, wearing army fatigues. He's got a big beard, he looks like Fidel Castro, but he's about six-foot-four, a gigantic guy. And, as he's leaving with the pizzas to take them down the hall, he says, 'That song sounds like it could use a piano!'"

Bachman was weary. He wasn't prepared to deal with this intruder. He blinked, did a double take, and said, "It's two in the morning . . . I can't play the piano."

"The pizza delivery guy said, "I can. Gimme a shot!' He took the pizzas down the hall. He took the lid from the pizza box and said, 'Let me write down a little chart.' It wasn't the chords, it was stopping and starting and that little thing in the middle that Ralph Murphy and I did years earlier. So he wrote down this little chart, played the piano, got up, and left. I thought, 'Well, we'll wipe this tomorrow.'"

That piano solo, played by the pizza guy that knocked on the wrong door at 2 a.m., is the solo you hear on BTO's *Takin' Care Of Business* to this day. No wonder it became a rock anthem, a favorite in hockey rinks from coast to coast. The song had been nailed in one take and then dialed up a piano player from the ozone all on its own. As Randy recalls, "We came in the next day. Played it. The piano isn't bad. It gives us a different sound. We were getting tired of two guitars, bass and drums. The head of the record label came in and said, 'This thing really cooks, leave the piano on. Who's the piano player?' We said, 'We have no idea.' We had to wait 'til War and Steve Miller came in and ask them, 'Where did you order that pizza from?' We ordered pizza again. The same guy came. We got his name, Norman Durkee, wrote it down, gave him double scale, and put his name on the album. It was amazing.

He did one take and left. So that whole thing is one guitar take, one vocal take, one piano take. The song speeds up and slows down. It's a very imperfect song, but in it people hear what rock & roll really was: a bunch of guys playing for fun and not for perfection."

And we've been	
Takin' care of business (every day)	
Takin' care of business (every way)	
Takin' care of business (and it's all mine)	
Takin' care of business and workin' overtime	

From the session that produced his first hit onward Randy Bachman has preferred spontaneity and "feel" over perfection. During his time spent in New York he had learned to recognize a hit when he heard it, and he is proud as punch of his spontaneous and imperfect track *Takin' Care Of Business*. "It's a terrible, terrible recording," he admits, "but so are 20 or 30 other great records. You can't even hear what the guy is saying in *Louie Louie*. But there is some magic in the grooves. When I was doing that tour with The Kingsmen, everybody was complaining that the lyrics were 'dirty' or obscene or suggestive and the label wanted them to remix it. *Louie Louie* was recorded on a three-track. So, they went back and redid the vocal, but it wasn't the same song. The magic wasn't there. So, they went back to the original. You can't mess with that chemistry. You are only too grateful that it happened to you and you accept it."

Over the years, *Takin' Care of Business* has been used in many TV and radio commercials. Television and radio spots often lack spontaneity and sponsors were willing to pay for a taste of it in order to sell a few thousand more cars, trucks, or hi tech widgets. Normally, hijacking Top 40 hits is a risky business for ad companies. It has not always translated into sales. Sometimes it does. Sometimes it doesn't. *Takin' Care Of Business* was a different kind of rock anthem in 1974, though, a Blue Collar anthem for working class men and women, not a drug-induced head-trip or a jet-propelled love song. It was a celebration of rock & roll, and, at the same time, provided an occasion for normal working class people to celebrate their lifestyle while singing along. Sticking with what had worked since day one kept Randy Bachman vital during his

BTO days, and has been a contributing factor to his career ever since. In 2004, he released Jazz Thing, a tribute to his mentor, Lenny Breau, featuring harmony vocals by Denise McCann, not because he believed he was going to sell a zillion jazz albums, but because he wanted to do it and knew he would have fun touring the jazz material.

Takin' Care Of Business has become the most licensed song in Sony Music's publishing catalog, part of the sound tracks of our lives, used in major advertising campaigns organized by powerful corporations like K Mart, Office Depot and the Australian chain of office supply stores, Officeworks. It's been used to sell beer, played at hockey games and by the King of Rock & Roll, Elvis Presley. Elvis liked the phrase so much that he changed the name of his band to the TCB band and had the logo painted on one of his jets. For years there was a rumor circulating that claimed that the King had named his band after Randy's song, but it was unconfirmed. "Many years after his death," Bachman told Spinner, "I saw a Special on HBO or Showtime or something like that, when they were interviewing Priscilla Presley at Graceland. They asked her where Elvis got 'takin' care of business,' and she said, 'Oh, we were driving in our Cadillac to the airport in LA, going to fly back to Memphis, and a song came on the radio by a Canadian band Takin' Care Of Business, and Elvis said, 'Quick, turn that up I love that song.' I was blown away. Elvis was the reason I started to play Rock 'n' Roll guitar in the first place. I was a kid playing classical violin from the age of five to 14, and, I saw Elvis on TV and went, 'Wow that's Rock 'n' Roll!'"

In the new millennium Bachman continues to host his Vinyl Tap radio show on CBC Radio One, and to perform with Burton Cummings, Chad Allen, Fred Turner and Denise McCann. He is also keenly involved in writing songs with European guys like Michael Saxell and local songsmiths like Ron Irving and Mike Shellard.

In the fall of 2003, Shellard, lead vocalist of the country group, One Horse Blue, was driving back from a gig in Alberta and was critically injured in a highway accident. Right away, Randy rallied the troops and staged a benefit at Roosters, a roadhouse in Pitt Meadows. Streetheart, the Guess Who (with ex-Mother Tucker's Yellow Duck vocalist Donnie McDougal singing Burton Cummings' songs), Chilliwack, One Horse Blue, the Suzanne Gitzi Band, and country star Rick Tippe all played sets. Prism guitarist Lindsey Mitchell put on a great show sitting in with a couple of the acts. I spent some time backstage with Lindsey, Randy, and Denise and was struck by Bachman's good health and his youthful gait. He told me he had lost a lot of weight and that his daughter, Callianne, was responsible for his new fitness program. Mike Shellard had just finished doing some song demos with Randy, and we were both concerned about his condition. He had sustained multiple fractures but was no longer in intensive care.

The good news was that the benefit raised several thousand dollars for his wife, Mavis, and his kids. Later that night, during Randy's set, Callianne joined her father for a couple of songs. The crowd went bananas, of course, when he got around to *You Ain't Seen Nothin' Yet*, *Hey You*, and *Let It Ride*. We all sang along when he finished up with his signature song. Bachman came off the stage sweating and wiping himself down with a towel. He was happy. He had taken care of business.

Sundown

Gordon Lightfoot

Words & Music by Gordon Lightfoot

© 1974, Moose Music, Songs of Universal

I can see her lyin' back in her satin dress

In a room where you do what you don't confess

Sundown, you'd better take care

If I find you bin creepin' round my back stairs

On May 22, 1976, Gordon Lightfoot was playing the opening chords of *Sundown* on *Saturday Night Live* when his performance was suddenly interrupted by John Belushi, who was dressed in the "Samurai Tailor" costume he had worn for his recurring character, Futaba, in a sketch in which he had taken a pair of shears to *SNL* host Buck Henry's tuxedo. Now it was the Canadian singer-songwriter's turn, Lightfoot's indiscretion being that he had agreed to perform two songs, but despite Buck Henry's protests had launched into a third. As the sound of the music died, a camera close-up showed the TV audience that Futaba had cut Lightfoot's guitar strings with a pair of wire cutters.

Of course, the mock violence was all in good fun, and the boisterous studio audience roared its appreciation as Lightfoot looked stunned, Futaba bowed, and Buck Henry stood triumphantly by his side. It was a marvelous moment in the first season of a TV show that has survived to the present day because of the foundation laid by John Belushi, Dan Aykroyd, Bill Murray, Chevy Chase, Steve Martin, Jane Curtain and Roseanne Rosannadanna, a.k.a. Gilda Radner.

In retrospect, the sketch seems an odd example of serendipity or synchronicity or sheer coincidence that Lightfoot's *Sundown* lyrics had been partially inspired by his turbulent on-again-off-again affair with hardcore groupie Cathy Evelyn Smith, who would subsequently be accused of injecting John Belushi with a fatal dose of heroin and cocaine in his bungalow at the notorious Sunset Boulevard hotel, Chateau Marmont.

There was no way that Lorne Michaels, the producer of *SNL*, could have foreseen that there would be anything at all going on between Gordon's ex and Belushi in the future. In fact, it wasn't widely known at that time that Cathy Evelyn was the subject of Lightfoot's song.

Cathy Evelyn Smith definitely had some strange effects on the men she hung out with, for example, Canadian singer-songwriter Dan Hill, whom she dated sometime after Lightfoot, Hoyt Axton, and Tom Paxton. Having dragged Hill out to California, she ditched him at a Laurel Canyon party in favor of a marquee movie star. Then a year later, she ended up in Hill's Hollywood hotel room and proceeded to put out some lines of heroin on top of his hotel room television set. "It was her way of making it up to me for going upstairs with the actor," Hill told *Writing Gordon Lightfoot* author Dave Bidini. "She always used to call me a wimp, but I said, 'You're right, Cathy. I'm a Don Mills wimp but there ain't no way I'm snorting heroin off the top of a TV set.' This was 1979, before John Belushi died . . . Cathy was beautiful, charismatic and smart. I was at a stage in my life where I was drawn to the bad girl, and maybe she had the same allure for Gord.... As a groupie," Hill explained," she'd take your kids to school, go shopping, do your books because she was bright, and then she'd [make love to you]. In the music business, that wasn't thought of as strange at all."

Smith, a native of Hamilton, Ontario, was not present at the *SNL* theater when Lightfoot and Belushi were briefly featured together; she was driving Hoyt Axton's tour bus down that *Ribbon Of Darkness* on an endless string of one night stands that Lightfoot had chronicled in song for Marty Robbins. It had become a number one country hit a decade earlier.

By this time, Lightfoot had begun to develop a reputation as a hard-drinking, womanizing performer who played rough. When Cathy Smith got around to writing her autobiography, she accused Gordon of hanging her out the window of an LA apartment building by the ankles. Belushi met her briefly when she was part of the Band's entourage during their 1976 appearance on *Saturday Night Live,* but he would not get to know her personally until she had become a serial groupie and begun hanging out with the Rolling Stones. According to legend, Smith had first been the girlfriend of Hawks' drummer Levon Helm and mother of Helm's son, Tracy Lee.

Lightfoot met her at the Riverboat club in Toronto, and they spent a lot of time in rented hotel rooms and her tiny apartment, where she lived with her son, Tracy Lee. When his marriage to Brita, his Swedish wife, had begun to melt down, Gordon rented a 28th floor bachelor pad in one of Toronto's exclusive new high-rise buildings, where he lived the life of a high-rolling jet-setter.

Cathy Smith was an orphan raised by foster parents. By the time that Gordon and Cathy began hanging out together, they were both acknowledged substance abusers. While Lightfoot was fond of wine, beer, and whiskey, his situation was said to have been somewhat exacerbated by Cathy's abuse of hard drugs and he was more than a tad jealous of her staying out to all hours of the night with male acquaintances.

Gordon Lightfoot was born in Orillia, Ontario, the birthplace of Stephen Leacock, on November 17, 1938. He was a child prodigy, winning singing contests and recording records before he graduated from high school. Upon graduation, he studied music composition and learned how to sight-read sheet music in Los Angeles. Moving to Toronto, he worked as a bank teller by day and at night began to worm his way into the music business, composing freelance arrangements for CBC productions, playing drums under the pseudonym Charles Sullivan, and harmonizing with the Gino Silvi Singers.

In 1960, he joined the "Swinging, Singing 8" chorus line of the CBC TV show *Country Hoedown*. Paid $100 per week to support stars like Tommy Hunter on the network's most successful entertainment show, he was quickly nicknamed "Leadfoot" because his dancing skills left much to be desired. "I was the only one who was always doing a do-si-do instead of an aleman right," he admits. "The only reason they kept me was that I was so damned good at sight-reading." Many years later, he would look back fondly on those days spent working with comedian Gordie Tapp and country singer Tommy Hunter. As he told Jean Somnor, "I was so happy in that job. I was very shy. They were all very funny and all I had to do was just watch them."

Hearing Ian & Sylvia at the Village Corner in Yorkville awakened Lightfoot to the potential of a career as a folk artist. In 1963, he got his first break when Art Snider got him a job producing eight episodes of a corny British television variety show, *The Country & Western Show*.

Marrying Swedish embassy publicist Brita Olaisson and spending his honeymoon working in England inspired Lightfoot to write no less than 60 new songs during his five-month stay in the UK. His lyrics now had a clarity that appealed to audiences when they heard him perform in Yorkville coffeehouses and local bars. Years later he would say, "Playing in bars had its advantages. You could try out all kinds of new things and make all kinds of mistakes and hardly anyone noticed. Sometimes you could hold the audience by throwing in some off-color humor and following it with a good up-tempo country tune or a bawdy ballad. Sometimes they'd be watching the hockey game on TV with the volume turned up so you couldn't sing over it, so you just sat down, waited for the period to end, and got a few songs in during the intermission."

These working conditions might have frustrated some people, but Lightfoot accepted his situation philosophically. "There was lots to do just staying out of trouble. I knew six guitar chords and some variations. I played everyone else's songs and a few of my own. I saw a lot of my friends go down the tubes in those days, but somehow I managed to survive. The excesses of all-night partying were taken for granted, but most of all I remember getting people off by singing. At some point I decided to make a go of it, and there were people who gave me a hand up the ladder."

| I can picture every move that a man could make |
| Getting lost in your lover is the first mistake |
| Sundown you better take care |
| If I find you bin creepin' round my back stairs |

Despite his British sojourn, Lightfoot's new songs owed far more to Bob Dylan than they did to the Beatles. Ian & Sylvia were impressed. "They were immediately struck by the quality of Lightfoot's songs," Nicholas Jennings notes, "especially *For Lovin' Me* and *Early Morning Rain*, which Ian said evoked 'the old tradition of Canadians working in the far north on construction jobs then heading to the city to blow the money.' Sylvia was haunted by the line 'You can't jump on a jet plane, like you can a freight train,' which she thought beautifully contrasted the rural past with the urban present."

The popular folk duo recorded the two songs for their next album. Their manager passed them on to his folk supergroup Peter, Paul & Mary, who scored a Top 30 hit with *For Lovin' Me* in February 1965. Albert Grossman dispatched his assistant, John Court, to Toronto to meet Lightfoot in person. Court was impressed. He thought Lightfoot was "a heck of a songsmith" and that he had "one of those wonderful voices."

Sometimes I think it's a sin
When I feel like I'm winning when I'm losing again

Ultimately, though, Grossman appeared to be more interested in exploiting Lightfoot's song catalog than making him a star in his own right. An unsuccessful early deal with Warner Brothers was replaced by a less than satisfactory one with United Artists, who insisted Lightfoot record Dylan's *Just Like Tom Thumb's Blues* as a single instead of one of his own compositions. Meanwhile, Marty Robbins took his *Ribbon Of Darkness* all the way to the top of the *Billboard* country chart. Commissioned to compose a Canadian epic, Lightfoot came up with *The Great Canadian Railroad Trilogy*, which he debuted on New Year's Day 1967, performing the song with a 40-piece orchestra on a CBC TV Special that kicked off Canada's centennial celebrations. In September '67, Lightfoot was featured on "Lightfoot Forward" a special production of the CBC TV program *Telescope*, which opened with a shot of a jet plane revving its engines to the tune of *Early Morning Rain*. Other segments featured his mother and sidemen Red Shea and John Stockfish.

Bernie Fiedler had paid Lightfoot big money to play three and four week stands at his Riverboat club, and beginning in 1968, they began to stage an annual series of shows at Massey Hall, where Lightfoot had won a singing contest at age 12. The 2800 plush seats of the prestigious theater were not enough to house all of Lightfoot's fans for merely one show per year, and the promoter and performer added more and more dates as the years passed by. Already an icon in his native land, Lightfoot's career didn't take off in the United States until he signed with Warner Reprise in the early '70s and began to work with producer Lenny Waronker.

If You Could Read My Mind became his first Top 40 hit on the

Billboard Hot 100, hitting the number 5 spot and topping the Adult Contemporary chart. The lines "I don't know where we went wrong / but the feeling's gone and I just can't get it back" referred to his marriage breakdown. Many Canadians could relate. Lightfoot was made an officer of the Order of Canada that same year. He and Anne Murray owned the Juno Awards during the early '70s, being named Best Male and Female Vocalist year after year. His run as top male chanteuse only ended when Terry Jacks' *Seasons In The Sun* became a gigantic *Billboard* hit in '74. In 1975, Jacks and Lightfoot both received Junos, Terry for Male Vocalist of the Year and Gordon for Male Artist of the Year. From '75 on, Lightfoot was awarded a Juno as Canada's Best Folk Singer, winning no less than 15 Junos during the decade.

By all accounts, the parties following Lightfoot's annual Massey Hall concerts were the best thrown in Toronto during those years. Murray McLaughlin was a bosom buddy. Liona Boyd regularly attended. And when Bob Dylan's Rolling Thunder Revue came to town for two shows, Dylan paid tribute to Lightfoot, invited him on stage, and partied till the wee hours of the morning at Lightfoot's Rosedale mansion. Lightfoot was a swashbuckling, romantic figure cutting a swath through the entertainment world.

I can see her looking fast in her faded jeans
She's a hard lovin' woman got me feelin' mean

Sundown was a bit of a departure from Gordon Lightfoot's usual faire, a *noire* ballad laced with the turmoil of sexual jealousy that percolated ambiguously beneath the shimmering surface of his most danceable groove put to vinyl. Released in the spring of 1974, *Sundown* spent 23 weeks in the Top 40 and became his only number one hit on the *Billboard* Hot 100. Even though John Belushi biographer Bob Woodward claims that Cathy Smith did not develop a heroin habit until several years after her involvement with Lightfoot, in retrospect, "Sundown" is an uncannily accurate designation for a woman junkie, a simple extrapolation of Neil Young's line "every junkie is like a setting sun."

| Sundown, you'd better take care | |
| If I find you've been creeping 'round my back stairs | |

The song also describes her lovers, which included no less than three members of the Band and at least two of the Good Brothers, who were opening shows for Lightfoot and were rumored to have been the number one candidates to be guilty of sneaking around Lightfoot's "back stairs." When questioned by interviewers, Lightfoot has been uncharacteristically unwilling to say much about the song. "All it is," he told *Crawdaddy* in '75, "is a thought about a situation where someone is wondering what his 'live one' is doing at the moment. He doesn't quite know where she is. He's not ready to give up on her, either, and that's about all I've got to say about that." There definitely were some questions that Gordon was not willing to answer at the time, but nobody cared because Sundown was so good, with its liquid electric guitar riffs and seething bass and drum rhythms. Lightfoot's lyrics held so many double entendres and hinted interpretations that you'd need a codebook to decipher them.

Lightfoot was far more comfortable speaking about the rest of the album. "SUNDOWN came out on schedule," he said in the same interview. "It was maybe a month late. We put that album together over a three-month period and I was very happy to sit down and listen to it. It didn't give me any bad moments. Musically, it was strong. The songs were good, and all of a sudden we got a hit single off of it, and then *Carefree Highway*." The origins of that song, he says, came from a freeway sign he saw on the outskirts of Flagstaff, Arizona. "I thought it would make a good title for a song," he told Nancy Naglin. "I wrote it down, put it in my suitcase, and it stayed there for eight months." He eventually crafted it into a song about a girlfriend he had dated when he was 22. The song's easygoing tempo, bright melody, and romantic imagery furthered the image of Lightfoot as a gypsy balladeer, a troubadour.

| She's been looking like a queen in a sailor's dream | |
| And she don't always say what she really means | |

In Dave Bidini's unauthorized biography, *Writing Gordon Lightfoot*, he poses "questions he is not supposed to ask" in several chapters written as if they are letters addressed directly to Lightfoot, and comes up with a bare bones description of *Sundown*. "There are times in Cathy's book (*Chasing The Dragon*)," Bidini writes, "when she describes sleeping with you in the beginning, and her memories seem, I dunno, kind of sweet . . . But things got bad fast, foreshadowing your portrait of her in *Sundown*, which, if it wasn't such a well-crafted country rock song, would be regarded as one of the toughest and maybe meanest sets of lyrics ever written about anyone. It would be regarded as plainly misogynistic, I think, if the narrator the narrator being you didn't come across like such a mess. But even if you didn't hang her out the window (by her ankles), your relationship started to blacken. You did terrible things to your girlfriend, and she did terrible things to you."

Whatever catharsis Lightfoot found in writing and performing his most successful single release, the immediate benefits he reaped from its success were undeniable at the time. "Lightfoot's is the voice of the romantic," a critic wrote in *The Village Voice*. "For him (as for *Don Quixote*, one of his chosen heroes) perfection is always in view and always slipping from his grasp." When both the SUNDOWN album and single hit number one on the *Billboard* charts in June 1974, Gordon expanded his band to include a pedal steel player and a drummer. He toured Europe as a headliner.

An indication of just how popular *Sundown* was during the summer of '74 is shown by the fact that it was his only Top 40 country hit in the US. Like Anne Murray, he had amassed a lot of middle of the road airplay, beginning with his breakout 1971 hit *If You Could Read My Mind*. *Sundown* also spent a couple of weeks atop the Adult Contemporary charts. Lightfoot's record label followed it up with *Carefree Highway*, which hit into the Top 10, and *Rainy Day People*, a number 26 hit in 1975. Even though his personal life was a shambles, and he was taken to task for his womanizing and boozing by *Rolling Stone*, his career was at its peak. So, apparently, were his songwriting abilities, which he approached with a Puritan work ethic that was singularly different from the way that many of his fellow singer-songwriters went about their business. He soon wrote his masterpiece, *The Wreck Of The Edmund Fitzgerald*, a surprisingly gothic chronicle of a contemporary tragedy. And although he later bonded with some of the survivors of the tragedy, for the present he remained footloose and fancy free.

As he later revealed, his cavalier attitude had almost cost him one hit song. "*Carefree Highway* was almost left in the glove compartment of a rental car we had for a day," he confessed in the liner notes for his boxed set SONGBOOK. As the years passed by, being able to write songs on a regular basis became an indicator that all was still well in his life. "I'm still interested in songwriting," he said in 2000. "I don't have as much time as I would like to do it, but I'm still doing it. I can think about lyrics when I'm in the show. I can think about lyrics when I'm tuning up in the dressing room. I can think about it while I'm driving in my car. I write things all the time on slips of paper and all sorts of crazy things like that. Then I go back to the room where I work and get it together."

If songwriting was of this much importance to Gordon Lightfoot's sense of well-being, performing was not far behind. To some people who were in a position to know, it was even more important. As his manager, Al Mair, told Dave Bidini, "Gord wasn't the easiest person to know, which is why those nights on stage were so important to him. He lived for performing. It was his air, his food, his reason for living."

Over the years, Lightfoot evolved a unique approach to surviving in the music business. Prior to recording SUNDOWN in the fall of 1973, he embarked on a 500-mile canoe trip in the Canadian north, a ritual that he had employed in the past to clear his mind. Critics like Robert Everett-Green have claimed that he "captured a romantic national vision even in the moment it was being lost." No doubt, roughing it in the Canadian bush had kept things real for Lightfoot in ways that most urban Canadians no longer experienced.

About this time, Lightfoot resolved to revitalize his marriage to Brita, but this effort failed and Cathy Smith returned to his 28th floor apartment. Lightfoot had more in common with Smith than he did with his wife. As Al Mair later told biographer Dave Bidini, "Being famous isn't easy, not for anyone, even though it might look like it from the outside. Cathy was beautiful and smart, but she was a tramp. During that time, she was all that Gord had. And for a few years, they were virtually inseparable. Whether this was good or bad for him depends on your perspective."

Sometimes I think it's a shame
When I get feeling better when I'm feelin' no pain

When the questions about the lyrics to *Sundown* persisted, Lightfoot let interviewers know in no uncertain terms whom the song was *not* about. It was not about his ex-wife, Brita. "My former wife and I realize what we had to do and we got it done, and it's nobody's business," he told Naglin. "I'm sick and tired of it and so is she. We're friends."

Lightfoot chronicled his grief at being estranged from his children in the gut-wrenching ballad *If Children Had Wings*, which was prompted by his ex-wife's decision to move to France and take their offspring with her. As he told *Crawdaddy*, "Most of the relationships I have been in have failed. My personal life leaves something to be desired, but I'm trying to get it together now." Still, he often overreacted to criticism in the press, especially when accused of being an alcoholic. "I am definitely not overweight and I am definitely not an alcoholic," he told Naglin. "All I've been eating lately is papaya juice and lecithin." However, he would not give up his boozing until it affected his most important activity his ability to write quality songs.

Sometimes I think it's a shame
When I get feeling better when I'm feelin' no pain

In the 1980s, when his songwriting dwindled for a protracted period of time, Lightfoot quit drinking and womanizing, married a second time, and settled down to a happy domestic existence in an even bigger Rosedale mansion. He began to work with producer David Foster and toured relentlessly throughout the decade. He also leant a hand to many causes, including the Stein Valley watershed concert, an Alberta concert with Ian Tyson to protest the erection of a dam on the Oldman River, a Temagami Wilderness protest in Toronto, and a trip with Sting to view the devastation of the Brazilian rainforest. In April 1985, Lightfoot recorded the opening lines of *Tears Are Not Enough* in aid of the U.S.A. for Africa Trust, joining Bryan Adams, Joni Mitchell, Neil Young, and many other Canadian celebrities. That November he was inducted into the Canadian Music Hall of Fame by Bob Dylan during a Juno Awards show ceremony and later appeared as a special guest during Ian & Sylvia's Reunion Concert.

In a typical spirit of benevolence, he is said to have paid for Cathy Smith's legal fees when she ran afoul of the LAPD. However, he did not welcome her back into his life. Nor was he willing to discuss with journalists whether or not she had indeed been the woman he had immortalized in his biggest hit, *Sundown.*

> Sometimes I think it's a shame
> When I get feelin' better when I'm feelin' no pain
> Sundown you better take care
> If I find you bin creepin' round my back stairs

From the outset, Lightfoot had been a grisly interview, especially for rookie journalists like two *Georgia Straight* novices in 1971 who asked him how many interviews he had done that day. "Well," he had told them, "my throat hurts. I should be in bed. I've been boogyin' all night long, and I had to get up and come down here and I want to be back in bed by three." He had maintained throughout his career that he was a simple man, a claim that is born out by his serious approach to songwriting and his loyalty to his musicians.

Over the years, Lightfoot has made few personnel changes in his band, and contrary to trends has also employed his road musicians to record most of his album tracks. In the '60s, he performed with guitarist Red Shea and bassist John Stockfish. Rick Haynes replaced Stockfish in '68 and Terry Clements replaced Shea in '72. Since 1976, Terry, Rick, keyboard player Mike Hefferman and drummer Barry Keane have formed a nucleus that has also embraced pedal steel player Pee Wee Charles.

Lightfoot has always been a consummate professional, dressing in boots and jeans for his concerts but always donning a stylish freshly pressed shirt. His guitar playing is often overlooked, perhaps because he also composes and performs on the piano. "I use Travis-style finger-picking for various time signatures," he recently told Ben Elder. "I've found that it's best without any picks at all. I've adapted to it and cultivated nails. You do get some flesh, but you try to land right in between the nail and where the flesh is. If you get them just the right length, you can get a real good purchase on a string. And if you're using pick-ups on the guitar, you can get a lot of accents that make the playing more interesting."

Other than a bout with Bell's palsy, which had numbed his facial muscles during a Massey Hall concert and forced him to cancel a number of concert dates in '72, Gordon Lightfoot enjoyed relatively good health throughout the first 64 years of his life. In September 2002, however, he was unable to perform a concert in his hometown and was flown from Orillia to McMaster University Medical Centre in nearby Hamilton. He first complained of stomach pains and later learned that he had suffered a near fatal aneurysm. A team of doctors had fought to stem the flow of blood into his abdominal cavity, and he was in a coma for six weeks before beginning a slow recovery.

By the summer of 2004, Lightfoot was well enough to perform a song at the Mariposa Folk Festival, a surprise special guest during a tribute to his songwriting. By November 2004, he had recovered sufficiently to stage two full concert benefits for the hospital that had saved his life. "The family atmosphere in that hospital is remarkable," he told a CBC reporter. "It goes right through the staff and the people who go there. And, believe you me, I've seen lots of people, lots of people in pretty bad shape, come in through those doors." It is not known whether or not Cathy Smith, who has returned to Hamilton, visited him during his convalescence.

Sundown you'd better take care
If I find you've been creeping 'round my back stairs
Sometimes I think it's a sin
When I feel like I'm winning when I'm losing again

Wondering Where the Lions Are

Bruce Cockburn

Words & Music by Bruce Cockburn

© 1991, Golden Mountain Music Corp (SOCAN), Songs of Universal

Sun's up, uh huh, looks okay

The world survives into another day

And I'm thinking about eternity

Some kind of ecstasy got a hold on me

On May 10, 1980, comedian Bob Newhart was in New York City to host NBC's popular *Saturday Night Live* TV show. His special guests were the Amazing Rhythm Aces and Canadian newcomer Bruce Cockburn, who was being introduced to an American audience for the first time. Bill Murray joined the Rhythm Aces, shaking a tambourine during their performance of *Third Rate Romance*, and the *SNL* Band backed Cockburn on *Wondering Where The Lions Are*. The song was already bubbling up on the *Billboard* charts, an acoustic reggae track he had recorded in Toronto with Leroy Sibbles' Jamaican rhythm section.

Bruce Cockburn had toured the folk circuit in Canada for many years as a solo act. He was a dazzling guitarist and an accomplished multi-instrumentalist, and many of his Canadian fans had come to believe that he didn't need a band at all. Additional musicians would most likely get in his way, although, many of those same fans had begun to admit that he appeared to have found an extraordinarily vital groove with his latest hit. He was also a poetic lyricist who had read Rimbaud and T.S. Eliot and been inspired by Bob Dylan and John Lennon, but the clear, free-flowing imagery of his best songs was very much his own.

> I had another dream about lions at the door
> They weren't half as frightening as they were before
> But I'm thinking about eternity
> Some kind of ecstasy got a hold on me

The first time I saw Bruce Cockburn in concert was in Vancouver in the early '70s. He was opening for former Luke & the Apostles front man, Luke Gibson, who was trying to establish a solo career after his Toronto band had failed to agree with Albert Grossman on a management deal in the Big Apple. Few of the locals had any idea who the headliner was, but many of us had already heard a buzz about Cockburn. A privileged minority had actually purchased or listened to one of his three albums put out by True North Records, a company run by his manager, Bernie Finkelstein, that has continued to issue his releases and those of many other fine Canadian acts down through the years. Bruce began his opening set standing in a semi-circle of musical instruments that were spread out on the floor of the Egress nightclub stage before him. He told us that he was learning to play all of them, had mastered some better than others, and then proceeded to blow us away with every selection he performed.

I had simply never heard better tone or brighter guitar strings before. My only comparison would have been the first 20 or 30 minutes or so after I had put new strings on my Martin D-28. Much longer than that and the clear bell-like resonance diminishes in most cases no matter how carefully we wipe those strings after each time they have been assailed with human sweat from a picking session. So it actually occurred to me while I was listening to this early Bruce Cockburn concert that he might very well have strung every single one of those six or eight instruments with new strings prior to going on stage and performing. It was a remarkable approach that you didn't see very often in those days. Strings cost too much and musicians were paid too little. Nevertheless, Cockburn's records, and especially the instrumental track *Sunwheel Dance*, exemplify the best six-string guitar tone you will ever hear on a record or a CD. And getting to hear him in concert in the intimate Beatty Street venue near the old Greyhound Bus Depot on West Georgia remains one of the musical highlights of my life.

Combining the techniques of blues pickers like Mississippi John

Hurt with his own modal jazz licks, Cockburn recorded ten remarkable Canadian folk albums before Bernie Finkelstein was able to secure a good enough deal with American labels like Island, Millennium and Columbia that his music had a chance of breaking in the U.S. His May 1980 *Saturday Night Live* performance propelled *Wondering Where The Lions Are* into the *Billboard* Top 25 and sold a lot of copies of DANCING IN THE DRAGON'S JAWS. It was a remarkable track, not only because of its marvelous melody and striking imagery, but also because it was one of the most danceable grooves recorded anywhere in the '70s. In the '80s, Cockburn followed it up with a series of similarly songs, including *Rumours of Glory, Lovers in a Dangerous Time,* and *If I Had A Rocket Launcher,* which also featured politically insightful lyrics that reminded some rock & roll fans of a time in the '60s when rock and pop lyrics had been more adventuresome.

> Walls windows trees, waves coming through
> You be in me and I'll be in you
> Together in eternity
> Some kind of ecstasy got a hold on me

Bruce Cockburn was born on May 27, 1945 in Ottawa, and raised on a farm near Pembroke, Ontario. From an early age he studied piano and composition and took clarinet and trumpet lessons. In 1956, Elvis rocked his world and he began to play rock & roll. His grandmother presented him with his first guitar in '59. When he showed an aptitude for the instrument, his parents bought him a better one, a Kay arch-top with an electric pickup. By 1963, he was in a band called the Jades.

Upon graduating from high school, Bruce headed for Europe and spent the summer of '64 busking on the streets of Paris. He liked the life of a troubadour but returned to North America and enrolled in classes at the exclusive Berklee College of Music in Boston. "I wanted to compose jazz music for big bands," he later told *Acoustic Guitar* magazine. "I studied as much theory as they were able to pack into the couple of years I was there." He played in jug bands in the Boston area, and when he was in Ontario he played with the Esquires, who are credited with making the first Canadian music video in 1964.

In 1965, he acquired a Gibson electric guitar and recorded his first record, the Esquires' *Love Made A Fool Of You*, which Capitol Records released as a single in Canada. By 1966, Cockburn had hooked up with Bill Hawkins' folk-rock band, the Children, and began writing songs with Hawkins. He also played organ and harmonica with a band called Heavenly Blue. He credits Hawkins as an important influence. "Bill taught me about using words," he told Nicholas Jennings. Three of his compositions from this era were recorded by Donna Warner, Brent Titcomb, and David Wiffen's folk-rock group Three's A Crowd on their CHRISTOPHER'S MOVIE MATINEE album, which was produced by the Mamas & the Papas' Cass Elliott. While Cockburn was working with the Children, the band opened for both the Rolling Stones and the Lovin' Spoonful.

When the group disbanded, Cockburn joined the Flying Circus, a psychedelic band that opened for Jimi Hendrix and Wilson Pickett. However, by this time he'd tired of being in bands. As he told Jennings, "I'd acquired a body of original work that I liked singing alone better than with a band; plus, I was getting a little sick of self-indulgent, noisy rock." He made his first appearance as a solo artist at the Mariposa Folk Festival that same summer.

By 1969, Bruce was married, and he and his wife Kitty had moved into a Yorkville flat they shared with Murray McLaughlin and his wife, Patty. Cockburn taped 26 TV shows with Three's A Crowd; however, only one of the shows aired before the series was canceled. Life in Yorkville had deteriorated from the happy hippie days of the Summer of Love, when there was said to be 1400 bands in Toronto, more than 400 of them playing union gigs. Many of the flower children and music business pioneers like Bernie Finkelstein, who had managed both the Paupers and Kensington Market, had moved to the country.

Sharing an urban apartment with his pal McLaughlin was cool, though, as Bruce told Jennings: "He had great songs, good lyrics and music, played guitar well and sang beautifully. On top of that, he had charisma." McLaughlin was less generous in his appraisal of Cockburn, telling Jennings "He was an odd buzzard. Sometimes on stage he used to wear these little Catholic choirboy shirts with a little tie. It was very weird."

"There were a lot of things we didn't have in common," Cockburn admits. "I wasn't really a drinker. I'd get stoned and sit there for an hour without saying anything." However, it was a spate of supernatural occurrences and a bad dream that broke up their happy little home. After a night in which Cockburn had a nightmarish dream, he and his wife packed their belongings and their dog, Aroo, into a camper and headed for the country. "It was really psychodrama stuff," McLaughlin recalls. "Someone said they'd had a dream where they flew disembodied through the apartment and saw everyone else hacked to pieces, all bloody and disemboweled in our beds. It turned out that all of us had had the same dream."

Cockburn began performing shows with his dog at his feet. His relaxed, down-home style was totally in sync with the back-to-the-land movement and the *Whole Earth Catalogue* lifestyle that was in vogue. When Bernie Finklestein heard Bruce sing his new song *Going To The Country* at the Pornographic Onion Club, he was intrigued. Bernie wanted to get back into the music business, and their meeting led to the formation of True North Records and a lifelong partnership. By December of '69, Bruce was in a Toronto studio recording songs for his first album with Gene Martynec producing. The time was ripe for the enterprising impresario Finklestein to launch his debut album. CBC-TV had just featured his artist in a documentary about the Mariposa Folk Festival, Cockburn was asked to provide music for the sound track of the feature film *Going Down The Road*, and Prime Minister Trudeau and Pierre Juneau would soon announce legislation that would increase the Canadian content on radio airwaves from coast to coast.

The themes of Bruce Cockburn's early albums were a concern for the environment and an appreciation of the vast Canadian landscape. In 1975, a conversion from agnosticism to Christianity brought new themes and a growing audience, but he never became a bible thumper. By 1979, 10 years and 10 albums after his debut, Bruce was recording material that Bernie could use to break his career in the bigger American market. With his *Wondering Where The Lions Are* single and his DANCING IN THE DRAGON'S JAWS album, he provided Bernie with music that the whole world would soon embrace.

Up among the firs where it smells so sweet
Or down in the valley where the river used to be
I got my mind on eternity
Some kind of ecstasy got a hold on me

And I'm wondering where the lions are . . .
I'm wondering where the lions are . . .

Wondering Where The Lions Are was written on January 12, 1979, one of the last songs that Bruce composed before heading into Manta Sound in May to record his 10th album. The song had its roots in a poem he had published in Nelson Ball's *Weed* magazine in 1967. That poem, "The Black Pope's Brittle Sermon," had begun with the line: "When the only reality is lions in the street." This image of hungry lions roaming the streets came from a dream he had had the year before. Dreams would inspire songs in years to come. In fact, DANCING IN THE DRAGON'S JAWS opens with the spiritual *Creation Dream*. His *Wondering Where The Lions Are* dream happened when he was told by a relative involved in counterintelligence that the planet was on the brink of a nuclear war between Russia and China. As he recalled in his *All The Diamonds Songbook 1969-79*, first published in 1986, "I had dinner in Ottawa with someone who worked in defense research. He and his colleagues were really scared because, at that time, while the Soviets and Americans had 'an understanding' by which they would avoid surprising each other, China was the wild card in the deck. That night I experienced a re-run of a dream I'd had some years before in which lions roamed the streets in terrifying fashion, only this time they weren't threatening at all. When I woke up in the morning some things connected and I wrote the beginning of this song while driving out of town along the Queensway."

Huge orange flying boat rises off a lake
Thousand-year-old petroglyphs doing a double take
Point a finger at eternity
I'm sitting in the middle of this ecstasy

Young men marching, helmets shining in the sun,
Polished as precise like the brain behind the gun
(Should be) they got me thinking about eternity
Some kind of ecstasy got a hold on me

And I'm wondering where the lions are . . .
I'm wondering where the lions are . . .

In 1994, he told *SongTalk* magazine's Paul Zollo that "I had dinner with this relative of mine and he said, 'we could wake up tomorrow to a nuclear war.' Coming from him, it was a serious statement. So I woke up the next morning and it wasn't a nuclear war. It was a real nice day and there was all this good stuff going on and I had a dream that night which is the dream that is referred to in the first verse of the song where there were lions at the door but they weren't threatening . . ."

From his "Sun's up, uh huh, looks okay. / The world survives to another day . . ." opening, he moved on to his less threatening version of the dream about lions, and in the recording studio with a reggae rhythm section pulsing beneath his syncopated guitar chords, the effect was catchy as all get out. With a move away from folk to a World Beat feel, he was just "being joyful in the face of everything" on this his 10th album. He was also determined to "give a concrete expression of the suffering that's all too evident in the world." The appeal of *Wondering Where The Lions Are* is that it is wonderfully carefree and totally unfettered by the committed social commentary that would soon become the focus of his songs, a moment in time when he is taking a deep breath and just being grateful that the world has not come to a sudden end. Even the thought of "young men marching" off to war cannot bring him down.

The image of a "huge flying boat" rising off a lake he took from memories of a visit to Vancouver Island where he saw Mars water bombers taking off from Sproat Lake before dumping their load on a forest fire. The petroglyphs were also glimpsed on this same trip to the West Coast. While these images have nothing directly to do with being warned that "we could wake up tomorrow to a nuclear war," they continue a feeling of tension that is present when you are near a natural disaster, such as a forest fire that is raging out of control. Seeing the pre-written-language symbols on a cave wall provides a thread that somehow connects the singer with eternity, with a bigger picture than merely the mundane freighters anchored offshore. It's a message of sorts from the distant past when human existence was very different than it has become today, a message that is comforting because it tells the songwriter that the earth has existed for a very long time and will very likely continue to exist long after he and his temporary fears have faded away.

But it is from the melody and exuberant hopeful tone of Bruce's vocals that we sense his feeling of ecstasy and oneness with eternity most powerfully. The lions are linked with armies on the brink of war, but suddenly even the lions are no longer determined to destroy his world.

Freighters on the nod on the surface of the bay
One of these days we're going to sail away
Going to sail into eternity
Some kind of ecstasy got a hold on me

And I'm wondering where the lions are . . .
I'm wondering where the lions are . . .

A similar, pulsing energy propels *Rumours Of Glory*, which also became a concert favorite. Cockburn's reaction to seeing helpless, unarmed refugees shot down by helicopter gunships in Central America moved him to write the more aggressive lyrics to *If I Had A Rocket Launcher*. This song brought him worldwide recognition and the admiration of a generation of environmentally conscious fans who also embraced his outraged reaction to the violence perpetrated by 'Irangate' and the arming of Central American dictators. Of course, by this time in 1984 representatives of the Reagan administration were already in Afghanistan supplying Osama Bin Laden with rocket launchers and plenty of rockets to shoot down Russian helicopter gunships, an activity that was lauded by most of the free world at that time and would only be regretted a decade and a half later when Bin Laden organized a vicious airborne terrorist attack on the World Trade Center and the Pentagon.

"*Wondering Where The Lions Are* was the first song I'd had that got big time national airplay in Canada," he told *Guitar Player* magazine, "and it got on the *Billboard* chart in the US. But whereas it was the start of something in Canada, in the sense that the next few records I put out also got a lot of airplay, in the States that didn't happen, so with 'Rocket Launcher' it was like starting all over again. And that time it did take, and it's been progressively better since then."

By this time Bruce had also become as good an electric guitar player as he was an acoustic guitar player, and fans looked forward to hearing the instrumental aspects of his new releases as well as his lyrics and melodies. Eventually, he released an entire CD of instrumental tracks. Fans also came to anticipate interviews that he did with magazine writers because he was a lot more willing to communicate what was going on with his music than a lot of the other rock and pop stars of the '80s and '90s. One of the things his fans liked the most about his music was that it continued to evolve.

"*If I Had A Rocket Launcher* was written about a particular time and place," he explained to Mike Ferner. "The situation that inspired it called for outrage. I'd spent three days in a couple of different Guatemalan refugee camps in Chiapas in southern Mexico. We could hear helicopters patrolling the border. The week before we were there and the week after we left this helicopter strafed the camp as if these people had not suffered enough with the incredible violence they were fleeing in the mountains of Guatemala. Their food ration was only three tortillas a day, no medicines, but they were still sitting there with courage and a capacity to celebrate. When they found out I was a musician, they brought a marimba that they had carried in pieces from their village. They all got out their best clothes, the kids danced, and they had a party. It just made me cry and still does when I think about it. That spirit that they showed in face of such incredible difficulty made me feel that the people in the helicopter had forfeited any claim to humanity and I just felt this incredible outrage."

Bruce Cockburn has issued many, many gold and platinum studio albums and compilations in Canada, won more than a dozen Juno awards, been inducted into the Canadian Music Hall of Fame by Gordon Lightfoot, and made an officer of the Order of Canada. He agonized over whether or not to release his rocket launcher song, a dilemma he had not had with his celebratory anthem *Wondering Where The Lions Are*. For many years, Bruce has been Canadian music's conscience, but in the new millennium he has once again become more introspective. "It's the wheel going around," he recently told *The Boulder Weekly*. "The stuff from the '70s was a product of inward-looking exercises. And then it got very much outward directed through the '80s and started to swing back so that you got some of both in the '90s, and by the end of the '90s it's back to internal again, but in what I hope is a deeper way. It's not my idea that love is at the center of everything, but I believe it is, and I understand a lot more about that than I did in the '70s."

Northwest Passage

Stan Rogers
Words & Music by Stan Rogers
© 1981, Fogarty's Cove Music

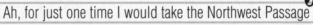

Ah, for just one time I would take the Northwest Passage
To find the hand of Franklin reaching for the Beaufort Sea
Tracing one warm line through a land so wide and savage
And make a Northwest Passage to the sea

In 2004, Stan Rogers' *Northwest Passage* was named the number 4 Canadian track of all time on the CBC's 50 Essential Canadian Tracks list, behind only Ian & Sylvia's *Four Strong Winds*, Barenaked Ladies' *If I Had A Million Dollars*, and Neil Young's *Heart Of Gold*. The song is an expression of such unabashed national pride that you might expect it to have been written in the decades leading up to Canadian Confederation or the years surrounding the Canadian Centennial, not 1980. It is Rogers' most inspirational composition, the title track for his first collection of songs that ventured outside the Canadian Maritimes for its subject matter. It was stirring imagery that sprang from Stan's emotional response to the vast expanse of territory beyond the densely populated regions of southern Ontario and Nova Scotia where he had spent the first three decades of his life.

After years of struggling with unsuccessful singles for major labels, Stan Rogers had taken the independent route and was beginning to make his mark with FOGARTY'S COVE in 1976 and TURNAROUND the following year. His celebration of Celtic music on these early albums focused on the Nova Scotian locales he knew best, and in 1979 the highly successful live album BETWEEN THE BREAKS brought interest in both the United States and western Canada. "We started touring even further afield, particularly in western Canada," he noted before his death in 1983, "and these new scenes had a profound effect on my writing."

Northwest Passage was to be the first of five albums celebrating

Canadian regions, a collection of songs that appealed to all Canadians the way that *Barrett's Privateers* appealed to Maritimers. The image of buckskin-clad Canadian explorers, fur traders, and finally settlers "tracing one warm line through a land so wide and savage" had massive emotional appeal. In the decades following Rogers' tragic death, *Northwest Passage* has become his most beloved composition. Incoming Governor General Adrienne Clarkson quoted a line from the chorus during her inaugural speech in 1999.

However, during the weeks of debate and voting leaded up to the completion of the CBC list in 2004, there was strong debate from many quarters concerning the inclusion or exclusion of Rogers' song. Ottawa caller Jeannette praised it, saying, "There is no song on your list that has an effect on me anywhere near close to *Northwest Passage* by Stan Rogers. The lyrics, the harmonies, and the soulful voice are unparalleled in Canadian music." Max Furlong disagreed vehemently. "Stan Rogers," he commented, "is one of the most overrated Canadian performers and a regrettable mention on your program. He is a writer by definition only, a sub-par singer, and is remembered mainly due to his grisly death. At a Thursday night open mic session he'd get two songs and a pint to go."

David and Sue Amatt-Flower defended the folk icon: "Nobody else has chosen to record the history of Canada in music better than Stan Rogers," they said during their call. "To exclude him from the best 50 list would be a travesty of justice." Still, what was one couple's cup of tea was poison to other listeners, as Toronto caller Ted Berezny stated, "If Stan Rogers were an American singer, many Canadians would think he was the worst kind of hyper-nationalist, and would find many of his songs ridiculous. What his work has to do with Canadian music in the 1980s is pretty marginal. Maybe the 1880s would be more appropriate."

No doubt Rogers' music is an acquired taste and not as well known out west as troubadours like Valdy and Gary Fjellgaard. Personally, I would far rather have seen Valdy's *(Play me a) Rock & Roll Song* on the list, a song that was pertinent to the rock versus folk debate and a ditty that brings the house down every single time Valdy performs it in concert. You can't help but be moved by some of the regional callers supporting their favorite acts, though, and Colin McAuley's plea was among the most heartfelt. "*Northwest Passage,*" McAuley said, "is our national anthem, for me anyway. I was driving this morning and had to pull over as my eyes teared up, like they always do. If there ever was an essential Canadian song, it *has* to be this one!"

Colin was not the first to call *Northwest Passage* our national anthem, nor will he likely be the last. When radio talk show host Peter Gzowski canvassed his *CBC Morningside* audience for a "second national anthem," *Northwest Passage* was a runaway winner. Nothing that Valdy or any of the Canadian recording artists garnering Top 40 air play during the late decades of the 20th century put out on record was as overtly nationalistic. There were plenty of obscure albums recorded as tributes to the Canadian Centennial but few could remember what they were, let alone recall or hum the melody of a single memorable song that might qualify as a second anthem. Baby boomers were into rock anthems, not nationalistic ones, and Canadians had come up with a few good ones. Tom Cochrane's *Life Is A Highway* comes to mind. Steppenwolf's *Born To Be Wild*, the Guess Who's *American Woman*, and BTO's *Takin' Care Of Business* have also become ingrained in our psyche. But Stan Rogers was only just stepping up to the plate where it comes to fame and fortune when his life was taken in a freak airplane disaster.

Stan Rogers has left us with a legacy of nearly 100 songs that many of us are only discovering in the new millennium. He also inspired a generation of Celtic artists, including the Rankins, Loreena McKennitt, Great Big Sea, Spirit of the West, and James Keelaghan. Some critics have been moved to claim that he created a whole new genre, Can Trad, or Canadian Traditional. While Joni Mitchell, Leonard Cohen, Neil Young, Bruce Cockburn, and even Murray McLaughlin were continually reinventing themselves and exploring widening gyres, Stan was spiralling inward toward a particularly Canadian song style. It is not over the top to claim that he was the first significant Canadian recording artist to concentrate most of his energy on becoming known throughout Canada rather than seeking fame and fortune south of the border and overseas. Storytelling was his game in both song and his personal life.

During his short, brilliant life Stan generated plenty of controversy and thrived on it. As biographer Chris Gudgeon notes, "Stan loved to argue. To him, it was better than drinking coffee. That's what got him going. That's how he related to people, how he connected. Those who never argued with Stan could not count themselves among his friends. He loved to argue and he loved the people with whom he argued." American folk icon Pete Seeger was moved to say that Stan was "one of the two or three most talented singers and songwriters on the North American continent." Tom Paxton suggested that "Stan Rogers was to Canada what Woody Guthrie was to the United States." Perhaps Stan's most amazing accomplishment is that he rose to prominence in folk circles without the opposition that folkies like Seeger and Guthrie thrived on during the Peace marches and anti-war protests of the late '50s and '60s. In fact, his songs are not overtly political; nor are they based in appealing to a ready-made fan base of likeminded protestors. In an era of increasing political correctness, he did not even embrace the woman's rights movement to the hilt as was almost mandatory in those days. As Sylvia Tyson notes, "It's the contradictions that make Stan Rogers fascinating to so many people. You can see it in his attitude towards women. Stan Rogers took great delight in his own particular brand of male chauvinism, and yet the two women in his life whom I knew his mother and his wife are extraordinarily strong. His persona was tough, but his songs could be tender and poetic."

When all is said and done, it may be more helpful to regard Stan as a great Maritime songwriter in the lineage from Wilf Carter and Hank Snow to Stan's contemporary, Gene MacLellan. Wilf had wandered to Alberta, hooked up with the Brewster family, and entertained on trail rides in Alberta before hitting on the radio and making it big in New York City as Montana Slim. Hank had gone to Nashville and recorded the classic *I'm Moving On*, which stuck at number one on the *Billboard* country charts for a record 21 weeks in 1950. He continued on as a star of the Grand Ole Opry into the '70s. Hank Snow and Wilf Carter were still touring across Canada to sold-out concert audiences while Stan Rogers was blazing his own modest trail in coffeehouses and pubs. Gene MacLellan had been less successful as a performer but had written Anne Murray's signature song, *Snowbird*. And, speaking of Canadian Maritime women, there is Rita MacNeil, to whom it is even more useful to compare Stan.

Rita's career had just started to bloom when Stan's was plucked from his grasp, but her 1979 Maritime anthem, *Working Man*, often performed with the all male miner's choir Men of the Deeps, is cut from the same cloth as Stan's catalogue of songs. Rita was catapulted from regional to international stardom almost overnight due to her shows at Expo 86 in Vancouver. We can only guess what might have transpired had Stan Rogers been booked to play Expo 86 and never boarded the ill-fated Air Canada Flight 797 in May 1983.

> Westward from the Davis Strait, 'tis there was said to lie
> The sea route to the orient for which so many died
> Seeking gold and glory, leaving weathered broken bones
> And a long forgotten lonely cairn of stones

Stan Rogers was born on November 29, 1949 in Hamilton, Ontario, the first son born to Nathan Alison "Al" Rogers, a former RCAF pilot, and Valerie Bushell Rogers. Both of his parents had been born and raised in Nova Scotia, where the family had long enjoyed a rich history. According to biographer Chris Gudgeon, Stan's first memories were of "sitting in his grandmother's kitchen in Hazel Hill, Nova Scotia, in his hand a slice of still-warm bread lathered in peanut butter. The room is hot, filled with the loamy warmth of the wood stove and the smells of the kitchen birch wood burning, bread baking, and a giant and perpetual pot of stew. Around him sit his mother and grandfather and grandmother and various aunts and guitar-playing uncles every-one singing and laughing. In years to come, Stan would recognize the songs by Hank Williams, Jimmie Rodgers, and Nova Scotia boys Wilf Carter and Hank Snow but for now the sounds blend together and that is enough. Other children had fairy tales, Stan had country & western." Growing up in southern Ontario, where he heard both country and classical music, Rogers would enthusiastically tell anybody who would listen that he was raised on "a diet of Mozart and Hank Williams."

Stan romanticized the Canso-Hazel Hill area of Nova Scotia in his song and album, *Fogarty's Cove*. As he explained in the liner notes: "Mom's brothers, most of them, played or sang or both and I guess it followed naturally that one of my first memories would be of my uncles sitting around in my grandmother's kitchen 'half shot', playing guitars (some of them home-built) and singing old tear-jerkers by Wilf Carter, Hank Snow, and Hank Williams, with aunt June and Mom and all the rest joining in, in more-or-less harmony, while dad looked on and smiled, and played referee."

Stan was eager to join in, and by the time he turned five he had his first guitar, home-built by his uncle, Lee Bushell. "The frets are cut from brass welding rods," he recalled, "the nut and saddle were carved from an old toothbrush, the bridge pins are brass beads, and the top, back, sides, neck, fret-board and strap pin were all hand-cut from hardwood birch. It weighs nearly 20 pounds, has tone vaguely resembling that of a small Martin . . . I still play it often, keep it near me in the living room, and will never, never part with it."

By the time Stan was fully-grown he presented an imposing figure for a troubadour. At six-foot-four and 235 pounds, he was an unlikely Leprechaun, but his rapidly receding hairline quickly fleshed out the image. Flanked by his equally tall, fiddle-playing brother Garnet Rogers and bass players like David Woodhead or Jim Morison, they were called Stan Rogers and his Big Band. Stan's first brush with a major label was brief. Signed to RCA, he found himself being moulded to resemble a Ray Stevens clone and recording novelty songs like *Fat Girl Rag* and *Here's To You Santa Claus*. "They wanted to make me into a kind of Ray Stevens," he said during an early interview, "'Ahab the Arab' kind of thing." When the experiment failed, he moved on to become a fixture in the hotbed of folk activity that flourished for a few years in London, Ontario, where he began to write songs about an idealized childhood in the Maritimes. Stan's association with Vanguard Records was even briefer than his affiliation with RCA. Vanguard cut him loose before he had time to mix the rough tracks he and producer Paul Mills had recorded.

Deciding that he needed to secure bookings at prestigious folk festivals like Mariposa and Newport, Stan got a booking at the Northern Lights Festival in Ontario, where he found himself singing sea shanties sitting around with the traditional artists. But Stan didn't know any shanties with choruses where everybody joined in singing harmony with the lead singer. So he retired to his hotel room and wrote *Barrett's Privateers* in 20 minutes. Returning to the gathering, he introduced the song and reveled in singing lead while the others followed him.

Stan Rogers had found his niche writing traditional songs that had the same stirring choruses that songs had 200 years ago. His success owed a lot to his thorough research of his subjects. *Barrett's Privateers* chronicles the adventures of a crew of legally sanctioned Halifax pirates during the American Revolutionary War when Britain encouraged Nova Scotians to plunder American cargo ships. Sailing a route that took them as far south as the haunts of real pirates like Captain Henry Morgan in Montego Bay, Jamaica, his inept amateur pirates and their ill-equipped ship run afoul of superior American firepower. The sorry story of *Barrett's Privateers* is told by a survivor who lost both his legs on the ill-fated mission. The song has been recorded by dozens of pub bands and Celtic groups in several countries. Ironically, many of the musicians who perform this song still believe the song to have been written during the 1770s during the final days of high seas piracy rather than in the 1970s by a Canadian from Hamilton, Ontario.

The song's authenticity is compelling, but it made Stan Rogers a contemporary to the founding fathers of the American constitution not Bruce Cockburn, Valdy, or Bob Dylan. At the same time, it was convincingly authentic and deliriously fictional evoking the adventures of Hollywood pirates like the one-legged Long John Silver from the animated film *Peter Pan* and then squashing the glory into gore. Canadian Maritimers chose to embrace it as a celebration of their heritage, about which very little had been written in recent years. Stan Rogers had hit a vein of gold and he mined it industriously until his death seven years later.

Stan Rogers has said that *Barrett's Privateers* and the equally compelling and popular *Wreck of the Mary Ellen* were written spontaneously in a few minutes. Such was not exactly the case with his masterpiece, *Northwest Passage*.

Stan Rogers had intuited that writing about this topic could be a rich and rewarding endeavor. After all, the whole reason North America had become populated was a European desire to seek a spice route to the East. Sure enough, this had become diverted by the fur trade and the discovery of gold in the New World, and, subsequently, tobacco in Virginia, but throughout the early years of Canadian history the allure of finding a northwest passage had driven explorers to push westward toward that same spice route to the east. The quest had gone on until the Panama Canal had been constructed and the *St. Roche* had sailed the difficult northern route to the Pacific, proving that it was possible but precarious, and not at all commercially viable. After that, the significance of the "Northwest Passage" had gradually diminished until it flourished only in documentary films and the tedious pages of high-school textbooks.

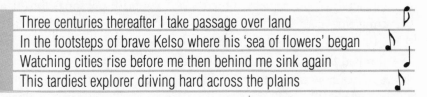

Three centuries thereafter I take passage over land
In the footsteps of brave Kelso where his 'sea of flowers' began
Watching cities rise before me then behind me sink again
This tardiest explorer driving hard across the plains

Stan had a good working title and the recording sessions went smoothly. The only problem was that the day before the sessions were to end, he still didn't have a title. As he recalled, "I was helpless with fatigue at that point and I remember at one point I was lying on the floor of the studio looking up. Everyone else had gone to bed and I was completely alone in the place and I was lying there and I could hear the sort of machinery cooling that had been heating up during the day, some sort of electronics. I could hear the cabinets sort of cooling or clicking or something, and just dead silence. And I started thinking about the silence of the north and what John Franklin must have felt on that last fatal voyage of his, where he got so close to breaking into the Beaufort Sea. He had got within 40 miles of breaking through and he would have been the first man through the Northwest Passage, but instead he and all of his men and both ships were lost and it was kind of a terrible saga. And I got thinking again of the first people who went across Canada. There was an explorer by the name of Kelso or Kelsey, depending on where you thought he was from, who first saw the Canadian prairies and described it as a 'sea of flowers,' and that always stuck in my head. David Thompson was the first person to accurately survey and map the Canadian Rockies. Alexander Mackenzie was one of the first people to reach the Pacific through the Canadian Rockies, Simon Fraser, another. The Fraser River that runs into Vancouver was named after him. All of these great explorers who were equally intrepid as Lewis and Clark or Kit Carson or any of them you know. Canadians don't know much about these people. I mean, we study them in grade five or six history and that's the last we hear of them. Canadians don't know how Canada was developed. I mean they have a smattering of history from the time of Confederation, the founding of our country in 1867. They know who John A. MacDonald was. He was the first Prime Minister, in many ways the father of our country. But they don't know who the other fathers of confederation were. I'm descended from one of them, so I take an interest in them. At any rate, in my songs for the past couple of years, I've been trying to satisfy my own lust for dramatizing these things or perhaps injecting them into popular culture. But I've also had the motive of trying to make my countrymen a bit more aware of just how fascinating their history is, and to sort of help them become a bit more small 'n' nationalist. I wrote *Northwest Passage* with all of that in mind, lying on my back on the floor of the studio at 3:00 in the morning."

And through the night behind the wheel, the mileage clicking west
I think upon Mackenzie, David Thompson, and the rest
Who cracked the mountain ramparts and did show a path for me
To race the roaring Fraser to the sea

Over breakfast, Stan played the song for Paul Mills, bringing tears to his producer's eyes. The song was recorded an hour later. Mills had told his artist that *Northwest Passage* was "a very stirring and strong piece." He was right. Folk music critic Emily Freedman declared that Stan's new album was "another brilliant and innovative record from the emerging genius of Canadian songwriting." While the live album BETWEEN THE BREAKS had brought Rogers national interest, NORTHWEST PASSAGE opened up the international market and got Stan a booking agent and pal, Jim Fleming, who might have become his manager had he lived longer. They got as far as drafting a business plan, which is what managers do. Fleming was impressed that Stan had come a long way without a major label, agent, or manager. He was the darling of the revitalized folk festival circuit in the early 1980s. "There was something happening with Stan," Fleming told biographer Gudgeon. "His career was just growing by leaps and bounds, primarily through word of mouth."

Before his death, Stan Rogers recorded two more albums. FROM FRESH WATER was the second of his planned five regional albums, based in the Great Lakes region. FOR THE FAMILY was an album of cover versions of traditional Nova Scotian songs. It included three his uncles had written and was recorded during the sessions for his fifth album of original material on his own Forgarty's Cove label. Stan had championed making it in Canada and downplayed becoming a star in the United States, but now he was being booked into better clubs and festivals and had a real chance of selling significant numbers of records to a larger audience. Being a star outside of Canada now no longer seemed unappealing.

A trip to Scotland was poorly planned, but Fleming was able to get Stan booked to play the prestigious Kerrville Folk Festival in Texas. In fact, he was heavily booked in the spring of 1983, although he began the tour with a working holiday in Bermuda and a booking at the Bermuda Folk Club. Then he and his band embarked on a cross-country tour that took them all the way to Vancouver, Victoria, Seattle, San Francisco, and Los Angeles before flying to San Antonio. All the hustle and bustle meant that he was away from his wife and children for long stretches of time, but it was the price he had to pay.

> How then am I so different from the first men through this way
> Like them, I left a settled life, I threw it all away
> To seek a Northwest Passage at the call of many men
> To find there but the road back home again

By most accounts, Stan's performance at the Quiet Valley Ranch in Kerrville began poorly. Some say the band had become inebriated. Others claim they were sabotaged by feedback from the sound system. They finally got it together during the rousing chorus of *Northwest Passage*. "Stan later said it was the worst show he'd done in years," Winnipeg comedian Al Simmons recalls. "But I was absolutely blown away, and they had the audience absolutely hypnotized. I'd never seen anything like it before. When he sang, and when he performed, the power coming off the stage was incredible." Stan and his band came back for one encore, *The Mary Ellen Carter*, finishing much stronger than they had begun. It was not exactly a triumphant entry into the US Festival circuit, but Stan was enjoying the camaraderie of a widening circle of performers and decided to stay on, although his brother Garnet beat a hasty exit, flying back to Canada to be with his wife.

An excursion to a game ranch, where the tour bus was attacked by a ten-foot ostrich, provided some levity. Stan, of course, sided with the bird's attempt to disrupt their journey. He might be gaining stature within the folk music pantheon, but he was still champion of the underdog. Fellow Canadian folk artist, Connie Caldor, recalls that Stan was "unusually reflective" during a dinner the performers shared that evening. "He was almost eulogizing himself," she told Cudgeon. "He was talking about his life, and what he felt strong about, and what he felt good about, and he said how wonderful it was to have tasted success. He was basically saying, 'If I die tomorrow, I'll be content.'"

It was not unusual for Rogers to talk about himself, but the content of his conversation proved to be a tragic foreshadowing of the events that followed. Stan hung around one more day and night and joined the others in the usual grand finale before heading off to the campground for informal sing-a-longs and farewells. No doubt, one of the songs that Stan sang clustered 'round one of the campfires that final night in Texas was his own *Northwest Passage* with its stirring chorus.

And if should I be come again to loved ones left at home,
Put the journals on the mantle, shake the frost out of my bones
Making memories of the passage, only memories after all
And hardships there the hardest to recall

Since recording the song, Stan had written an additional verse, which like the comments he made that Connie Caldor has recalled, speak eerily of a foreboding of his own mortality at a time when he was just hitting his prime. Stan Rogers never did "come again to loved ones left at home." He died in a freak airplane accident, a fire that killed 23 of the passengers on Air Canada Flight 797 even though the pilot managed an emergency landing at an airport in Cincinnati. Stan Rogers succumbed to intense smoke aboard the ill-fated flight and rescue teams were not able to evacuate his prone form before the fire exploded with deadly intensity. Canada's newest rising star was dead at age 33.

Turn Me Loose

Loverboy

Words & Music by Paul Dean and Duke Reno

© 1981, BMI April Music (Canada), EMI BlackwoodMusic Inc.

I was born to run,

I was born to dream,

The craziest boy you ever seen,

I gotta do it my way,

Or no way at all.

Turn Me Loose was written as a response to the combined misery of Mike Reno and Paul Dean. Writing it and recording it changed their fortunes, and the incredible worldwide popularity of their splendidly crafted stadium rock track put them on the map. By the late '70s, a second generation of Canadian music stars was beginning to emerge with new energy from new studios in Vancouver. Local producers like Bruce Fairbairn were entertaining rock royalty in the form of Bon Jovi, Aerosmith, AC/DC, Metallica, and Kiss, while managers like BTO's Bruce Allen were putting their fledgling acts (Prism, Trooper, Bryan Adams, and, eventually, Loverboy) on the road, fronting for these visiting, multiplatinum-selling mega stars.

Despite the national and international success of Vancouver artists like Terry Jacks, BTO, Valdy, and Heart, the road to the top was still rocky. Bands like Sweeney Todd lay in wreckage along the way. It was much the same on the other side of the Rocky Mountains. A Calgary-based band, the Stampeders, rivaled the Winnipeg-based the Guess Who by releasing their number 8 *Billboard* smash, *Sweet City Woman*, in the summer of '71, and followed up with a string of Top 5 Canadian hits. Winnipeg had long been a music hotbed, home to Randy Bachman and Neil Young, where bands like Streetheart rose periodically out of the prairie dust. Plenty of bands played in bars in the late '70s, with far too few of them selling many records. Musicians throughout Western Canada were heartened by all of the activity on the Coast, but were dispirited in too many instances by creeping corruption, playing tough

Winter-bound clubs, freezing half to death in woefully maintained band houses, and all around lackadaisical management.

Thus it came to pass that when two talented, disenchanted musicians met by chance in a Calgary warehouse in the summer of 1978, they soon discovered they had a lot more than talent and a love of good music in common. As Mike Reno recalls, "Loverboy came at a time in my life when I was a bit disillusioned with the music business, having left a very popular recording group in Ontario called Moxy."

Reno, who was still known by his given name Mike Rynoski at the time, had replaced Moxy's original frontman, Buzz Sherman, two years after the band issued its debut album and had been treated like a second-class citizen by everyone involved. "Management of this band was a stiff; the record company was a stiff; and even the band guys just didn't care anymore," he told *Voices of Classic Rock*. "I remember recording with Moxy. I'd just laid a track down and didn't really like how it sounded — I think I was a little flat on a few of the notes. So, I suggested we do another take and the reply was something to the effect of 'just relax and go get yourself a cup of coffee.' I suggested it was a minor change, a few words, just one take . . . and it would make it perfect. 'After all, we're making an album here, right fellas?' They told me to stop making trouble or they were going to 'kick me out of the band.'"

The guitar player Reno was about to meet, Paul Dean, had been kicked out of a band he really cared about, the Winnipeg based Streetheart. "That was a serious time for me," Dean recalls. "I left my girlfriend of eight years sitting in Edmonton to be in that group. I was very depressed."

Mike had decided to give his own notice and walked away from Moxy before they could give him the boot, deciding he'd head for LA where his older brother was living and check out the action in Sunset Strip clubs. However, he wouldn't make it that far before he found a kindred spirit. "As I was heading west through Canada," he explains, "I stopped in Calgary to see friends. We went out to a nightclub; I think to see Johnny Rivers. As we got to this club, I heard music coming from the back. To be more accurate, it was coming from this building behind the club, which was like an old Greyhound bus repair shop. It sat closed, with lots of windows, some of which were broken, and one light hanging from a cord, flickering. It was kind of an 'On The Waterfront' type of place."

His curiosity got the best of him. He wandered into the warehouse and discovered "Paul Dean sitting on a soda pop case, electric guitar in hand, amp about 20 feet away, and he's just pounding away . . . the only guy in there. I said, 'Hi,' and we ended up playing and talking together all night. It was kind of a sad time for Paul. He'd come home for Christmas and the band that he was playing with basically told him not to come back. It was the first time he'd been fired. Of course, I was pretty disillusioned with the music business, so between the two of us we had some serious attitude going . . . we had some things to say."

| And I was here to please, |
| I'm even on knees |
| Makin love to whoever I please, |
| I gotta do it my way, |
| Or no way at all. |

That night, Mike Reno and Paul Dean wrote a song together about doing things their way, for a change. They were inspired to believe they could make some pretty good music if they put a band of their own together and stuck to their guns. As Mike recalls, "I guess the song we wrote that evening reflected our feelings, our desires to be free of the politics and the bad management and people jerking us around. It inspired us to work together."

Lou Blair may have had a hand in setting up that fateful warehouse jam, making sure that Reno went to the club where Johnny Rivers was playing and Dean was rehearsing nearby. Paul's recollection of meeting Mike Reno that night is worth noting. "This real straight-looking guy with short hair and a tweed jacket walks into the room and starts playing drums. I didn't think he was much of a drummer, but he turned out to be a good singer and I liked his personality." Soon after, they put together a band of local musicians and started recording demos in the basement of a church, directed by Johnny Rivers' road manager, Walter Stewart, who happened to be a friend of Lou Blair and had already produced some Stonebolt tracks. In addition to producing Loverboy's early demo sessions, he went on to produce some great Stonebolt albums and a Fosterchild album. The music scene in Vancouver was hopping.

By all accounts, the first Paul Dean/Mike Reno sessions in that church basement were a hoot. Before they left Calgary to work more closely with their agent, Lou Blair, and new manager, Bruce Allen, in Vancouver, Mike and Paul enlisted the talents of keyboard player Doug Johnson, who had just left Fosterchild. Ex-Streetheart drummer Matt Frenette was recruited on the Coast, where he was hanging out at a local beach and improving his tan after being let go from the Winnipeg band not that long after Dean had been fired.

> And then you came around,
> Tried to tie me down,
> I was such a clown,
> You had to have it your way,
> Or no way at all.

Working at Bullfrog Studios in Kitsilano on the newly installed, synchronized, dueling eight-track decks that provided the tiny facility with 16-track mixes and masters, Reno and Dean put together the ten demos for an album. Studio manager Maggie Scherf remembers fondly the time that the boys were at the studio, especially the extra work that Paul put in on *Turn Me Loose*. "He kept coming back in and working on that track until he had it honed to perfection," Maggie told me recently. Until the mid-'90s when Bullfrog closed its doors, studio owner Fred Koch used to pull a reel to reel copy of the 10-song Loverboy demo tape out of the vault once a year at the annual Bullfrog Birthday Party and play it proudly for his employees and guests.

The band's sound was coming together and now they desperately needed a name because they had been booked to open for Kiss at Empire Stadium, the home turf of the CFL football squad, the BC Lions. Paul's mother is partly responsible for the catchy name Loverboy. As he recalls, "My mother used to call me 'lover boy' when I was a teenager. I can't remember whether she was teasing me because I was always trying to pick up girls or saying, 'Come on, 'lover boy,' it's time to wash the dishes.'" The memory came to him as he was leafing through his girlfriend's fashion magazines, which had beautiful girls on every cover. "Cover girl . . . Cover boy," he mused, thinking he was on to something. "Then," he explains, "the light came on 'Loverboy!

People are going to hate it or love it!'" It was a fitting designation for a band that played original hard rock music with a glam rock flair and wore leather costumes on stage.

> Well I've had all I can take,
> I can't take it no more,
> I'm gonna pack my bags and fly . . . baby,
> Or no way at all.

The same love it or hate it ethic would apply to their song lyrics. "We talk about boygirl things," Paul told *Seventeen*, "but I like to put a twist into it. A little irony, 'I love you, but I hate you.' We try to ring a common note, although I don't want to go over anybody's head or write about things that only older people are concerned about, like car payments and mortgages."

"We write about honest feelings," Mike asserted. "*Turn Me Loose* came about because of an earlier band I no longer wanted to be in as well as a long time relationship I had with a girl that I didn't think was fair to continue. I still love her very much, and she's one of my best friends, but I'm hardly ever home, and I didn't want to tie up somebody that way. Now I'm sharing my life with everybody in the world as well as the guys on the road."

"It's the fun aspect of this band that's made it all worthwhile," Paul told *Music Express* in 1983. "When I was writing songs for Streetheart with lead singer Kenny Shields, we'd write all these really heavy tunes like *Action* and *Look At Me*, which seemed appropriate at the time. But Reno is such a happy spirit that my writing style with him is totally different. We write more positive material, which seems to be more acceptable to current trends."

As luck would have it, the final member of Loverboy came on board mere days before their first gig, a November 1979 opening slot for Kiss, when bass player Scott Smith quit Lisa Dalbello's band and joined Loverboy. It wouldn't be long before Bruce Allen had them signed to Columbia/CBS Records Canada in Toronto and turned them loose with producer Bruce Fairbairn and fledgling engineer Bob Rock in the number one recording facility in town, Little Mountain Studios, to record their first album. Little Mountain was a sizeable complex with two rooms large enough to record orchestras for jingle sessions and numerous smaller production areas, located in the bustling warehouse district above False Creek and below West Broadway. The thoroughly modern studio was owned by CKNW Radio and Griffiths, Gibsons Productions, and designed by veteran British engineer and studio designer, Geoff Turner. Turner had left early on to found Pinewood Studios but young producers like Howie Vickers, Claire Lawrence and Bruce Fairbairn had begun churning out hit album after hit album by both local acts and multiplatinum-selling visiting superstars, making the studio the most successful of all recording studios in the history of Vancouver music.

In the '80s, studio manager Alison Glass, who was a friend of Bullfrog manager, Maggie Scherf, told me that she was proud of Little Mountain's ability to keep up with the rapidly changing technological advances being made that would soon put an end to the half century magnetic tape age when CDs, digital recording machines, and computer mixes became the latest rage. Maggie envied Alison's budget. And Alison had another swig on her martini and mentioned their gross revenue for the past calendar year, and the two friends shared a laugh and yet another martini. To me, working as a journalist and jack of all trades in those days, people like Maggie and Alison were the heart and soul of the music biz in Vancouver and we were all frequently thrown together with all of the musicians and songwriters and sweaty managers and cigar smoking agents at numerous record launch parties, awards show banquets, and the inevitable studio Christmas parties. We were all collectively proud of our growing family of cool, young pop and rock stars, all being recorded right here in Vancouver. Alison was proud of those multiplatinum albums that Metallica, Foreigner, Bon Jovi, et al were cranking out when they block booked her whole facility and rocked on at all hours of the day and night. For beginners, though, 24 tracks can sometimes be a few too many.

So why don't you turn me lose,
Turn me lose,
Turn me lose,
I gotta do it my way,
Or no way at all.

"The first album was overdub city," Paul Dean admitted to *Guitar Player* magazine of their adventures recording the album tracks in the spanking new 24-track room at Little Mountain. "There were six keyboards on every track, and *Teenage Overdose, Always On My Mind*, and *The Kid Is Hot Tonight* had six or seven guitars apiece. On the second album, I overdubbed the rhythm track on *Lucky Ones*, and the guitar solo on *Jump*. Everything else I used only one guitar. I prefer to record live in the studio because things are clean and you can hear the expression of things. *Turn Me Loose* took hours to get right. We were having problems because there was a lot of hum in the studio. I found that the only way to get rid of it was play while standing on a four-foot stool; the hum disappeared when I was in that position. It must have been quite a picture."

Why don't you turn me lose,
Turn me lose,
Turn me lose,
I gotta do it my way,
I wanna fly.

To this day Paul Dean will tell you that his biggest break was meeting Mike Reno. "When it comes down to writing," he told Jim Ferguson, "we do everything together. For instance, he wrote the bass line to *Turn Me Loose*, as well as some of the lyrics. Nothing really gets written down. We just memorize everything. If I'm writing a song, I need to have the tape recorder on. That's the way I construct all of my stuff."

I'm here to please,
I'm even on my knees,
Makin love to whoever I please,
I gotta do it my way,
I gotta do it my way,

The Kid Is Hot Tonight was chosen as the first Canadian single, which put the band on the domestic map, and *Turn Me Loose*, their first collaboration as songwriters, broke the band in the United States. Loverboy sold millions of copies of their first album Loverboy and followed up with three more multiplatinum releases: GET LUCKY, KEEP IT UP, and LOVIN' EVERY MINUTE OF IT. They disbanded briefly in 1989 to pursue solo careers, but reunited in 1993 for a benefit for their guitar slinger pal, Brian "too loud" MacLeod (Chilliwack, Head Pins). They had so much fun they decided to get back together. In November 2000, the band lost their bass player Scott Smith in a tragic sailing accident, but was able to regroup and continue, although their days of multiplatinum albums and Top 40 *Billboard* hits were behind them.

Loverboy celebrated their first 25 years of recording together by releasing a digitally re-mastered GET LUCKY, complete with bonus tracks. Two years later, they released a new studio album, JUST GETTING STARTED. In March 2009, Loverboy was inducted into the Canadian Music Hall of Fame. They'd set album and concert ticket sales records, taking their music to the people for coming on 30 years. CARAS president, Melanie Berry, declared that "they are an iconic band who owned the radio waves in the '80s, dominated MTV video play, and sold over 20 million albums worldwide. Twenty-eight years since their self-titled debut I'm sure you'll agree that Canada still loves Loverboy!" Bob Rock shared the stage with Mike, Paul, Doug, and Matt during their induction.

And when you came around,
You tried to tie me down,
I was such a clown,
You had to have it your way,
Well I'm sayin no way,

So why don't you turn me lose,
Turn me lose,
Turn me lose,
I gotta do it my way,
Or no way at all.

Still hometown favorites to this day, the band was chosen to play during the Winter Olympics 2010 in Vancouver. Their best tracks,

Turn Me Loose and *Working For The Weekend*, have become arena rock anthems featured at major sporting events. *Turn Me Loose*, the rebellious song that got it all started, is featured on the soundtrack of the Jason Statham action flick, *Crank*.

In 2012, the band returned to their roots to celebrate three decades, since they hit the Top 20 of the *Billboard* Hot 100 albums chart and sold two million copies of their self-titled debut, by working again with Bob Rock, who engineered that magical first album. The result was a new Paul Dean Loverboy single, *Heartbreaker*, to go along with Reno's *Flying High*, which became the theme song of the Vancouver Canucks' run to the Stanley Cup in 2011. In July 2012, the band hit the road with Journey and Pat Benatar, kicking things off on a "loving every minute of it" jaunt expected to last the duration of the year.

"It's great coming full circle 30 years later," Paul Dean said in a press release. "We first toured with Journey in '82 on the success of our GET LUCKY album. It was an amazing package then, and it's an amazing package today." Over the decades, Loverboy have sold more than 20 million albums, but they continue to stay in touch with their roots by playing their signature tunes *Working For The Weekend* and *Turn Me Loose* every chance they get.

New World Man

Rush

Lyrics by Neil Peart & Music by Geddy Lee and Alex Lifeson

© 1982, Core Music Publishing

He's a rebel and a runner

He's a signal turning green

He's a restless young romantic

Wants to run the big machine

New World Man is Rush's only Top 40 *Billboard* hit. It is also their most accessible track. By the time the band went into the studio to record SIGNALS, lyricist Neil Peart's eclectic arsenal of references had elevated Rush above their heavy metal beginnings to international stardom as a progressive rock act, a "thinking man's hard-rock band" according to *Rolling Stone*. However, in this hastily written last track, Peart kept things simple and inadvertently provided Canadians from all walks of life access to their music.

As Geddy Lee points out, "It wouldn't have been on the album if we didn't have four minutes of space available. I think what it really boiled down to was that we'd worked so hard getting all these slick sounds that we were all in the mood to put something down that was real spontaneous. In the end, the whole song took one day to write and record."

Most important of all for an album whose main theme was communication versus alienation, *New World Man* was a vehicle that provided Rush the opportunity to be heard for the first time by people who didn't listen to album oriented rock (AOR) radio stations. "I guess that SIGNALS had more to do with writing about people than ideals," Neil admitted. "PERMANENT WAVES was probably our first album that was in touch with reality it was about people dealing with technology instead of people dealing with some futuristic fantasy world or using symbols for people. Now I'm trying to make those symbols into real people and real conflicts in people's lives."

The 1982 cut also benefited from vocalist Geddy Lee's decision to return to his normal vocal register after a decade of imitating Robert

Plant's falsetto screech. Guitarist Alex Lifeson glued himself to the churning new wave reggae track working in tandem with Lee and Peart to fashion a sound that is similar to the radio-friendly music that the Police were making during the early '80s. Coincidentally, the Police recorded their first Top 5 hit, *Every Little Thing She Does Is Magic,* at the same facility, Le Studio, in Morin Heights, Quebec, shortly before Rush recorded *New World Man* there.

A companion piece to the group's signature song *Tom Sawyer, New World Man* represents Rush's most successful effort to move beyond the extended AOR radio format that works so well in their live performances. Both singles won over legions of new Rush fans who had previously found Neil's fantasy and science fiction references as obscure as his fascination with the work of doctrinaire novelist Ayn Rand. While Rush has never depended on singles for their album sales or their continued popularity, their three most successful chart entries, *Closer To The Heart, Tom Sawyer* and *New World Man,* have remained in their repertoire in the new millennium.

Before the release of *New World Man,* Rush had been the kind of rock band that people either loved or hated, and despite the momentary wider interest, their cult status kept on growing. By the mid-'90s, critics who had previously hated them accepted the fact that they had carved out their niche in the rock world. As *Chicago Tribune* critic Greg Kot noted in October 1996: "The ultimate rite of passage band, Rush remains a primarily testosterone-laden enterprise. At the sold out United Center on Monday, the Canadian trio's audience was, at least, 75 percent male, and most of them appeared to know every lyric and chord change with the accuracy of lifetime obsessiveness. Like the Grateful Dead, Rush is among the biggest cult bands in the world reviled, misunderstood, or dismissed by the uninitiated, but virtually the only band that matters within its tight circle of worshippers."

In the lyrics of *New World Man* and *Digital Man,* from Rush's 1982 album SIGNALS, Canadians found typical Neil Peart heroes. Young suburbanites who sounded familiar to the generation of kids that grew up playing computer games and rapidly became leaders in the digital revolution that took place in the early '90s. No matter to teenage computer geeks that the hero of *New World Man* was supposed to be an idolized leader; he also fit the profile of the soon to be self-empowered hackers, crackers, and nerdy dot com millionaires of the digital age.

> He's got a problem with his poisons
> But you know he'll find a cure
> He's cleaning up his systems
> To keep his nature pure

Rush's music is a fusion of Geddy Lee's vocals, synthesizer, and electric bass playing, Alex Lifeson's guitars, and Peart's percussion. All three players are virtuosos in their own right. Peart has been named the most influential rock drummer of all time by at least one trade magazine. Their live performances are so passionate and masterfully executed that, to some people, their lyrics are often merely the frosting on a very well baked cake. However, those same, seemingly innocent song lyrics have also come under fire.

Misinterpretation of Neil's lyrics by fundamentalist Christian zealots provided sufficient controversy that he gained considerable press defending himself. More recently, overeager acid-heads have attempted to attribute a psychedelic mysticism to nearly every phrase and nuance of Peart's lyrics that was simply not intended when he wrote them. Net culture debates of the band's philosophical directions has spawned a new generation of Rush fans and scholarly essays and books that endeavor to explicate in detail nearly every phrase that Neil Peart has written and Geddy Lee has sung. Meanwhile, when fused into song and appreciated solely as a trigger for individual imaginations, their records continue to entertain Canadian radio audiences simply because they are so open to interpretation that we can all find some elements to relate to. As intellectual as most Rush songs seem to be, their singles also work very well because they are some of the best churning rock & roll records of all time.

> Learning to match the beat of the Old World man
> Learning to catch the heat of the Third World man

Teenagers Neil, Geddy, and drummer John Rutsey formed the first incarnation of "the Rush" in the late '60s in homage to the Cream, the Who, and the Beatles. Their first regular gig was playing the Coff-in, a teen drop-in center in an Anglican Church basement in Sarnia, Ontario. Soon after this, Geddy was inspired to explore his falsetto vocal range by hearing Led Zeppelin's Robert Plant. In the beginning, his vocals became screams simply because the band played so loud. "My grandmother would be yelling about the noise and the band were playing so loud they couldn't hear her," Geddy's brother Allen told biographer Bill Banasiewicz. "They just kept jamming while she kept yelling and cooking . . . since volume was as important as skill," Banasiewicz writes, "the band could be heard for blocks around. Allen would catch neighborhood kids sitting outside the basement window and chase them away. Many of these kids would later show up at the Coff-In."

He's got to make his own mistakes
And learn to mend the mess he makes
He's old enough to know what's right
But young enough not to choose it
He's noble enough to win the world
But weak enough to lose it --

He's a New World man...

Alex Lifeson was born Alexander Zivojinovich in Fernie, British Columbia in August 1953, and moved to Toronto when he was only two years old. He got his first guitar at age 12, an acoustic that he amplified by attaching the pickup from a record player. His first electric guitar was a Japanese-made Canora that he painted "psychedelic" because he "had to have a guitar that looked like Eric Clapton's Gibson SG." He chose to call himself "Lifeson" because that is what Zivojinovich meant in Croatian. His first band was the Projection. He borrowed Geddy's Traynor amplifier, which was bigger than his little Kent amp, for rehearsals.

Geddy Lee was born Gary Lee Weinrib on July 29, 1953, in Willowdale, Ontario. His Polish parents had survived internment at Auschwitz before moving to Canada. They insisted he take piano lessons. His mother's thick, Yiddish accent is the source of the pronunciation of his first name. "When I was quite young," he told *TV Guide Online*, "she called me Gary, but my friends thought it sounded like 'Geddy' so they called me 'Geddy'. When I was about 14 or 15 and joined the Musicians Union, I joined as Geddy."

Alex and Geddy first met at Fisherville Junior High School, where they began playing their guitars together. "My earliest influences," Alex told *Guitar Player*, "were Clapton, Jimi Hendrix, and Jimmy Page. Page was probably my greatest influence early on. Rush started just a little before the time Led Zeppelin came out, and when I first heard the album, I thought, 'they're doing just the things we want to do. They have the sound we want to have.'" Along with keyboard player Lindy Young and drummer John Rutsey, they played their first paying gigs while they were in grade eight.

Sixteen-year-old high-school dropout Ray Danniels became their manager. Ray had a knack for managing and soon had his own stable of bands, including the highly successful Beatles tribute act, Liverpool. But Rush was the only group he was working with that wrote their own original material. By 1970, they were a trio again, sounding better than ever, and were already experiencing the problem of finding venues where they were welcome to play their original material. As Alex recalls, "About a third of our repertoire was original tunes, and this held us back from playing a lot because people wanted to hear stuff they could relate to songs on the AM radio and things like that. Some of the cover versions of the songs we did like *Fire, Purple Haze,* and *For What It's Worth* we had our own arrangements for, so they didn't sound just like the originals."

By 1971 they had graduated from high school and Ray had begun booking them fulltime. As Alex recalls, "After I finished high school the band really started happening. It wasn't just two gigs on weekends; it was six nights a week, five sets a night. We got a pretty strong following in Toronto, and we made lots of friends."

In 1973, they cut their first record, a cover of Buddy Holly's *Not Fade Away* backed with a Rutsey-Lee original *You Can't Fight It*. Released on their own Moon Records label and distributed by London Records, it failed to get much airplay. "Nobody wanted to pick us up," Alex recalls. "They said we were too heavy and there was no market for the music the band was playing. So all the record labels in Canada passed on us."

Ray Danniels employed a unique strategy that had not been explored by most Canadian bands. As he told Banasiewicz, "Canadian managers would send their acts 1,400 miles to Winnipeg, not even considering that New York City was only 500 miles away. My theory was the reverse, why go 1,400 miles to Winnipeg when you could play in Cleveland or Detroit, which were just a few hours drive from Toronto." Their second American show was a set at a pop festival staged at a drive-in theater in East Lansing, Michigan, where they were not regarded as anything special by the 1400 rock fans who showed up on a rainy day. However, extending their travels beyond Ontario into the United States would eventually expose them to more receptive audiences than they encountered in northern Ontario, where, Geddy recalls, "They don't care what you do. They don't care if you play the greatest original material in the world if their ears haven't heard it before. They just want to get drunk and hear their favorite tunes."

> He's a radio receiver
> Tuned to factories and farms
> He's a writer and arranger
> And a young boy bearing arms

Ray Danniels financed the band's independent debut album recorded after midnight at Toronto Sound and produced by Terry Brown, who had previous experience mixing cuts for the Who, Procol Harem, Donovan, April Wine, and Thundermug. "We were going in when the rates were a little cheaper," Alex told a BBC interviewer. "We'd finish a gig at 1:30 a.m., pack up, go to the studio until about 8:00 or 9:00 a.m., and the crew would take our gear back to the club, set it up, and we'd go down and play. I think we had two nights off in a row a total of three times in the course of six months."

Local deejay David Marsden was the first to play the lead single on the radio when he aired it on CHUM-FM Toronto. "Rush was very influenced by Led Zeppelin and Black Sabbath," Alex acknowledges, "but I'm very fond of that first album." Their similarity to Led Zeppelin paid off when Ray Danniels' pal, Bob Roper, got a copy of the album to Donna Halper at WMMS-FM in Cleveland and she began to play *Working Man*. The radio station got an enthusiastic phone-in response from Ohio fans who thought the cut was a new one by Led Zeppelin. This aroused the interest of Mercury Records' Cliff Burnstein, who called Halper. She told him that *Working Man* was the cut, and, as he recalls, "I hung up the phone, put it on, and sure enough it was a motherfucker." Burnstein had signed BTO and he quickly signed Rush to a two-album deal with Mercury. Ray Danniels was immediately able to book Rush onto a Toronto show opening for ZZ Top, where they experienced their first incident of being bullied by headliners. "We opened with *Finding My Way*," Alex recalls, "and the crowd went crazy. They obviously knew the material. We got an encore, but before we could go back up for another encore somebody ordered the lights turned up."

The band was teetering on the brink of commercial success. However, Geddy and Alex had to react quickly because John Rutsey picked this pivotal moment to tender his notice. Acting on a tip, they drove to St. Catherines and auditioned Neil. As Alex recalls, "he had a very small set of Rogers (drums), I think, and he pounded the crap out of them. He really hit them hard. Incredible power and strength even back then. Of course, Geddy and Neil just hit it off. They were the rhythm section and just got into a groove, and they were playing like mad." Ironically, Neil had been playing drums in a cover band named "Hush."

"At the time," Geddy recalls, "he had never written any lyrics. We had a date, like, eight days later, to play the Pittsburgh Civic Arena opening for Uriah Heep and Manfred Mann. So that was first and foremost in our minds; we were just looking for a drummer. We never thought about lyrics or anything like that." As Geddy and Alex got to know Neil better, they wondered if he might not be the perfect choice for a permanent member who they could co-write with like they had with John Rutsey. "He was a very different person for us, a person full of ideas and very verbose," Geddy acknowledges. "Alex and I just looked at each other — this is the guy to solve all our problems."

"I came into it by default," Neil admits, "just because the other two guys didn't want to write lyrics. I've always liked words. I've always liked reading. So I had a go at it. I like doing it. When I'm doing it, I try to do the best that I can. It's pretty secondary; I don't put that much importance on it. A lot of times you just think of a lyrical idea as a good musical vehicle. I'll think up an image, or I'll hear about a certain metaphor that's really picturesque. A good verbal image is a really good musical stimulus. If I can come up with a really good picture lyrically, I can take it to the other two guys and express to them a musical approach." Ray Danniels would be moved to form a new company, Anthem Records, named after the title of a book by Neil's favorite author at the time, Ayn Rand.

When they hit the road to promote the album they had recorded with Rutsey, they got some good reviews, but critics expressed concern about their mundane lyrics. Jim Knippenburg writing in *The Cincinnati Enquirer* wanted better lyrics, but praised them for a "more polished sound, complete with a variety you hardly ever find in heavy metal." *LA Times* critic Dennis Hunt was less encouraging, calling their music "flagrantly derivative." Marc Shapiro dismissed their set as "heavy metal tedium."

Writing new material for their second album while on the road was difficult. As Geddy recalls, "We had exactly 26 minutes to be onstage and offstage. We had two people on our road crew. We were traveling maybe 200 to 500 miles a night. We wrote songs in cars while moving, we wrote songs in hotel rooms, wherever we could get a minute alone." Back home in Toronto, they were rewarded for their efforts by being named Most Promising New Group at the 1975 Juno Awards.

He's got a problem with his power
With weapons on patrol
He's got to walk a fine line
And keep his self-control

Trying to save the day for the Old World man
Trying to pave the way for the Third World man

Most Rush fans would probably shudder if they heard their favorite band's name uttered in the same sentence as the words "new age." However, Rush would soon evolve from a Zeppelin-like heavy metal band to become as "new age" as the writings of Carlos Castaneda and dolphin researcher John C. Lilly, who explored the farthest reaches of human consciousness floating in sensory depravation tanks. In the anonymous audience sanctuary at Rush concerts, fans immersed themselves in the obliterating volume the band generated and floated buoyantly on Geddy's streaming vocals. It was a safe, fantasy environment, an immediate disconnect from the fetters of the increasingly complicated world of the late '70s. Unlike the prancing superstars of the Glam Rock bands, Geddy, Alex, and Neil provided fans with heroes who were serious musicians in a world where rock stars were often regarded as airheads, egomaniacs and shallow pretty boys.

FLY BY NIGHT has come to be regarded as a Canadian classic. CARESS OF STEEL followed. 2112 won the band their first wave of hardcore fans in the US, but it didn't crack the Top 40 album chart, stalling at number 61. Meanwhile, Rush concert performances were getting better. In fact, their live shows were so good that Mercury issued the double live album ALL THE WORLD'S A STAGE, featuring performances taped at three sold-out Massey Hall shows, which put the band over the top, selling a million copies in the US alone. A FAREWELL TO KINGS followed suit, and in November 1977 Rush was awarded three gold albums in Canada for 2112, ALL THE WORLD'S A STAGE, and A FAREWELL TO KINGS, signifying that all three had sold 50,000 domestically. In early 1978, Rush was awarded their second Juno as Group of the Year, an award they collected again in '79. PERMANENT WAVES hit the number 4 spot on the Billboard album chart and MOVING PICTURES peaked at number 3 and sold more than 4 million albums in the United States. Without much chart success other than Closer To The Heart, a number 77 Billboard single, their sales were phenomenal with only one glitch, the atmospheric HEMISPHERES, which failed to rise into the Top 40 on the album sales chart.

Meanwhile, critics sharpened their knives for their reviews. Most often maligned were Geddy's falsetto vocals. Circus published one review that declared that if Geddy's voice "was any higher and raspier, his audience would consist entirely of dogs and extraterrestrials." Montreal Gazette critic John Griffin's description of Geddy sounding like "a guinea pig with an amphetamine habit" was coupled with the double insult of calling Alex's guitar playing "ordinary." Some writers were not as inventive and merely vitriolic. "If I had a nickel for every insult about my voice," Geddy quipped, "I'd probably be a millionaire." Nevertheless, by the time Rush went into the studio to record SIGNALS, he had begun to explore lower notes. "You'd have to be a fool to ignore constructive criticism," Geddy told *Rolling Stone*. "We've changed things in our music that were pointed out years ago, things about feel or a tendency to feel forced. But a lot of critics believe they are the resident experts and they make the decision on what's valid and what isn't. I think that's horse shit." It seemed that nothing the band did pleased all the critics and few of the critics said anything that pleased the band. Neil wasn't comfortable with the term "power trio," either. "If a visitor from another planet would ask me to define Rush," he told Mats Rydstrom, "I would definitely *not* say we were a power trio. A band with three members, guitar-bass-drums, is the classic power trio, but would you call the Police a power trio?"

Besieged by allegations that they played "Nazi Rock" and held Aryan beliefs, charges that Neil's lyrics were demonic, and the usual nonsense about Geddy's falsetto vocals, Rush also regretted agreeing to record the live EXIT STAGE LEFT album. They had "retouched" several passages and came under criticism for that, as well. Meanwhile, *Tom Sawyer* had stalled at number 44 on the *Billboard* chart, although a live version had hit number 25 in the UK. It was with these issues in mind that they set about recording SIGNALS. Geddy's trademark falsetto voice would be heard for the last time on record that decade in a guest vocal on Rick Moranis and Dave Thomas' (as Bob & Doug McKenzie) GREAT WHITE NORTH album. He graced the high registers of human hearing capability on their Top 20 novelty hit, *Take Off*.

There would be many changes as Rush sought to streamline their music. *Chemistry*, culled from sound check jams, was the first track on which all three members contributed lyrics. Their avid interest in NASA and space shuttle launches was built into *Countdown* with sounds from an actual launch provided by scientists who recorded them at the Space Centre. *Subdivisions* dealt with alienation.

New World Man was a last minute addition to the album. In order to preserve the continuity of the eight-track and cassette format, they needed nearly four minutes more music and the hastily assembled track became known as "project 3:57." Where the opening track *Subdivisions* and the fourth track *Digital Man* had been developed over an eight-month period leading up the sessions, *New World Man* appears to be a succinct distillation of all of the ideas they had been developing to include in the project. Neil's lyrics were among the most straightforward he had written for the band. They were precise, poetic and, perhaps, even personal and autobiographical definitely less dramatic and all encompassing than his epics had been.

It was a trend that had begun with the move to Le Studio for the PERMANENT WAVES sessions. From that time onward, their intention had been to return to simplicity. As Geddy notes, "We sort of tried to get back to our original desires as songwriters. I think we wanted to become a little more concise and get our ideas across in a more concise and contemporary manner. Music was changing; rock music was changing dramatically . . . reggae and white reggae and more sort of aggressive punk music that was coming out. We wanted very much to be part of that. We wanted very much to learn what was going on and reflect the times as opposed to being left behind."

He's not concerned with yesterday
He knows constant change is here today
He's noble enough to know what's right
But weak enough not to choose it
He's wise enough to win the world
But fool enough to lose it

He's a New World man . . .

Even Geddy's decision to return to a lower register was a calculated move. "That's a conscious decision," he maintained, "because I want to use my voice more. I want to sing more, and it's real hard to sing when you're using all your energy to stay two octaves above mortal man." Inviting Ben Mink into the studio to experiment playing his electric violin on the *Vital Signs* track was another move the band made in order to keep up with the times. There were fewer power chords and passages where Alex flexed his virtuoso guitar playing muscles. Geddy stepped up to play more melodies and synthesizer pads on his keyboards, providing Alex more room to create atmospheric rhythm guitar tracks. "Basically," he explains, "we didn't want to go in and make another MOVING PICTURES." They would be accused of "betraying their heavy metal roots," but as Alex argued, "We never considered ourselves a heavy metal group, anyway. We feel we have much more to offer than that." Rush was one of the very first groups to record and mix their albums digitally, beginning with MOVING PICTURES. SIGNALS was so hip that it was chosen as the basis (with *Tom Sawyer* and *Spirit of the Radio* as bonus tracks) for one of the first Laserium productions to present the music of a single rock band, and viewed by millions of visitors to planetariums around the world. While the Police wailed about the "ghost in the machine," Rush was fully immersed in the digital age long before most people purchased their first personal computer. They were in many ways the ultimate "New World band."

Over the years, Rush has won a raft of Juno Awards and was inducted into the Canadian Music Hall Of Fame in '94. In 1996 the trio were made members of the Order Of Canada. Their album sales rival the Beatles and Stones for total sales by a rock band, and they continue to record and tour to the present day. In the late '90s, they quit performing after the tragic death of Neil's daughter Selena in an automobile accident; however, after a five year hiatus, they reunited in the early years of the new millennium and soldiered on touring and recording with renewed energy.

During interviews for the award-winning 2010 documentary film *Rush: Beyond The Lighted Stage*, all three band members appeared convincingly relaxed and comfortable with their collective place in rock & roll history. And, after the band's Time Machine Tour ended in the summer of 2011, Rush fans were delighted to learn that the band was back in the studio recording their 20th studio album, CLOCKWORK ANGELS, which was released in June 2012. In the fall of that year, Geddy, Alex, and Neil embarked on their latest tour, and, even though they still hadn't been inducted into the Rock & Roll Hall Of Fame after many years of being nominated they had truly become the New World Men of the Rock & Roll world.

Summer of '69

Bryan Adams

Words & Music by Bryan Adams and Jim Vallance

©1984, Irving Music Inc., Adams Communications Inc., Almo Music Corp,
and Testatymemusic

I got my first real six-string

Bought it at the five-and-dime

Played it 'til my fingers bled

It was the summer of '69

The summer of 1969 was indeed a great time to be alive. In July, astronaut Neil Armstrong stepped onto the surface of the moon and uttered his famous words heard around the world: "That's one small step for man, one giant leap for mankind . . ." In August, half a million souls showed up at Max Yasgur's farm in up-state New York to celebrate peace, love, and rock & roll at the Woodstock Music & Art Fair. And in September, the Beatles' last and best studio album, ABBEY ROAD, was released. But the two young men who would eventually become Canada's Lennon & McCartney, Bryan Adams and Jim Vallance, were only 10 and 17 years old, respectively.

By this time, at the end of the second decade of rock & roll, no Vancouver artist had managed to score a Top 40 *Billboard* hit. Tom Northcott's *Sunny Goodge Street* had come close, becoming an underground FM radio classic that had been played on radio stations around the globe. Many West Coast music fans remembered local bands like Mock Duck, the Collectors, the Seeds of Time, Papa Bear's Medicine Show, the Painted Ship, the Nocturnals, My Indole Ring, the United Empire Loyalists, Black Snake Blues Band, Hydro Electric Streetcar, Night Train Revue, Mother Tucker's Yellow Duck, and Little Daddy & the Bachelors with fond nostalgia. In 1970, Susan and Terry Jacks and their Poppy Family band finally hit the number 2 position on the *Billboard* chart with their *Which Way You Goin' Billy*, and the race was on.

Me and some guys from school	
Had a band and we tried real hard	
Jimmy quit and Jody got married	
I shoulda known we'd never get far	

Tom Northcott, signed to a contract by Warner Brothers' LA division, recorded his A-sides in San Francisco and LA and his B-sides in Vancouver. He received a surprising amount of worldwide airplay with his covers of Donovan's *Sunny Goodge Street,* Dylan's *Girl From The North Country,* and Leonard Cohen's *Suzanne,* but was not able to generate sufficient American chart numbers to make the *Billboard* Top 40. Bill Henderson's sixties band, the Collectors, morphed into Chilliwack in the early '70s, with vocalist Howie Vickers leaving to pursue a solo career, and sax and keyboard player Claire Lawrence moving on a few years later to become an independent producer. Chilliwack scored Canadian hits with Henderson's songs, notably *Lonesome Mary, Crazy Talk, California Girl,* and *Fly At Night,* but like all of the other Vancouver bands vying for airplay in the early '70s, they struggled to gain international recognition.

By mid-decade that would begin to change. Randy Bachman's BTO relocated to Vancouver. Doucette, Trooper, Hammersmith, Heart, D.O.A., Bim, Valdy, the Pointed Sticks, the Payola$, Pied Pumkin, the Bruce Miller Band, the Jim Byrnes Band, the Powder Blues Band, Billy Cowsill's Blue Northern, Doug & the Slugs, Prism, and Loverboy all enjoyed at least a fleeting taste of big time success and some of them would become bona fide international superstars.

Tom Northcott used the profits from his early successes to buy a fishing boat, and his profits from fishing to finance a law degree at the University of British Columbia. He also partnered up with Jack Herschon to build Studio 12 on West 12th Avenue in a move to begin creating the infrastructure needed for a successful local music industry. Herschorn also purchased Aragon Studios, a Sixth Avenue facility formerly used by the CBC to record orchestras, equipped it with a state of the art mixing console that had been previously used in a Sunset Strip studio to record Hollywood stars like Bing Crosby, Frank Sinatra, and Ray Charles, and renamed it Can Base Studios.

The Poppy Family had split into solo projects in the '70s. Terry

Jacks scored the number 4 North American record of 1974, *Seasons in the Sun*, which is said to have sold more than 11 million records, worldwide, built a studio, and began producing new artists. Susan Jacks scored national hits with Bruce Miller's *Anna Marie* on her domestic A&M releases. Across town, Mushroom Records' young impresarios Howard Leese and Shelley Siegel made a big splash in '75, signing Chilliwack, Jerry Doucette, and Steve Fossen and Roger Fisher's band Heart to record deals.

Fossen and Fisher had just hooked up with foxy Seattle singers Ann and Nancy Wilson, who immediately bonded with guitarists Fisher and Mike Flicker (the head engineer at Mushroom Studios, the old, renamed Aragon/Can Base facility). Offstage and on stage, Heart was hot! Leese and Flicker produced the band's debut album, DREAMBOAT ANNIE, and the breakout hits *Crazy On You*, *Magic Man*, and *Barracuda*. Mushroom Studios and Mushroom Records continued to be a hotbed of hit-making activity until the untimely death of Siegel due to a brain aneurysm in 1979, after which Mushroom was converted to a facility for recording film scores.

> Oh when I look back now
> That summer seemed to last forever
> And if I had the choice
> Ya – I'd always wanna be there
> Those were the best days of my life

By the early '80s, Vancouver had its own music mafia with agents, promoters, producers, record label executives, and managers like Cliff Jones, Paul Hovan, Peter McCullough, Terry Jacks, Ray Pettinger, Bruce Fairbairn, Bob Rock, Gary Taylor, Roger Schiffer, Maureen Jack, Lou Blair, Sam Feldman, and Bruce Allen working out of Kitsilano and Gastown office complexes. The head offices of the Canadian subsidiaries of the major American labels were still located in Toronto, but the playing field was tilting. The good news for musicians was that the situation had improved to the point where you no longer had to hang onto your day job. There were plenty of club gigs and studio work available, and new bands were touring every week of the month.

As the '80s progressed, it would be independent producers and engineers working at nearby Little Mountain Studios who would begin to host mega projects by out-of-town bands like Bon Jovi, Aerosmith, Blue Oyster Cult, and AC/DC. Bruce Fairburn emerged as one of the most savvy rock producers on the planet. He cut his teeth on albums for Prism, Loverboy, and Krokus before establishing Little Mountain as one of the premiere rock studios in the world with his work on Bon Jovi's blockbuster sophomore album SLIPPERY WHEN WET, which sold 11 million copies in the U.S. alone. After that, the word was out and big name bands were flocking to Vancouver to rejuvenate their careers under his guidance.

The Payola$' Bob Rock began to work at Little Mountain as a recording engineer and assistant producer, following in Fairburn's footsteps to produce big albums for Metallica, the Cult, Motley Crew, Bon Jovi, and many others. However, a young local songwriter by the name of Bryan Adams, who rivaled Robert Redford's rugged good looks, became Vancouver's first superstar solo artist.

Bruce Allen, who had recently masterminded the successful careers of BTO and Prism, was Adams' personal choice for the role of manager, and the persistent teenager pursued Allen relentlessly. "He wore me down," Allen says. They sealed their deal with a handshake, the only contract that they have made during their long and successful association.

"We've been together now since I was 18," Bryan later told Q magazine, "and we've never had a contract. We did it all on a handshake. Anytime I've signed a contract with anyone there's been trouble." Bruce Allen put the full force of his influence and expertise into breaking his new client worldwide, not merely in Canada and the United States. He later told Rolling Stone that Adams was "his own best promotion guy. He remembers people. He's polite. I've never had to slap him around to get him to do something. He can be stubborn, and sometimes we scream and yell at each other, but it's one on one and he will listen."

Adams and his songwriting partner Jim Vallance had a bottom line slogan that they often quoted to each other, a slogan that eventually became yet another song title: Kids Wanna Rock. Not surprisingly, they wrote songs that appealed to Woodstock generation kids like themselves who had grown up in the '60s.

Ain't no use in complainin'
When you got a job to do
Spent my evenin's down at the drive-in
And that's when I met you

"Looking back," Jim recalls, *"Summer Of '69* was Bryan and I at our best. We hadn't had any real success yet that would come when RECKLESS went number one on the charts and sold 12 million copies. But that was a year away. In January 1984, Bryan and I were still writing songs for all the right reasons, for the pure love and joy of it. We had nothing to prove, and even less to lose. We wrote songs to please ourselves."

By the time they sat down to write the songs for RECKLESS, Adams and Vallance had been working together for six exciting years, ever since they met serendipitously in the winter of '78 in a Long & McQuade music store in Vancouver's trendy Kitsilano neighborhood. As Vallance told *Beatology,* "I had just quit a band because I didn't enjoy touring and for about a year I wasn't involved much in writing or recording, mostly just doing session work, playing on MacDonald's commercials, and so on. And then in January 1978 I was at a store buying guitar strings or something and Bryan Adams was there, too. The girl I was with knew him and she introduced us. Bryan had just quit his band, Sweeney Todd. He was living with his mom, and wasn't doing much." Vallance had actually been looking for a vocalist to demo up his songs, but Adams arrived at their first session in Vallance's basement studio armed with ideas and half-written songs of his own. "I tried to be very tactful," Vallance told *Rolling Stone* in 1987, "but Bryan was an unruly young fellow, and the song ideas were just unstructured. So we pretty much scrapped anything he and I had been working on independently and started writing together."

They sent out dozens of demo tapes, but only received interest from one record label. A&M offered Adams one dollar to record four of his songs. "I couldn't find anyone else to give me a break," he recalls, "so that's the one I took."

Jim had come up with the initial idea for a song titled *The Best Days Of My Life*. He ran his idea by Bryan, and, as they usually did when they wrote songs together, they set out to develop the scenario and fill in the blanks. Beginning with Jim's memories of playing in teenage bands in the late '60s and Bryan's memories of playing in garage bands in Ottawa and Lynn Valley in the early '70s, they proceeded with the song lyrics. Together they remembered details from their early experiences, like playing your first guitar until your fingers were bleeding and having teenage crushes on your high school classmates, and pasted these together with coming of age images like actually getting lucky for the first time. Adams later claimed he was also alluding to the sexual position "69."

"It took a few weeks to realize that *Summer of '69* was a better title," Jim recently told *Top 100 Canadian Singles* author Bob Merserau, "so we literally shoehorned that phrase into a few gaps in the arrangement. In 1966, John Lennon and Paul McCartney challenged each other to write a song about their childhood in Liverpool. Paul came up with *Penny Lane* and John wrote *Strawberry Fields Forever*. Bryan and I decided we'd try something similar and wrote about growing up in Canada in the '60s."

"My songs are love fantasies all the way," Bryan told an interviewer from *Hit Parader* magazine in the early '80s. "I haven't had that many intense love affairs. I have had my share of flings that have made me able to talk about it."

"It's a song about our youth," he explained to another interviewer, "both Jim and I, growing up as musicians. The year is immaterial, although it was a great year. I was only ten, of course, but I remember the moon landing, the Beatles breaking up, Woodstock . . . That song took more rewrites than any of the others." Jim was seven years older than Bryan, but they had a lot in common, and, in the end, it wouldn't matter what lyrics they left in and what lyrics they left out, because by the time the song was released as a single in the summer of '85 Adams was the hottest young rocker on the planet and everything he touched turned to gold and platinum.

Bryan Guy Adams was born on November 5, 1959 in Kingston, Ontario. His British-born father was a Canadian military diplomat. Bryan and his younger brother, Bruce, were raised in Ottawa and the capital cities of countries like Austria, Portugal and Israel, where his father was posted, and educated in the best boarding schools in England and the United States until his parents broke up in the early '70s. One day when he was crossing the English Channel on a ferry, he heard the Beatles for the first time and was inspired to follow in their footsteps. His middle name was an acknowledgement that he had been born on the anniversary of Guy Fawkes' failed attempt to blow up the British Parliament buildings. He would eventually explode on the international rock scene himself, but not before he got his first after-school job while living with his mom and brother in the quiet, semi-rural community of Lynn Valley, a suburb of North Vancouver.

With his mom working fulltime and Bryan working part-time, the family's lifestyle changed, but after being moved from one foreign posting to the next, one boarding school to the next, Adams was happy to settle down to having his own garage band and attending a regular Canadian high school. He bought some real guitar amps and a Fender Stratocaster with money he earned himself, and he pestered the living daylights out of a number of local promoters and managers until he finally, at the ripe young age of 16, got hired as the lead singer of a cover band called Shock.

Bryan preferred playing electric guitar, but began fronting his own bands because he couldn't hook up with a better vocalist. Playing in Vancouver nightclubs proved to be a distraction that encouraged him to quit his high school classes and buy a piano with tuition money that had been intended for his post-secondary education. When none of his own bands, including the nearly successful "Shock," seemed to be going anywhere, he pestered the manager of a successful band that had scored a number one Canadian hit with *Roxy Roller* but had lost its lead singer. He was rewarded for his efforts with an audition to replace Nick Gilder as the lead vocalist of the Vancouver based Sweeney Todd. He got the job, re-recorded the *Roxy Roller* lead vocal for an American release, and new vocals for the band's second album, *If Wishes Were Horses*.

"I couldn't believe it," the band's manager, Martin Shaer told reporters. "He sang the songs better than Nick." However being 16, and a high maintenance teen at that, Adams never really fit comfortably into the older band personnel while they were out on the road touring. At times, his antics drove his band mates nuts. Eventually, it would come out that the most frustrating aspect of his time spent with the group was the lack of input he was granted during the recording of the sophomore album. "The group was put together and run by one guy," he recalls. "It was a fabrication. It was totally unnatural. In the studio, I came in, sang, and split, and that was all there was to it. Nothing sincere, nothing really musical about the whole trip; it was really forced."

> Standin' on your mama's porch
> You told me that you'd wait forever
> Oh and when you held my hand
> I knew that it was now or never
> Those were the best days of my life
>
> Back in the summer of '69

Jim Vallance was born on May 31, 1952 in Chilliwack. He grew up in the smaller town of Vanderhoof in the central interior of the province, where he played in teenage bands. When he turned 18, he enrolled in first-year classes at the UBC School of Music, where he studied piano, cello, and other instruments. However, after a year, he dropped out of university, spent some time kicking around Europe, and joined the jazz-blues-rock band Sunshyne, where he met and befriended trumpet player and arranger, Bruce Fairbairn. Vallance wasn't in the band long, but Fairbairn persevered, securing a government grant for the band that saw some members of the act become clowns and street musicians while the rock band project continued under a new banner.

With a revised lineup that was now called Prism and featured former Seeds of Time guitarist Lindsay Mitchell and vocalist Ron Tabak, Fairbairn set out to secure a record deal. When Mitchell's songwriting faltered, Vallance was brought in to help out, eventually becoming the band's drummer and chief songwriter. Fairbairn used demos of more than half a dozen of Vallance's songs to secure the band a record deal. Managed by Bruce Allen, the band was an immediate success, and Vallance's *Open Soul Surgery, Spaceship Superstar,* and *Take Me To The Kaptin,* published under the pseudonym Rodney Higgs in an attempt to preserve the elite status of his career as a classical musician, all became Canadian rock classics. Vallance, who couldn't handle the roadwork, quit the band and bonded with Adams. For trivia fans, he was replaced by drummer Rocket Norton, who'd played in the Seeds of Time with Lindsay, and has chronicled their colorful history together as West Coast music pioneers in his excellent biography, *Rocket Norton: Lost In Space,* which is a fascinating read. While Prism was on the road in America with the energetic Bruce Allen often along for the ride on the band bus, Jim and Bryan were churning out songs that would soon become hits for Prism and many other local acts. As their collaborations blossomed, they came to have a healthy respect for each other's talents, even though they didn't become the kind of bosom buddies that Steven Page and Ed Robertson became while they were writing the hits that propelled the Barenaked Ladies to the top of the charts a few years down the road.

"We are two different people," Vallance later told biographer Sorelle Saidman. "Bryan always had his set of friends and I had mine. On a day off I'd stay home and play with my computer whereas Bryan would go skiing or to a hockey game." There were other contrasts, as well. For example, Vallance was classically trained and Adams completely self-taught. "I had two piano lessons and hated it," he told *Rock* magazine. "I had two guitar lessons and hated that. And I took one vocal lesson and really hated that. So, I decided to figure it out for myself."

On the other hand, they were both deliberate workaholics and for long periods of time they would be at it working in the mini studio that Jim had built in the basement of his house in Kits from noon until midnight seven days a week. "Our songwriting is quite methodical," Adams has said, "we really have to sit down and work at it. I don't want to be a rock casualty. Doing drugs for the sake of trying to become inspired would be really foolish. We are very disciplined. Our songs don't just pop out of thin air. Hard work is what makes us successful. We work hard and put in long days."

In addition to pestering Bruce Allen, Adams had pestered A&M Records Toronto A&R guy, Michael Godin, and the head of the label's Irving-Almo Music publishing division, Brian Chater. His persistence eventually resulted in a publishing deal that led to a recording contract. "He . . . told me he was playing with Sweeney Todd at the Gasworks," Godin told biographer Saidman, "but that wasn't something he was interested in. He wanted to talk to me about his career. He played me a few songs (off his demo tape) and they were okay but they weren't great. He sent me a letter the following March saying he'd met this guy named Jim Vallance, and, shortly after, we got a couple of demos, which were pretty good."

Bryan impressed a lot of people when he performed some last minute surgery on a Lindsay Mitchell song that Lindsay sent him the night before a final master tape had to be sent to Toronto. Meanwhile, Bryan and Jim were really churning out the song demos. "If we start writing a song," Vallance told an interviewer, "we can tell pretty early on if is going to be a good one or not. If it doesn't feel good after writing the first minute, we'll go on to another one. We rarely argue or disagree. If Bryan puts forth an idea and I don't like it or vice versa there's no discussion, we just move on."

One of the good ones would be Bryan's first single *Let Me Take You Dancing*, a dance mix that was released before he signed with Bruce Allen, a guy who hated disco with a passion. "That song was written in August of '78," Bryan recalls, "released in February of '79, and it became a hit in the summer of '79. Disco was such a happening thing that year. Jim and I recorded it as a pop song, then disco started to take off. I didn't know anything about it before that so we figured we'd make a twelve-inch of it, and it just took off in the clubs. Studio 54 was worth it alone, the ultimate human orgasm. I went through the ultimate disco experience, dancing and hearing your song at Studio 54."

Canadian sales of the disco mix were more than 30,000 with American sales topping the 150,000 mark. Meanwhile, people were beginning to record their songs. Bonnie Tyler recorded *Straight From The Heart*, and, after Bryan co-wrote *Jump* with guitarist Paul Dean for the second Loverboy album, Adams and Vallance found themselves being asked by elite bands like Kiss to co-write songs.

Bryan's self-titled debut album, recorded in Toronto, didn't light many fires at radio but it encouraged A&M to send Adams to New York to work with producer Bob Clearmountain. The match-up proved to be a winner, yielding the much more promising YOU WANT IT, YOU GOT IT. Adams remembers the time spent in Manhattan fondly. As he told *Rolling Stone*, "Making that album was the most fun I ever had. I had no home. I had no house. I had no car. I owned nothing. There I was a free man in New York City. It was spring and it was beautiful. I'd walk to the studio every day."

This humble routine became his trademark, an approach he has followed throughout his career. "He is so determined not to turn into a product or a 'rock star,'" Bruce Allen told *Rolling Stone* in 1987. "There's no entourage of bodyguards, no flunkies running to do stuff. When he played Madison Square Gardens a few years ago, he took the subway to the shows." Adams would also adopt a workingman's stage wardrobe — sneakers, jeans, and a t-shirt. A rock steady rhythm section and guests like the Doobie Brothers' Jeff "Skunk" Baxter and Hall & Oates' guitarist G.E. Smith resulted in an a more dangerous sound than the Toronto sessions, and Adams' singles from this second album got a lot more air play. Before he headed out on the road to open for the Kinks, Foreigner, and Loverboy, Adams let the guys from Remote Control go and formed his own band. Guitarist Keith Scott and bassist Dave Taylor became mainstays and joined him in the studio on future projects. Adams also enticed New York session musicians Tommy Mandel and Mickey Curry to join his touring band.

In August 1982, Bob Clearmountain came to Little Mountain Studios in Vancouver to produce Adams' third album. Bryan was beginning to get a lot of respect from people in the business that knew about the great songs he and Vallance were penning for BTO, Prism, Loverboy, Ian Lloyd, Lisa Dal Bello, Tim Bogart, Bob Welch, Bonnie Tyler, Rosetta Stone, and Kiss. With his new band lineup, he and his band had begun to create a buzz on the road. Vallance joined him on drums at the Yamaha Music Festival in Japan. The year ended on a positive note with Adams and Loverboy rocking the LA Forum on New Year's Eve.

In January 1983, A&M released CUTS LIKE A KNIFE and the lead single *Straight from the Heart*, which became Bryan's first Top 10 *Billboard* hit. The album was his first million-seller, yielding two more hits, *Cuts Like A Knife* and *This Time*, before the end of the year. Jim

Vallance remembers that "*Cuts Like A Knife* was the breakthrough single. Things really took off from that point." Steve Barron was hired to direct music videos for release on MTV, where Adams was openly endorsed as one of the bright new stars of the music video era.

Standin' on your Mama's porch
You told me that you'd wait forever
Oh and when you held my hand
I knew that it was now or never
Those were the best days of my life
Back in the summer of '69

With the momentum from CUTS LIKE A KNIFE, there were now legions of Bryan Adams fans eagerly awaiting the arrival of his fourth album. Jim and Bryan were on a roll, writing prolifically, but the song that has become his most popular Canadian hit of all time didn't come easily. As Jim later told a British interviewer, "We had that title kicking around for a while and we actually wrote a completely different song called *Summer of '69*, which wasn't very good, so we scrapped it. But we liked the title, so we came back to it a few months later. We re-wrote it and did a demo, but it didn't quite hold together, so we did another recording, tried a different approach, and that didn't work either. So Bryan took it into the studio and recorded it with his band a third time, and it still didn't sound right. We came very, very close to leaving it off the album, but at some point it made the final cut. And to be honest, all these years later, when I hear it on the radio, I can't remember what I didn't like about it."

A&M released RECKLESS on December 1st 1984 and immediately provided a video for the lead single *Run To You*, which rose to number 5 on the *Billboard* chart in early '85. The album was a step forward on all fronts, bristling with songs that had hit potential, including a duet with Tina Turner. *Somebody* hit number 11. *Heaven* became Bryan's first *Billboard* number one. *It's Only Love* was released to coincide with his opening slots on Tina Turner's European tour. He cut a dashing figure slashing away at his electric guitar and leaning in to share a microphone when he joined Tina on stage for their duet. Video footage of their performances was cut into a live music video for MTV. Thus far, he had not been engaged or linked to any celebrity females, and his association with the sexiest woman in rock & roll furthered his image as one of the sexiest young millionaires on the planet.

The press had already learned that Bryan was intensely protective of his private life, able to compartmentalize his rock star persona. However, it was becoming more and more difficult to avoid the paparazzi, and the previous sanctuary of his modest West Vancouver home was no longer the safe bastion of privacy it had been before he toured with Tina Turner. Until 1987, when *Rolling Stone* began knocking on his front door, he had successfully kept his relationship with Vicki Russell, daughter of British filmmaker Ken Russell, private. Compartmentalization wasn't all that difficult for him. Music had always been a consuming interest. Girls had always come second or not at all. As he told *Rolling Stone*, "If it wasn't for the fact that people were making up rumors about me, I'd have kept my private life to myself." To clarify his position, he confessed that: "In high school I was too far into my music to even pay attention to girls. I'd run after the occasional girl, but music and rock & roll bands were far more interesting to me."

The lyrics to *Summer of '69* were not factually autobiographical. He had only been 10 years old and living in Europe at that time. However, the year fit the experience for most of his Woodstock generation audience perfectly, and the emotions and events were something his fans could relate to. The girls liked the references to first love. The boys liked the bands and guitars. The part that rung true the most was that he had been in plenty of teenage bands that didn't amount to much before he made his first hit record.

| Man we were killin' time |
| We were young and restless |
| We needed to unwind |
| I guess nothin' can last forever forever, no |

And now the times are changin'	
Look at everything that's come and gone	
Sometimes when I play that old six-string	
I think about ya wonder what went wrong	

However, the success of the cut would hasten Adams' decision to move on to songs that talked about more than teenybopper love and garage band guitar exploits. As Jim Vallance explains, "One of the things we decided was that we'd have to abandon the scenarios we were using in the past. We were using relationship scenarios to write lyrics and we decided not to do that." The result of their changing gears, however, was the disappointing Into The Fire, where the title song was about a moment of choice. They would soon admit that they were washed up as a songwriting team. Vallance would later say, "With Adams and I, it was 'familiarity breeds contempt'. We spent an enormous amount of time together over an 11-year period, sometimes 12 hours a day, just the two of us in a room writing songs. It was stupid, really, because eventually we just burned out. Bryan's a total workaholic who doesn't know when to give it a rest. I'm the one who pulled the plug."

Standin' on your Mama's porch	
You told me it would last forever	
Oh the way you held my hand	
I knew that it was now or never	
Those were the best days of my life	
Back in the summer of '69	

Before their collaboration ended they had written songs for artists from here, there, and everywhere, including *Tears Are Not Enough* (with David Foster), the song that anchored the All-Canadian Northern Lights benefit record and video that raised $3 million dollars in aid of African famine relief. Adams recorded an entire album with Daniel Lanois that was scrapped before he settled down to a second successful professional relationship with producer and songwriter, Mutt Lange.

The transitional album INTO THE FIRE was recorded in his house in West Vancouver, where waking up the neighbors would lead to a great future album title. "It started out as a home studio," Adams confided to *Canadian Musician*, "and when I was on the road I would let it out to bands to overdub and mix." Some of those bands were among the loudest on the planet. "I remember coming back from the road," he reminisces, "and AC/DC was recording at the house. From the kitchen I could hear Brian Johnson singing *She's Got You By The Balls*. Sometime, during all of that, I bought this burnt-out old warehouse in Gastown with the thought that one day I would build a studio complex there. It was finally ready just as Nirvana was finished mixing their FROM THE MUDDY BANKS OF THE WISHKA album in the house."

Moving his operation to the downtown core worked for Adams' clients and pleased his neighbors, but he would seek evermore private and exotic locations for his own album projects. A mobile studio, built at the same time as the Gastown complex, led to his most memorable recording experience. As he told *Canadian Musician* magazine, "For the recording of 18 'TIL I DIE, we set it up in a house in Ocho Rios, Jamaica. It was fantastic! I have some of the best memories from that experience. Mutt and I went there and wrote the whole CD, bit-by-bit, day-by-day when we weren't snorkeling, of course. The drums and band stuff was overdubbed later onto the original demos. It was a lot of fun!"

The lyrics of 18 'TIL I DIE represented an attempt to recapture the youthful defiance and celebratory spirit of *Summer of '69*, but it did not surpass the electrifying exuberance of what many Canadians regard as Bryan Adams' signature song. "I always knew I'd be in music in some sort of capacity," he noted in *Bryan Adams: The Official Biography* in 1995. "I didn't know if I'd be successful at it, but I knew I'd be doing something in it. Maybe get a job in a record store. Maybe even play in a band. I never got into this to be a star. The idea of being famous wasn't part of the plan. When I was 15 or 16 listening to the Who was all the escapism I needed. Nothing else seemed to matter."

His passion for music, which is so effectively expressed in the lyrics to *Summer of '69*, stems from the days before he was rich and famous and the road was long and winding. "School seemed unimportant," he declares in his biography, "music being the only thing that gave me something to look forward to. There were a lot of years sitting on a bus or in a station wagon, slipping on black ice, touring across America and Canada before things started to happen."

Bryan eventually relocated to a comfortable home in the Chelsea district of London, where he immediately purchased seasons tickets for his favorite soccer team. It was a passion he and Mutt Lange had in common. A change to a vegan diet resulted in the added bonus that his lifelong skin problems cleared up right away. Journalists regularly mention that Bryan Adams has won numerous Juno awards, several Grammies, and has been nominated for Oscars, too. However, awards and even the money he has made from the sale of well over 50 million albums are not the reasons Bryan Adams will likely never retire from the music business. He quit school to play music and he isn't about to give it up just yet. As he told *Bop* magazine, "I guess you could say that I'm the 'Dennis the Menace of rock & roll'. What's important to me is having a good time with my music, which is what I love to do. And this may sound strange but something that's also important to me is breakfast I really love it! It's the one meal of the day that has got to be great."

RECKLESS sold more than 12 million copies worldwide. Bryan performed with Peter Gabriel and U2 on the Amnesty International Conspiracy of Hope Tour, which provided Adams with the confidence that he had done about as much as he could accomplish as a teen idol. He moved on to collaborate with Mutt Lange, a liaison that produced his triple platinum *(Everything I Do) I Do For You*, which spent seven weeks atop the *Billboard* Hot 100 (and a record-setting 16 weeks atop UK charts). Adams and Lange also came up with Adams' number one hits *All For Love* (with Sting and Rod Stewart) and *Have You Ever Really Loved A Woman*, which spent 5 weeks atop the *Billboard* chart. These singles were also featured in the soundtracks of Kevin Costner's *Robin Hood: Prince of Thieves*, *The Three Musketeers* (starring Martin Sheen and Kiefer Sutherland), and *Don Juan De Marco* (starring Johnny Depp). This resulted in worldwide sales of more than 10 million copies of WAKING UP THE NEIGHBOURS and 13 million copies of Adams' "best of" package SO FAR SO GOOD before CD sales tapered off with the release of 18 'TIL I DIE in 1996.

While these sales numbers are impressive, Bryan Adams has never merely been about selling records. He has always been an exciting performer and has shown considerable support to a variety of charities while maturing into a fully rounded complete artist whose intelligence and emotion shine through every project he becomes involved with. In the new millennium when he could easily have become a cranky, petulant rock recluse, he has shown tremendous support for various cancer research organizations and contributed the complete proceeds of some benefits to these charities. He has also shown personal insight into the issues involved and not merely shown up to strut his stuff on the day of the show. He is still active writing and recording, sometimes working with his old pal, Jim Vallance, and has not been content to merely haul out his superhits at concerts. Of course, many of his fans still favor his early hits that he wrote with Jim: *Straight from the Heart, Cuts Like A Knife, Run to You*, and *Heaven. Summer of '69* captures the all-consuming passion that young rock and rollers from all walks of life experience whether they go on to become superstars or not.

If I Had a Million Dollars

Barenaked Ladies

Words & Music by Steven Page and Ed Robertson

©1991, H&S Express, WB Music Corp, Treat Baker Music

If I had a million dollars (If I had a million dollars)
Well I'd buy you a house (I'd buy you a house)

On Saturday, July 2, 2005, Barenaked Ladies performed a joyous rendition of *If I Had A Million Dollars*, at Live 8 in Barrie, Ontario. Neil Young and his wife, Pegi, were next, performing *Four Strong Winds* together, just like Ian & Sylvia did back in the '60s. Then Neil moved to the piano to deliver a solemn new song, *When God Made Me*. He strapped on an electric guitar for the finale, *Keep On Rockin' in the Free World*, joining a cast of thousands all riffing away on a ragged but rugged version of the rock anthem that earned him his honorary degree as the godfather of grunge. It was heartwarming to see Gordon Lightfoot up rocking along with young performers all of them eager to bend a guitar string and sing along with Neil. Before the dust settled, Steven Page led the assembled throng in a spontaneous a cappella performance of *Oh Canada*.

"*Keep On Rockin in the Free World* is always, always, always a train wreck," Page told *BNLblog.com*. "*Oh Canada* was Neil's idea, but he made me start it. We sang it as a reminder of what our country's core values are." The irrepressible BNL front man never misses a beat. He once quipped, "You can never trust a Canadian ... next thing you know we'll be supplying your natural resources." He has a keen eye for details, and his take on just about everything under the sun can be counted on to be wilder and wackier than most everybody else. "Watching Neil Young's set," he recalls, "I noticed a woman in the crowd remove her top to the cheers of hundreds of men around her. I turned to Gord Downie and said, 'Neil's lovely new song about his country has been hijacked by a pair of tits.' Gord gritted his teeth, shook his head in disappointment, and then looked up and said, "No. Augmented, Steve. Augmented."

And if I had a million dollars (If I had a million dollars)
I'd buy you furniture for your house (maybe a nice
    chesterfield or an ottoman)
And if I had a million dollars (If I had a million dollars)
Well I'd buy you a K-Car (a nice, reliant automobile)
And if I had a million dollars, I'd buy your love

Scarborough high-school students Steven Page and Ed Robertson first began jamming together at a summer music camp in 1988. Both teenagers already had their own bands, Scary Movie Breakfast and the Rage. While attending a Bob Dylan concert together they were cracked up by a reference to a bare-naked lady. Dylan is famous for shooting from the hip and spewing out a stream of weirdness stuff, and he may have used the expression in his introduction to a song.

Most likely, this was his early talking blues, *I Shall Be Free*, in which he "hot-footed it out the window bare-naked" and later hooked up with a woman who was the "great granddaughter of Mr. Clean" and took "15 baths a day." It is one of Dylan's funniest compositions with plenty of absurd situations and zany references in a similar vein to some of the songs that Steve and Ed later came up with themselves.

Page and Robertson thought that the idea of a "bare-naked lady" was a hoot. Not a bad name for a band, eh? Not long after that Ed was reminded that he had promised a food bank organizer that the Rage would play a benefit, but the band had already broken up. As he recalls, "She called me a week before the event and said, 'So you're still on for the fund-raiser, right?' And I said, 'Uh, yeah, but now the name of the band is, um, Barenaked Ladies.' That was just a name Steve and I had bantered around, making each other laugh. I called Steve and asked, 'Do you want to be in Barenaked Ladies with me? I've got this gig; it's a fund-raiser." They made plans to rehearse some material, but when the day of the benefit arrived, they had nothing prepared. They decided to wing it.

Their impromptu performance at the October 1, 1988 Harvest Food Bank benefit was a smashing success. "We basically entertained ourselves," Ed admits. As a result of their gritty determination to do the best they could under the circumstances, the comedy troupe Corky & the Juice Pigs invited them along on a cross Canada tour. Barenaked Ladies had their first paying gig.

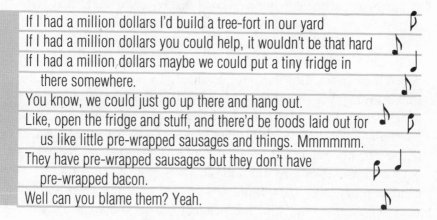

If I had a million dollars I'd build a tree-fort in our yard

If I had a million dollars you could help, it wouldn't be that hard

If I had a million dollars maybe we could put a tiny fridge in there somewhere.

You know, we could just go up there and hang out.

Like, open the fridge and stuff, and there'd be foods laid out for us like little pre-wrapped sausages and things. Mmmmmm.

They have pre-wrapped sausages but they don't have pre-wrapped bacon.

Well can you blame them? Yeah.

Page and Robertson fashioned a repertoire of original songs, Talking Heads, Madonna, and Proclaimers covers, and new songs they improvised along the way. Returning to Scarborough, they put together a demo tape, *Buck Naked*, which they recorded in Ed's parents' basement. Somewhere between Steven's estimation of 150 copies and Ed's memory of 500 tapes were dubbed and handed out. "I knew we needed a demo tape," Page told *Onstage*, "and at that time when it was two of us we had a 4-track recorder and taped every song we knew and wrote. I would call around to club owners and club managers in Toronto. I was terrified on the phone. I'm still not good on the phone, but I knew that if I wanted to get these gigs, I had to call these people." They started out in small clubs playing to audiences comprised largely of their friends, but the word spread rapidly that they were funny and entertaining. When they hooked up with bass player Jim Creeggan and his brother, percussionist and keyboard player, Andy, they recorded their second tape, *Barenaked Lunch*. This has become known as the Pink Tape, which was not sold off the stage because it was recorded poorly and slightly sped up.

Barenaked Ladies were still playing their acoustic guitars and working on their harmonies, but their performances had become as infectious as all get out. During Andy Creeggan's absence due to time spent in Ecuador, they added drummer Tyler Stewart to the lineup. "I just met them on the street at a buskers' carnival," Tyler recalls. "We were the most outgoing guys there, and we all just really hit it off in the sense of humor department." The new combination clicked and they were rewarded for their efforts by being named Band of the Year at YTV's Youth Achievement Awards.

By 1991, with Andy back in the fold, they had refined their act and honed their chops. This time they recorded in a professional recording studio so that they would have a product to sell off the stage. Steven's father, Victor Page, a retired schoolteacher, and his younger brother, Matthew, distributed their self-titled "Yellow Tape" from the basement of their family home and eventually sold 83,000 cassettes before the boys got themselves a record deal. This was quite a feat for an independent production that was only available in cassette format, and has since served as a model for independent Canadian acts. Songs from their tape were picked up by college radio stations from coast to coast, and they ventured as far afield as Austin, Texas, where they took part in the celebrated South By Southwest Music Festival. College audiences loved their irresistible acoustic hip hop and their irreverent off-the cuff banter. The Yellow Tape featured striking acoustic versions of four original songs and one cover. By the time they bumped into Sean Lennon, *Be My Yoko Ono* had become an alternative radio hit. Lennon played the song for his mom. He later told the boys from Scarborough how much she liked it.

Meanwhile *Brian Wilson* with its enigmatic refrain "lying in bed just like Brian Wilson did" had some Torontonians puzzled. Beach Boys fans were not sure they liked it either, but anybody that misconstrued the group's intentions had simply not seen Steven Page's mischievous grin or the gleam of a twinkle in his eyes. Even more controversial in some circles was their tongue in cheek *If I Had A Million Dollars*. It was the kind of song that you either loved or hated, and has received some nasty net culture posts from time to time, mostly from heavy metal addicts. Some adults believed Barenaked Ladies had no respect at all for women, and that their name was politically incorrect and in bad taste. Some folks just had no sense of humor.

This silliness came to public attention when Barenaked Ladies were dropped from the lineup of a Toronto concert at City Hall. Someone on Mayor June Rowland's staff had deemed the band's name inappropriate because it allegedly objectified women and might displease some citizens. Overnight, Barenaked Ladies were famous, featured on national network television news. They might be politically incorrect but they were the hippest band in the land, and their acoustic hip hop approach was endorsed by legions of young fans seeking an alternative to the high volume assault of the slick commercial grunge music that the major labels were all pushing.

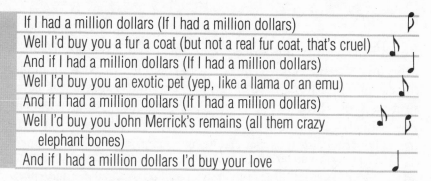

If I had a million dollars (If I had a million dollars)
Well I'd buy you a fur a coat (but not a real fur coat, that's cruel)
And if I had a million dollars (If I had a million dollars)
Well I'd buy you an exotic pet (yep, like a llama or an emu)
And if I had a million dollars (If I had a million dollars)
Well I'd buy you John Merrick's remains (all them crazy elephant bones)
And if I had a million dollars I'd buy your love

Heavy rotation airplay on Brampton, Ontario's CFNY-FM, a modern rock station, helped break the band in other modern rock markets. BNL also benefited from CFNY-FM's Discovery-To-Disk program and were handed $100,000 production money to record their first full-length album. A cover of Bruce Cockburn's *Lovers in a Dangerous Time*, and an accompanying video, bridged the gap between the Yellow Tape and the time they secured a deal with a major label. They went into a studio with producer Michael Phillip-Wojewoda to lay down the tracks that would eventually appear on GORDON before approaching any of the labels. It was the easiest way to insure absolute artistic freedom. Their manager, Nigel Best, negotiated a deal with New York-based Sire Records and a contract was signed on the steps of Scarborough's City Hall. Even though it failed to make much headway in the US, Gordon charted at number one on Canadian charts, sold 800,000 albums, and produced four Top 40 Canadian singles, *Enid, What A Good Boy* and new versions of *Brian Wilson* and *If I Had A Million Dollars*.

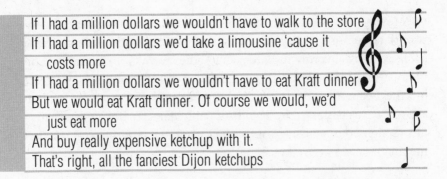

If I had a million dollars we wouldn't have to walk to the store
If I had a million dollars we'd take a limousine 'cause it
  costs more
If I had a million dollars we wouldn't have to eat Kraft dinner
But we would eat Kraft dinner. Of course we would, we'd
  just eat more
And buy really expensive ketchup with it.
That's right, all the fanciest Dijon ketchups

The initial album sales were encouraging, but the band's real strength was in live shows where zany antics and playful banter was tailor-made for each crowd and city. You could pretty much count on some cool moves from Steven Page, though. He was always willing to strut his stuff. There had never been anything quite like the Stephen Page School of Dancing in the rock & roll world. There were interactive activities too, the most popular being tossing boxes of Kraft Dinner onstage while the 'Ladies were singing *If I Had A Million Dollars*. While it was less threatening than the rubber rats that Florida Panthers fans showered down on their team every time they scored a goal during an unlikely 1995 Stanley Cup playoff run, some minor injuries were incurred. There was also the issue of what to do with all those boxes of uncooked macaroni. The band found a solution by returning to its roots that Food Bank benefit that Steve and Ed had played in 1988. As Page recalls, "When people started throwing macaroni at us, it got nuts. So we put boxes in the lobby and signs saying, 'Please donate to the Food Bank.' We got a couple hundred boxes per show and we played 200 shows a year, so do the math. It depended on whether the venue would let us set it up; some were 'suspicious of charities'."

Their second album, MAYBE I SHOULD DRIVE, didn't fare as well as its predecessor. Not much headway was being made introducing the act to American audiences. On top of that, Barenaked Ladies ran into the backlash syndrome that many Canadian bands have had to weather. There is just something about us Canadians that resents success, no matter how good the music is. There had also been corporate pressure to clean up their act, so to speak. Produced by k.d. lang's producer, Ben Mink, the second album was a dismal attempt at playing down their zany repartee a failed experiment. Page and Robertson had some hard decisions to make. They parted ways with Nigel Best and hooked up with Nettwerk Productions' Terry McBride and Pierre Tremblay, Sarah McLachlan's brilliant Vancouver strategists.

During Andy Creeggan's second hiatus, Kevin Hearn was brought in on keyboards and guitar. He would be a keeper. Even though the band's third album, BORN ON A PIRATE SHIP, was underwhelming, progress was being made on other fronts. Concert by concert Barenaked Ladies were worming their way into the hearts of American audiences. Behind the scenes, McBride was at work making things happen. *Beverly Hills 90210* star Jason Priestly had been showing up at their gigs. So they asked him to direct a video for their next single, *The Old Apartment*, which became their first Top 40 *Billboard* hit and led to a guest appearance on *Beverly Hills 90210*. "He's a fan of the band and directed our video," Page revealed. "So we bugged him enough to put us in the show." All of a sudden, Barenaked Ladies was in demand and playing to sold out houses. McBride dispatched engineers to tape shows, and the result was ROCK SPECTACLE, a live album to die for, which featured many of the songs that had been hits in Canada but had gone unnoticed in the land of the free and home of the brave.

Page and Robertson's sparkling wit also received recognition it had long deserved during an interview with *Billboard* magazine's Timothy White. "Most people don't realize it," Page told White, but our first three albums were conceived as a trilogy." "So, does that mean that ROCK SPECTACLE, as our first live album, would be, like, the long awaited sequel to *Return Of The Jedi*?" Robertson quipped. "Oh no!" Page shot back, expressing mock horror, "The live record is, like, our *Return Of The King* if you count *The Hobbit*." Timothy White loved their wacky presence and gave Rock Spectacle, their first album for Nettwerk/Reprise, two thumbs up.

Their next studio album, STUNT, sold four million albums in North America and provided the band with their first number one *Billboard* hit, *One Week*, which was also nominated for a Grammy award. Released in July 1998, Stunt benefited from a publicity campaign that saw Barenaked Ladies appear on *Saturday Night Live* and *The Tonight Show with Jay Leno*. They were included in the US HORDE tour along with Blues Traveler and Ben Harper and played to their biggest audiences, ever. Ten long years after Steven Page and Ed Robertson had improvised their first set together at a Food Bank benefit Barenaked

Ladies had finally turned their talent into a profitable enterprise. "We're actually making money now," Page told interviewers. "We've never been in a position where we were not surviving, but after Gordon everything was just a matter of breaking even, all along the way. Don't have the million dollars yet, so we can continue to sing the song."

> If I had a million dollars (If I had a million dollars)
> Well I'd buy you a green dress (but not a real green dress that's cruel)
> And if I had a million dollars (If I had a million dollars)
> Well I'd buy you some art (A Picasso or a Garfunkel)
> And if I had a million dollars (If I had a million dollars)
> Well I'd buy you a monkey (haven't you always wanted a monkey?)
> And if I had a million dollars I'd buy your love

Just when things were going great Kevin Hearn was stricken with leukemia. Thanks to recent advances in the treatment of cancer, he survived but would be out of action for two years before returning fully recovered in the new millennium. Jason Priestly directed the full-length video *Barenaked in America*, which was both fast paced and informative, providing a mix of live performances and behind the scenes personal stuff. In every market it was broadcast, it spread the word about the band and improved ticket sales. The documentary approach worked far better than a calculated image change and revealed the barenaked truth the boys who would be ladies had grown up to be daddies with more or less normal lives when they were not on the road.

Steven Page and Ed Robertson's lives came full circle while they were recording MAROON with producer Don Was in the same LA studio where the Beach Boys had recorded PET SOUNDS. One afternoon, Brian Wilson dropped by to say hello and play them a copy of his cover of the song they had written about his "troubled genius" and struggle to regain his former cheery self. When they had finished listening, Wilson asked if it was cool. "Of course it was cool!" Page says. "Just the fact that he acknowledged that he knows what we wrote is pretty exciting. To hear his voice is remarkable." Steven and Ed were not the only people on the planet who were happy to learn that Brian Wilson was alive and well and making music again. No doubt, all of those times that Barenaked Ladies and their fans had paid homage to Wilson in song had paid off. Music is good for healing, especially when it is sung as exuberantly and positively as the band from Scarborough, Ontario has always sung at their shows.

Steven Page would finally cave in to corporate pressure and sign a contract that permitted his beloved million-dollar song to be used in a commercial. Barenaked Ladies could always use the bucks, especially since the Loonie had been deflated to a shadow of its former self. To this day, the songs from that Yellow Tape they made so many years ago stick to them like old friends. "Songs like *What a Good Boy, Brian Wilson*, and *If I Had a Million Dollars*, we've done so many times over the last ten years, every show," Page admitted in an October 2000 interview with *The Cleveland Jewish News*. "But to see how much they mean to people I've never even met, that's pretty cool."

If I had a million dollars; if I had a million dollars
If I had a million dollars; if I had a million dollars
If I had a million dollars... I'd be rich!

Rich they were and the band was more prolific than ever. In 2004, they created their own record label, Desperation Records, and continued to put out best-selling albums. However, Ed and Steven had come to the part in the story where they run into the Lennon-McCartney syndrome and, after struggling to coexist when the thrill has gone, their band breaks up.

Steven put out a solo album in 2005 but continued to gig and record with the band. Both songwriters were as prolific as they had ever been, but now they were collaborating with others, and there simply were not enough tracks available on BNL albums for all of the material they were creating. When Ed got a request to write a theme song for a new Chuck Lorre sitcom, he came up with the campy song, *The Big Bang Theory Theme*, which the band recorded and network TV audiences heard in the luxury of their own homes every time Leonard Hofstadter, Sheldon Cooper, and their next door neighbor, Penny, regaled television audiences with their syndicated mirth. Along the way, the band taped a pilot episode for a variety show, but Fox executives turned it down. The band continued to put out an album a year, including Ed's Children's Album SNACKTIME!, which Steven had not wanted to release.

Then in July 2008 disaster struck. Steven was arrested and charged with possession of cocaine in Fayetteville, New York, and a month later Ed crashed the light plane he was flying. In December, Ed's mom passed away. In February 2009, the band and the singer separately announced that Steven had left Barenaked Ladies.

"Our relationship with Steve Page was great and very fruitful," Ed told reporters. "It lasted almost 20 years, but it was time to move on. Now we're doing something that feels really fresh and exciting to me. His departure left four singers and three multi-instrumentalists in the band, so we're not lacking for musical ideas, and now there's more room for the other writers in the band to bring songs to the table."

"We don't keep in touch," Tyler Stewart said on another occasion, "but we certainly wish him the best and there's good will there."

Page was less diplomatic, often revealing glimpses of the internal stress that had taken place behind closed doors. "The band was no longer the joyous place that it once was," he said in one interview, "but it hadn't been joyous for a long time before that. It wasn't that we didn't put on good shows; we still had a great time onstage every night. But it became a place where work was just about stress and not the end product." He has also let it be known that he feels it to be strange that the band continues to gig and perform the songs that he wrote and performed. Meanwhile, BNL fans wish the split hadn't happened. In September 2011, Rhino Records put out a new greatest hits package, HITS FROM YESTERDAY & THE DAY BEFORE. If I Had A Million Dollars is the first track.

Steven Page and Ed Robertson continue to sweeten our world with their infectious sense of humor and delightful songs, Steven as a solo artist, and Ed with the Barenaked Ladies. Together, they have sold more CDs than any other Canadian rock band. No doubt, they will continue to surprise us with more gems like Steven's A Different Sort of Solitude, which was written and recorded for the movie French Immersion and released in January 2012. That same year, Ed co-hosted Live! With Kelly. Kelly Ripa is the ABC network talk show host who has replaced Regis Philbin. Ripa told Robertson that BNL's One Week is the ultimate party song and a personal favorite. Robertson told Ripa that he was encouraged by all of the young talent that was bubbling up through televised talent shows. "I'm always blown away," he told Kelly, "by the people on these shows because I would be thrown off these shows . . . I would never make the audition, and I've sold 14 million records."

Any Man of Mine

Shania Twain

Words & Music by Shania Twain and R.J. Lange

© 1995, Universal, Songs of Polygram, Loon Echo and Out of Pocket Productions

THE STORY BEHIND

This is what a woman wants...

Any man of mine better be proud of me
Even when I'm ugly he still better love me
And I can be late for a date that's fine
But he better be on time

When Shania Twain returned home to Timmins, Ontario, in the fall of 2004, her every move was broadcast to the world. During her meteoric rise to superstar status, CMT Canada had devoted entire days of programming to her, calling them "Shania Sundays." She had become the most exciting Canadian since Wayne Gretsky starred for the Edmonton Oilers and Los Angeles Kings.

By this time, Shania's breakthrough album, THE WOMAN IN ME, had surpassed PATSY CLINE'S GREATEST HITS to become the best-selling album by a woman in country music. COME ON OVER had surpassed Garth Brooks' NO FENCES to become the best-selling country album of all time. In fact, with sales of more than 39 million worldwide, COME ON OVER had become the best-selling album by any female artist in any music genre, ever. Mercury Nashville had just released Shania's own "greatest hits" package, with four new singles added as an enticement for fans that already had every CD she had put out.

Amid all the hoopla, it was difficult to remember that Shania's first made-in-Nashville album had not spawned any Top 40 hits at all, mostly because her producers had ignored her own songwriting talent. Shania's fairytale romance and marriage to producer Mutt Lange had changed all that. As mediocre as her self-titled debut had been, her videos had always been stunning. It was her videos that first drew Lange's attention. She has said that he worked out to her CD before gathering his courage and phoning her management in Nashville. In retrospect, the fact that neither Mary Bailey nor Shania was familiar with his name or that he had produced album sales in excess of 100 million by the likes of Def Leppard, Foreigner, and Bryan Adams seems comical. They sent him a signed 8x10 photo.

According to legend, Shania had told incoming Mercury Nashville president Luke Lewis that "she wanted to be as big as Garth." Lewis "had looked into her eyes and knew she could do it." He had also told her about Mutt Lange's achievements, and soon they were running up phone bills chatting and singing their latest songs. Not long afer that, Mutt Lange and Bryan Adams were on a working vacation in Ocho Rios, Jamaica snorkeling and recording 18 'TIL I DIE. They packed up their recording gear and flew to Nashville to catch Shania's showcase set at Fan Fair '93. Shortly after that, Shania joined Lange while he was mixing Adams' album in Ramatuelle, near St. Tropez, in southern France. They fell in love, got married in Huntsville, Ontario and returned to Nashville to record THE WOMAN IN ME, which was overdubbed and mixed at Le Studio in Morin Heights, Quebec.

Shania's first two Top 40 singles encountered considerable resistance from some quarters. Choosing any single that is an outright manifesto from an album entitled THE WOMAN IN ME was bound to drum up some controversy. By 1995, the first year in which women outsold men in all music genres, country music was ready for a little emancipation and Shania thrived on all of the controversies that surrounded her.

In February 1995 I received Shania's CD and a promo kit, which included 8x10 versions of those now famous fashion shots and our first glimpse of her fetching navel as she posed beside Bo Derek's horse trailer. I was invited to breakfast with Shania, who was on her first coast-to-coast media blitz. I had interviewed plenty of Canadian country stars, including the reigning queen of Canadian country, Michelle Wright, but those interviews usually took place back stage at awards shows or on tour buses.

As I listened to the CD, I realized that Shania and Mutt had taken country music production to a whole new level. Mercury Polygram rep Ken Ashdown had told me that some radio guys were saying that

Whose Bed Have Your Boots Been Under was "not country." When I listened to the track, a bustling two-stepper brimming with fiddle, pedal steel, and traditional harmonies from Shania and Mutt, I was puzzled. Far more likely, I thought, the opposition was due to her strong woman's point of view. Shania may be hurting when she learns that her beau is "sneakin' around with Jill" and has spent a "weekend with Beverly Hill," but she tells him in no uncertain terms to take a hike. "*Whose Bed Have Your Boots Been Under*," she had said in a statement in the press kit, "is something I've been kicking around for the last couple of years. It's really cool to be able to come up with a hook that someone like Mutt believes in. He feels it's a hit song."

My breakfast interview with Shania turned out to be a pleasant surprise. Shania was as real as can be; the girl next door dressed tastefully in a brown sweater and skirt. Her beauty seemed to come from a confident inner glow. She didn't put on any airs. She didn't have "big hair." And she wasn't wearing an outfit that looked like she was about to make an appearance on the Grand Ole Opry. In fact, she was every bit a regular young Canadian woman pretty, polite, and genuinely pleased that I liked her music. When she learned which track was my favorite she began snapping her fingers and sang. "Am I dreamin' or stupid / I think I've been hit by Cupid / But no one needs to know right now."

The lyrics of the second single, *Any Man Of Mine*, lay out the ground rules that a man must accept if he is going to woo a post-modern woman. And while some country boys may have thought she was acting like a ball-busting feminist, Shania's manifesto is totally tongue in cheek. She is no flag-waving activist. She may be issuing ultimatums, but at the same time she is willing to pass out a few helpful tips to prospective suitors.

> Any man of mine'll say it fits just right
> When last year's dress is just a little too tight
> And anything I do or say better be okay
> When I have a bad hair day

Today I smile when I read the CD review I posted on the web that night. "This CD is infused with the deep love and affection felt between husband and wife team Lange and Twain who co-wrote all of the 12 tunes. From the opening strains of the tour de force ballad *Home Ain't Where The Heart Is (Anymore)* to the closing strains of the a cappella lullaby *God Bless The Child* we are treated to songs that inspire rather than the usual cheatin', hurtin', drinkin', tragi-comedy formula stuff. There are plenty of twisted cliché Nashvillisms, waves of twangy guitars and spicy Cajun fiddles, and even a number that has line dance mania served up with hand claps and drum programs *Any Man Of Mine.*"

Shania's country girl manifesto really rocked. The track was driven by biting edge fiddles, although Mutt Lange's production also featured those hand claps and searing electric guitar bursts that accentuated break dance sections that broke away from the up tempo two-step verses.

> And if I change my mind
> A million times
> I wanna hear him say
> Yeah, yeah, yeah, yeah, yeah I like it that way

At the very end she adds a saucy taste of rap poetry. Line-dancers loved the track. There is nothing that works better than a fiddle in the band to get people up on the dance floor. "I think the whole idea behind the fiddle on this CD is we wanted fiddle that really 'dug in', and was really aggressive," Shania told me, "not just the fiddle as a background instrument."

> Any man of mine better walk the line
> Better show me a teasin' squeezin' pleasin' kinda time
> I need a man who knows, how the story goes
> He's gotta be a heart beatin' fine treatin'
> Breath takin' earthquakin' kind
> Any man of mine

Shania Twain was born Eileen Edwards, the second of three daughters of Sharon and Clarence Edwards, in Windsor, Ontario, on August 28, 1965. Her mother fled an abusive relationship to live in northern Ontario, where she met and married Jerry Twain, a full-blooded Ojibwa. Jerry adopted Eileen and her sisters, and they became full members of his tribe. The family was not well off, and Shania later recounted stories of being raised in abject poverty, just like Dolly Parton. Shania's mother encouraged her from age four to sing for friends and family, and when Shania was a preteen, her mother took her to local bars after midnight, where she could get up and sing after last call. Sharon dreamed that Shania would become a country singer, but she soon gravitated to rock and pop. When her parents were killed in a tragic logging road accident, Shania quit her career in Toronto and returned to Timmins to raise her younger brothers. She worked in a musical revue in a Huntsville resort until her siblings were old enough to fend for themselves, then contacted Mary Bailey and asked if she would help her get a record deal in Nashville. Her stage name, Shania, was an Ojibwa word for "on my way."

During our interview, we touched briefly on the Cinderella aspects of her biography. "It is a Cinderella story," she admitted. "Not rags to riches, I'm not rich, yet. But certainly rags to something." When I asked about her tiny size and whether she'd been placed on a chair when her parents had encouraged her to sing at such a young age, she laughed and opened up. "The guitar was bigger than me," she confided. "I've been doing it for a very, very long time. I'm 29 years old now, and it has been 21 years that I've been singing professionally. I remember Gary Buck and Dallas Harms. I used to be on shows as the opener for Anita Perras when I was just a kid and she was a teenager. I opened for people like Carroll Baker. Ronnie Prophet was one. Mary Bailey, my manager, was an entertainer when I was a child."

As she continued, "I listened to all kinds of music, we had a multi-format station happening in our home town. I heard 'everything' through radio, but at home it was always country. And I only sang country music as a child. I had other influences. I was really enamoured with the Carpenters; their harmonies were so beautiful. I learned so much, at a very young age from groups like that. Her voice is just like silk; it is so gorgeous! There were many influences along the way. I think Dolly Parton is the one from the beginning right up until now, that has been the 'one'. Dolly has done everything. She's an exceptional writer. She's an actor. She's a great personality. She's everything." We soon found ourselves discussing the excellent production on her CD.

"A lot of people were pleasantly surprised," she said, "maybe even expecting it to be overproduced or too rock. I think what he has done is created a new standard for country music. What people don't realize is, of course, yes as far as Def Leppard is concerned he is a major contributor to that success. But to go from Def Lepard to Billy Ocean to Michael Bolton they are worlds apart."

"You are saying that he brings out the best in everyone he deals with?" I suggested. "He enhances the artist's music," she replied. "A lot of the success of this album has to do with the writing and what he has done with the sound of it. Right from the beginning he said, 'We need to go into your catalog. I want to know what you've been writing, then we'll go from there. You be the basis to the creativity of this album, because it needs to be you not me.' Ten out of the 12 songs on this album are songs that I was writing before I even met Mutt."

Shania told another interviewer that "*Any Man Of Mine* is also something I've been working on for quite a while. Mutt and I finished it together as well. I think it could be the impact song of this album. It is an excellent combination of the two of us. It's got everything that he's known for as a producer and writer, yet it's so me that it's not funny." The song would become a woman's anthem and yet be endorsed by emancipated men. Mutt encouraged Shania to sharpen the focus of the lyrics and radically changed its melody and arrangement.

Shania credits Sandy Neese, vice president of media relations for Mercury Nashville, for helping her name the album THE WOMAN IN ME. As she told James Dickerson, author of *Women On Top: The Quiet Revolution That's Rocking The American Music Industry*, "Mutt and I went through everything possible for the title. Then Sandy came one day and said *The Woman In Me* should be the one. Just the way she said it, I said, 'Yep, that's the one.'" Dickerson credits a network of women in the music industry with becoming her invisible support team. "Unknown to Twain," he claims, "Neese was a member of a loosely organized good ol' girl network in Nashville that years ago had pledged its membership to give breaks to female artists who were deserving of a helping hand." When male journalists bashed Shania in the media, legions of female journalists would feature her in interviews and cover stories for women's magazines.

"We really had a struggle with that first single," Neese admitted to Dickerson. "Radio didn't want to play it. It was too pop. It was too this, too that. Luke went back week after week and pounded on the promotions department. 'I know this is a hit. I know we've got something phenomenal going on here.' He wouldn't let go." During this intense promotion, Neese and Lewis learned that most of the phone calls that had been coming in to the stations that were playing *Whose Bed Have Your Boots Been Under* were made by women. "Unknown to Twain," Dickerson concludes, "the good ol' girl network fell in behind THE WOMAN IN ME. Behind the scenes women worked hard to make the album a success. Their hopes were riding high with Twain's hopes."

Shania's decision to promote THE WOMAN IN ME in malls and in the media instead of following the usual route of hitting the road and touring her buns off turned out to be a canny strategy. But it left her open to criticism that she couldn't sing and couldn't perform. Meanwhile, she was winning over millions of female and male fans with her spectacular videos and coyly claiming that she couldn't understand all the fuss that was being made about her bared navel. As she asserted in a VH1 interview, "So many other people bare their midriffs, I don't know why mine is such an issue." The controversial videos for *Whose Bed Have Your Boots Been Under* and *Any Man Of Mine* did far more for her career than anything she said in her own defense. What is not widely known is that they were made hastily when an animated video that featured cartoon boots cavorting to Shania's saucy vocal was scrapped and John Derek, who had contributed the fashion photography, was lobbied to rescue the project.

"Bo convinced John to do it," Shania told *Country Music Today*. "John Derek was the director and Bo Derek was the producer." The video began with a barefoot Shania strumming her guitar on a rural front porch, which was cut with images of her in a red dress table dancing in a roadside diner. There were some spectacular video moments, such as a flight of birds that swoops in and out of frame seemingly in perfect time with a glistening pedal steel guitar riff while Shania is dancing in her red dress at Bo's Santa Ynez ranch. Luke Lewis was frustrated when CMT at first refused to play the *Whose Bed Have Your Boots Been Under* video. "They thought it was redundant and too sexy," he recalls. "They never did play it like it was a hit."

At this juncture, the first cut of John Derek's video for *Any Man Of Mine* was rejected and veteran video producer Charlie Randazzo was called in. Randazzo is responsible for the barnyard dancing footage that was added to the second print, which CMT could not ignore, and it became her first number one CMT video. Shania plays directly to the camera as if she is a private dancer. Doing this with passionate abandon fulfilled every cowboy's dream. Steve Earle would quip that Shania was the "highest paid lap dancer in Nashville." "Even though I was kind of going against the grain at the time," she told *Country Music Today*, "in the end it was the best thing I ever did not being intimidated that it might be a little risqué."

Well any man of mine better disagree
When I say another woman's lookin' better than me
And when I cook him dinner and I burn it black
He better say, mmmm, I like it like that yeah

And if I changed my mind
A million times
I wanna hear him say
Yeah, yeah, yeah, yeah, yeah I like it that way

The video began with footage of Shania as a working cowgirl rounding up some heifers and moves on to the barnyard dancing sequence where she is turning up the sexual heat. When she steps out of her cowgirl duds and into a bubble bath it is as if she is responding to shouts of "shower, shower!" But the footage moves on to Shania dressing for a night on the town and emerging at the end as an urban Shania in an evening gown. Women related, men stared, and the patriarchy and matriarchy of the fundamentalist South whispered behind their hands. They were shocked! The ending foreshadowed videos in which she would leave rural settings behind, ride her horse past Egyptian pyramids, and boogie with a troupe of dancers in New York.

Shania's Mall Tour was a huge success with tens of thousands of fans turning out just to get a glimpse of her and, maybe if they were lucky, a personally autographed item. She would soon be featured on the cover of dozens of magazines, many of them fashion magazines, embraced by a legion of female journalists who encouraged women to go out and buy her records. "I'm not out to make a statement," she told Bruce Feiler. "Women are the people who read *Vogue*. "They're into the Calvin Klein ads, the Guess? ads if it wasn't for the music I would be the sort of person who wore the same thing for the rest of my life."

Any man of mine better walk the line
Better show me a teasin' squeezin' pleasin' kinda time
I need a man who knows, how the story goes
He's gotta be a heartbeatin' fine treatin'
Breathtakin' earthquakin' kind
Any man of mine

Let me hear you say yeah, yeah, yeah, yeah, yeah I like it that way

Any Man Of Mine hit number one on the country charts in the early summer and crossed over onto the pop charts. In September, Shania was in Hamilton, Ontario to appear on the Canadian Country Music Awards show and I was at her first press conference. Reporters wanted to know how many awards she thought she would win. "I'm not in the business of winning awards," she told them blithely. "I'm in the business of making music." She did win awards, of course, five of them, and I filed a feature story with *Country Music News* that reported her performance of *Any Man Of Mine* and *The Woman In Me* had been "spectacular." While this should have been clear evidence that she could both sing and entertain, critics continued to allege that she could do neither. Rumors of marital discord and impending divorce were equally spurious.

You gotta shimmy shake
Make the earth quake
Kick, turn, stomp, stomp, then you jump
Heel to toe, Do Si Do
'Til your boots wanna break
'Til your feet and your back ache
Keep it movin' 'til you just can't take anymore

By 1997, Shania had issued eight stunning music videos from THE WOMAN IN ME and dominated both the album and singles charts, proving that she could successfully challenge country norms, but she often faced the same old questions about her navel. The release of COME ON OVER and the announcement of Shania's upcoming world tour put everything on the line. If she packed arenas and stadiums and sales of her third Mercury album surpassed THE WOMAN IN ME, her detractors would be proved wrong.

For decades, country music had been a haven for male chauvinists and "girl singers" who played second fiddle to male headliners. Few country women had been successful touring on their own. Reba had managed to make it work mainly because her opening act was the hugely popular Brooks & Dunn. When Shania began touring all that would change. Her shows were sold out and her performances unprecedented. Fans from all walks of life celebrated her triumphant march across North America by singing along with their Shania. The entertainment skills she had developed at the Deerhurst Resort had been rehearsed for more than a month with her new band before she hit the road. To keep herself centered, she towed a horse trailer behind her bus and went for daily rides along the way.

In September 1998 during rehearsals for the CCMA Awards show in Calgary, I was impressed with just how hard Shania works to perfect her performances. After I had completed my green room interview with Randall Prescott and Tracey Brown, Tracey asked me if I'd like to slip into the theater with her to watch Shania rehearse. Seated in the third row we could see that Shania was in terrific shape. She needed to be for the rigorous workout that she and her band went through performing *Honey I'm Home*. I remembered all of those absurd critics' assertions that she couldn't sing and wouldn't be able to perform once she hit the road. And I marveled at how she stuck with it, taking charge and rehearsing their choreography time after time until both her band and the camera crew got everything just right. She wasn't upset a bit when awards show host Terri Clark had a little fun at her expense performing a parody of her moves. Terri is a big-boned gal from southern Alberta and would later quip while introducing Shania, who is a devout vegetarian, that she could benefit from eating a big steak.

Shania would soon eclipse everything that any Canadian country singer, including Hank Snow and Anne Murray, had done before her. The song that got her to the dance, *Any Man Of Mine*, has become the centerpiece of her "greatest hits" CD. Shania Twain has become a Canadian icon a little bit Karen Carpenter, a little bit Dolly Parton, and a whole lot Shania.

Come on everybody on the floor
A-one two, a-three four
Hup two, hum
If you wanna be a man of mine, that's right
This is what a woman wants...

You Oughta Know

Alanis Morissette
Words by Alanis Morissette &
Music by Alanis Morissette and Glen Ballard

© 1995, Songs of Universal Inc, Vanhurst Place,
Universal Music Corp and Aerospace Corporation

THE STORY BEHIND

I want you to know, that I'm happy for you
I wish nothing but the best for you both

On June 6, 2005, three generations of born-in-Ottawa singer-song-writers attended a gala show at Toronto's Elgin Theatre, where they were welcomed into Canada's Walk of Fame. Paul Anka received this long overdue national recognition, while Bruce Cockburn welcomed the new kid on the block, Alanis Morissette. "I've been a fan of hers ever since her first album came out," Cockburn said as he introduced Morissette. "Um, not the mall album," he added, hastily, "I mean JAGGED LITTLE PILL. It was intense and exciting."

Sporting a platinum blonde streak in her trademark brunette tresses, Alanis spoke of "continuity between Canadian artists. They are all very introspective and not afraid to be autobiographical." Indeed, Alanis has shown no reserve in telling us about her life. Nothing is held back in *You Oughta Know*, the first single off her JAGGED LITTLE PILL album, as she calls out an ex-lover using some of the most angry, bitter, and ironic lyrics ever written in rock or pop music history. She created quite a stir.

An older version of me
Is she perverted like me
Would she go down on you in a theater
Does she speak eloquently
And would she have your baby
I'm sure she'd make a really excellent mother

Alanis Morissette

228

These are lyrics that changed the vocabulary of women's music in the 1990s, opening a door that other candid young women artists, such as Joan Osborne, PJ Harvey, Sheryl Crow, Björk, and fellow Canadian Sara McLachlan, rushed through onto the *Billboard* charts. These women joined the ranks of the swelling alternative rock scene, which, since the mid-80's had mostly been composed of male bands signed to independent labels and distributors. They became an alt rock chick contingent with delightful band names like the Slits and Hole. Along with silver-haired alt country rock feminists like Emmylou Harris, alt country rockers like Lucinda Williams and Julie Miller, and folksingers like Nancy Griffith, these young rockers invaded the newly created Americana triple-A radio format and station ratings went up, up, up.

Women in rock had become a force to be reckoned with. The AAA format networks were immediately successful, attracted rafts of advertisers, and were quickly rewarded for their move to increase the richness of home-baked Americana pie music by the creation of a *Billboard* triple-A music category and Americana charts. These women spoke their minds and expressed their angst in whispers and shrieks. None of these feisty women of alternative persuasions got much play on the antiquated adult contemporary stations or any of the other easy listening networks at all.

Alanis Morissette was an unlikely leader of a postmodern feminist movement in rock music, often referred to as Grrrl power for its rough edge. She began her career in Ottawa singing dance tracks, and emerged in LA the unannounced ironic voice of Generation Y. She was branded the "angry white female" by *Rolling Stone* and "the first lady of rage" elsewhere. While grunge bands raged against the machine, these alt women fought back against a sexist attitude that permeated contemporary society and the recording industry. Their tactics disturbed not only male powers, but also their female predecessors, oddly enough.

"Tell Alanis she sucks," Courtney Love instructed a Maverick Records A&R representative. Alanis had displaced Courtney as the number one female act on the Maverick label, owned by Madonna. "While the media were lauding Courtney Love, the uncontestable yin storming rock's yang primacy," Mark Lepage noted in *The Montreal Gazette*, "The industry was sitting up and taking notice of the Canadian girl breezing past her to the spokeswoman podium."

Other complaints came from unexpected sources. Joni Mitchell, an outspoken rock feminist herself, complained that "Morissette writes the words, someone else helps set it to music, and then she's kind of stylized into the part." Morissette's producer and co-writer, Glen Ballard, came to her defense, denying these accusations. "It was real," he said, "truly the most uncalculated thing I have ever been involved with. There's no doubt it was a genuine and artistic awakening. We had hands on the Ouija board, man, and I'm telling you it took off. This is where it was supposed to be. The last thing we were trying to figure out was what we were supposed to be doing in terms of the marketplace."

Alanis was also accused of being as contrived as Milli Vanilli and the Spice Girls. No matter that Alanis wrote her own lyrics and spoke intelligently about the songwriting process in interviews. No matter that by 2004 JAGGED LITTLE PILL ranked second in American CD sales in the SoundScan era, second only to Shania Twain's COME ON OVER. No matter that, as subsequent singles from the album were aired, it became evident that there was far more to Alanis Morissette than a jilted lover. *You Oughta Know* was simply one of the most irresistible debut singles to hit the *Billboard* charts since a 16-year-old Paul Anka pranced into the spotlight with *Diana*, a song that had been tailored to make him a star by New York producer Don Costa.

"I sensed immediately that she was speaking to people and that she'd be understood," Guy Oseary, chief talent scout at Maverick, maintained from the moment he had signed her to the label. Madonna agreed. "She reminds me of when I started out," Madonna told *Rolling Stone*, "slightly awkward but extremely self-possessed and straightforward. There's a sense of excitement and giddiness in the air around her like anything's possible, and the sky's the limit."

'Cause the love that you gave that we made wasn't able
To make it enough for you to be open wide, no
And every time you speak her name
Does she know how you told me you'd hold me
Until you died, til you died
But you're still alive

You Oughta Know became a hit almost on its own. An influential LA deejay found the demo for the song on a compilation that had been sent out as a promotion with a music magazine. "We hadn't even shipped the single yet," Jerry Welch at Maverick recalls. "They started playing it. The phones lit up. And when the phones lit up, BAM, it went all across the country." Welch soon found himself besieged by requests for interviews. "I didn't twist anyone's arm," he insists.

You Oughta Know was chosen to be the lead single from JAGGED LITTLE PILL, which Alanis had co-written with her producer, Quincy Jones protege, Glen Ballard. Red Hot Chili Peppers' Flea and Dave Navarro were among the musicians accompanying her on the track. "Flea and I did that song together in the studio," Dave Navarro revealed recently. "It was already written with different instrumentation and we were asked to kind of rewrite the music . . . A lot like a remix. The structure of the song was in place but there were no guide tracks, we just had the vocal to work from. It was just a good time and we basically jammed until we found something we were both happy with. Alanis was happy, too."

> And I'm here to remind you
> Of the mess you left when you went away
> It's not fair to deny me
> Of the cross I bear that you gave to me
> You, you, you oughta know

As Alanis explained during an interview for a November 1995 *Rolling Stone* cover story, "That song wasn't written for the sake of revenge, it was written for the sake of release. I'm actually a pretty rational, calm person. The record is my story. I think of the album running over the different facets of my personality, one of them being my sexual self."

John Pareles at the *New York Times* got it. JAGGED LITTLE PILL was an autobiographical coming-of-age tale told in song. "The songs on JAGGED LITTLE PILL," he wrote in August 1995, "are tales of a young woman determined to make her own way, inventing herself as she leaves behind childhood indoctrination, manipulative lovers, sleazy business associates and, finally, her own self-doubt."

In 2005, Alanis made another effort to explain the dynamic of *You Oughta Know* and other songs on JAGGED LITTLE PILL during an interview published in *The Boston Globe*, "I think there's a timelessness to the songs. These were inward questions I was asking, and ten years later I still ask them."

Timelessness was more apparent on the singles that followed. *Hand in Pocket* revealed a more casual Morissette, a 21-year-old bohemian, to be sure, but not one caught up in revenge fantasies. *Ironic* and the accompanying video put her over the top, conveying in cinematic terms the ironic complexities of postmodern life where at least four Alanis Morissettes existed simultaneously. *Houston Chronicle* critic Tom Moon made the most insightful assessment of all when he wrote: "While the alternative rock world welcomes female artists, in the larger pop world the stereotypes tramp, high-minded singer-songwriter, dance-pop diva still prevail at the top of the charts. Morissette wants to challenge that thinking."

Vindication arrived in '96 when Alanis won two American Music awards, five *Billboard* awards, a British award, a German award, an MTV Europe award, four Grammy awards, five Juno awards, and three MTV awards. In concert, she was a whirling dervish amid a swirl of long hair and attitude laden vocals. Her first tour, begun in '95 in small clubs, continued for 18 months, moving to arenas before she collapsed from exhaustion and finally took time off to regroup and record SUPPOSED FORMER INFATUATION JUNKIE. She had become the anti-diva, but a superstar nevertheless.

You seem very well, things look peaceful
I'm not quite as well, I thought you should know
Did you forget about me Mr. Duplicity
I hate to bug you in the middle of dinner
It was a slap in the face how quickly I was replaced
Are you thinking of me when you fuck her

At least some of the notoriety that *You Oughta Know* enjoyed was due to the presence of the "f" word, which was bleeped out by some radio stations, and, when she was nominated in '96, during awards show broadcasts.

Alanis Nadine Morissette and her twin brother Wade were born on June 1, 1974 in Ottawa, the youngest children of schoolteachers Alan and Georgia Morissette. She spent her formative years on Canadian military bases in Europe before returning to the Canadian capital at age nine to audition for a role on *You Can't Do That On Television*. She was an instant hit on this locally produced TV series, which was syndicated on Nickelodeon in American markets. She liked being on TV well enough, but her passion for music encouraged her parents to set her up with her own record label and producers like Stampeder's veteran Rich Dodson. They had 2000 records pressed with *Fate Stay With Me* on one side and *Find The Right Man* on the other. Alanis continued her acting career, starring in a less than remarkable movie alongside future *Friends* star Matt LeBlanc, but her focus was on her music.

By all accounts, the Morissettes were a close-knit Catholic family that held daily family meetings to compare happy moments each of them had experienced. While her mom acted as her agent in the early days of her career, neither parent has been accused of pushing her into show business. If they have been accused of anything at all it, is that they encouraged their children to strive for perfection. "I don't think there's such a thing as a dysfunction-free family," Alanis told *Rolling Stone*. "My parents, I love them, I'd jump in front of a truck for them, but no matter what family you are in, there are going to be obstacles. And I'd be lying if I said there weren't any. I just wanted to do whatever it took to get the approval of my parents and the people I was working with at the time." Biographers have painted a picture of an 11-year-old Alanis traipsing from door to door hawking her demo record and shamelessly pushing sales by foisting it on her teachers in much the same way a precocious Paul Anka had persisted with his songs.

For Morissette, teen idol fame would not extend beyond Canadian borders. A deal with MCA Records led to two teenybopper pop albums and a Juno award as most promising new female artist. However, she felt compromised by the hoops that she had been encouraged to jump through in order to get to that point in her career. As she recalls, "I was working with all these people trying to control me and tell me what they thought I should be and what I should look like."

At first, Georgia Morissette promoted both Alanis and Wade, and they sang together on occasion, at festivals and other events, but it was

Alanis who had the most potential and Alanis who attracted the attention of producer Leslie Howe and promoter Stephan Klovan. Klovan had been impressed right from the start. "She sang this song called *Find The Right Man*," he recalls. "Here's this 11-year-old singing 'Gotta find the right man . . .' So I said to her, 'Alanis, that's quite a mature song for an 11-year-old-girl to be singing. Do you understand the words?' And she said, 'Understand them? I wrote them!'" Howe was less impressed but quick to realize her potential. "It wasn't like those songs are the greatest," he recalls, referring to an early demo tape. "I saw some raw talent there and thought we could develop it."

Both men would become obsessed with their protege and spend more and more personal time and money on her career. A video shot in Paris would add to their mounting debts but would be the clincher that convinced MCA's A&R director John Alexander to sign her. To defray costs, Klovan arranged for paying gigs, such as singing the national anthem at high profile events, and hooked Alanis up with sponsorship deals with women's fashions companies, airlines, and hotel chains.

Howe fabricated dance tracks and collaborated with her on new songs. "I normally get some musical pieces together," he explained at the time, "and Alanis and I would work out melodies together and work on the lyrics. For the most part, I wrote lyrics for the first album." With sales of ALANIS nearing 200,000 and a Top 10 Canadian hit, *Too Hot*, on the radio, Morissette was compared to Tiffany and Debbie Gibson, which may have irked her, but she was enjoying her instant celebrity, dating hockey stars and hanging out with the PM's daughter. In Paris, she rubbed shoulders with Diana Ross and Bob Hope. She was mobbed by autograph seeking fans after the release of her video *Too Hot*, which featured her with topless male dancers. She expressed dismay that her fans might think she was sleeping around. "Having a little sex thrown in there is okay," she said, "but there's no way I want people seeing me and saying, 'She's only 16? Oh that little slut, what is she doing?'" Dating 30-year-old TV actor Dave Collier definitely fueled speculation.

Morissette left an indelible impression upon her high school and her Ottawa peers. In 1995, in the midst of an epidemic of hometown backlash, Glebe Collegiate students were still obliged to listen to her teen version of the national anthem every morning before classes commenced. "All the time she was here everyone fawned over her, and treated her like a little queen," one student told *The Toronto Star*. "Alanis would be out at night with Alexandre Daigle or hanging around with Caroline Mulroney at some dance club, then be back at class where everyone would fawn over her."

When her second MCA album failed to repeat the success of its predecessor, Alanis cut her handlers loose and hooked up with American manager Jerry Welch, who had steered Paula Abdul through a transformation from LA Lakers' cheerleader to pop star. She nevertheless signed a publishing deal with MCA, and John Alexander helped her out with an introduction to Welch. He declined an offer to shop the Canadian albums in the US, but expressed interest in her future potential.

Two more years spent in Toronto, with forays to Nashville and Los Angeles in search of collaborators, didn't prove to be immediately fruitful. Her frustration at the manipulators she had encountered in the music business appeared later in the lyrics to *Right Through You*. Welch argues that the change of producers and time spent on her own in Toronto was invaluable. "She wasn't this 14 or 15-year-old pop girl, she was a young woman with her own sensibilities," he explains. "I said, 'Let's move her out of the house, away from Ottawa, some new surroundings, and let's get some life experiences, because that's where people write from.' So we moved her to Toronto and she got a really crummy apartment, just like most of us did when we were 18, and she got by on macaroni and cheese."

When a meeting with LA songwriter/producer Glen Ballard in February '94 was set up by her publisher, they quickly learned that they had a lot in common, not the least of which being that they were both ready to try something a little dangerous and less commercial. Alanis had been successful only in the limited Canadian domestic market,

Glen had worked on hits like Michael Jackson's *Man in the Mirror* and Wilson Phillips' *Hold On*. He got his start in the business as a staff writer in Quincy Jones' organization in 1978 and, although his methods differed from the maestro, he had learned a mountain of technique and a professional attitude during his apprenticeship. "Our production styles are actually pretty different," Ballard told *Sound on Sound*. "I'm in the trenches creating the songs first for most of the stuff I work on, but he had less of that. He would get really talented people, give them a context, and let them be creative, letting him mould that, and he was great at casting the right players for the right songs. Quincy always kept the right atmosphere in the studio. He was an encouraging and warm presence, and you wanted to do well for him, but not because he was intimidating, but because he genuinely loved people."

It was into a similar atmosphere where making songwriting "a joyful experience" was paramount that Alanis was introduced when she was invited to Ballard's home studio. "Glen had a certain history, as I had," she told *Rolling Stone*, "and when we met, we immediately connected. It was the most spiritual experience either of us ever had with music. The whole thing was very accelerated and stream of consciousness." "I just connected with her as a person," Ballard told David Wild, "and, almost parenthetically, it was, like, 'wow, you're 19?' She was so intelligent and ready to take a chance on doing something that might have no commercial application." Ballard had become disillusioned with making demos. He preferred to put the raw moment of creation right onto tracks that could then be overdubbed and mixed into final product. He also believed that the best way to proceed was to record her album before they sought a record deal. It was the only way to maintain independence. He employed an array of ADAT machines in his home studio that could be interfaced with a digital console in a fully equipped facility. "There was some question about what she wanted to do musically," he notes. "She knew what she didn't want to do, which was anything that wasn't authentic and from the heart."

| Cause the love that you gave that we made wasn't able |
| To make it enough for you to be open wide, no |
| And every time you speak her name |
| Does she know how you told me you'd hold me |
| Until you died, til you died |
| But you're still alive |

"We felt from the beginning that it was important to not try to gild the lily, and really let the rawness and the freshness of what we had captured in its initial form speak for itself," Ballard explains. "And it certainly found resonance out there in the listening public. It was completely spontaneous. It forced me to be a better player, because I would play my part one time, and that was usually the take. I didn't fix much of anything. She certainly didn't sing a song more than one or two times."

Over the years, Ballard had adapted to the technological changes that had revolutionized the industry. As he recalls, "When I was starting out as a staff songwriter in 1978, I had an office with no windows and a piano they'd pulled off the back lot somewhere. When it became possible to construct a drum part and a bass part in a sequencer it was so much more useful to me. I usually start by dialing up a beat, a guitar riff, or a keyboard idea, or a melodic line or title just to get something going." Recording engineer Chris Fogel recalls that "Glen and Alanis wrote everything between them and they'd help each other; it was a very good partnership. Sometimes Alanis would get a lyric at two or three in the morning and they'd lay the track down real quick just the basics: a loop, a couple of passes of guitar, a vocal and then I would come in and add any embellishments on top of that. We'd re-do some guitars on occasions, but rarely, because most were done in a single pass, and Alanis had grown attached to them. We added real drums to five of the songs, and did organ on all of them."

"They put us together thinking we'd probably come up with some more pop dance stuff," Morissette suggests. "We knew immediately that this was something very special. We both started with a clean slate. It was like a sanctuary for us. We were finally in this environment where we could do whatever the hell we wanted to do." Moving to LA and hanging out at Sunset Strip haunts, Alanis discovered a tougher world. She was robbed at gunpoint but was determined to persevere. She had endured more than 100 disappointing songwriting match ups before hooking up with Ballard. She had also endured numerous unsatisfactory relationships, many with older men who were "unavailable emotionally." Now all she wanted to do was to write songs and get a record deal. "Leaving Toronto to go to LA gave me a severe dose of disillusionment," she admits. "I was finally in a position where things weren't working out. And it was good for me. It made me realize that certain people I'd blindly trusted let me down."

She would later sum up her career and time spent before recording JAGGED LITTLE PILL by saying, "I have absolutely no regrets of anything that I've done, because had I not gone through that I'm not sure that this record would have come out."

> And I'm here to remind you
> Of the mess you left when you went away
> It's not fair to deny me
> Of the cross I bear that you gave to me
> You, you, you oughta know

Jerry Welch monitored her progress. "I hadn't seen her for a while, and we went to lunch," he recalls. "And she said, 'I've got a tape. I've got 15 things I want to play for you. And ten of them you could see . . . turn into Jagged Little Pill. You could see glimpses of things. I said, 'Man, you are on the right track. Just stay with it.'" Meanwhile, Alanis was undergoing "total culture shock." As she told *Playboy*, "LA is another planet compared to Toronto, where I recorded my first albums. Ever since I've been living here, I've felt part of a big musical family. Getting Flea and Dave involved wasn't even a big deal. Everybody hangs out in the same clubs and wants to do as much musically as they can." With the Red Hot Chili Peppers on bass and electric guitar, and Heartbreakers' Benmont Tench on Hammond B-3 on her tracks, Morissette and Ballard had managed to accomplish another Quincy Jones' trademark of finding the right players for the right songs.

Sometime during the sessions Fogel, who is credited with most of the mixing, began to realize that he was witnessing history in the making. As he recalls, "At that point in my career, I knew that they were good songs, but I didn't know that it was going to go any further. Then a buzz started in the LA recording community about what we were doing, and I remember saying as we were finishing the mixing that we'd be back next year, having sold two million copies, and everything would be great. That's the way we looked at it."

When Ballard and Morissette began to shop their tracks, they got their most encouraging response from Guy Oseary at Maverick, a Warner/Reprise subsidiary created exclusively for Madonna. Oseary wanted to see Morissette perform live before he inked a deal. Even Ballard's track record, which included writing and/or producing albums that had sold more than 100 million copies, was not enough of a credential to get the deal done without a showcase. Welch suggested the Maverick executives should come to Ballard's home studio. As he recalls, "Glen played acoustic and she sang right there in front of them. Then they put the tape up and she went into the booth and sang one of the tracks. After about half an hour they said, 'That's enough. Let's go outside. And we basically did the deal in the hallway.'"

> Cause the joke that you laid on the bed that was me
> And I'm not gonna fade
> As soon as you close your eyes and you know it
> And every time I scratch my nails down someone else's back
> I hope you feel it . . . well can you feel it

Following her 2005 induction into the Canadian Walk of Fame, Alanis Morissette launched her Jagged Little Pill Acoustic Tour, which let everyone know that she was less impetuous and somewhat wiser than when she first burst upon the scene at age 21. As she told *The Boston Globe*, "At 19, it's interesting to hear someone rage against the proverbial machine. At 31, it's sad. It's not very empowering to blame." The tour was unusual with the set designed to resemble her living room. Theresa Cano, reviewing Morissette's show at the Dodge Theatre in Phoenix, Arizona, was struck by the intimacy of her performance. "The stage replicated a comfy living room complete with couches, a grandfather clock, Persian and shag rugs, end tables, an easy chair with a stuffed-animal bunny rabbit plopped down on it, and swivel chairs," Cano wrote. "With the exception of the drummer and pianist, the six-member band moved about the 'room', at times spinning on the chairs and jumping on the couches as they played their instruments. Morissette mostly stayed center-stage during the show doing her signature, quirky rocking back and forth dance, occasionally prowling from stage left to right." As she progressed through a well-thought-out set-list, night after night audiences from coast to coast sang along and roared their approval when each song ended. By the time she got to her first encore, *You Oughta Know*, her fans inevitably raised their "sing-a-long with Alanis" routine to a boisterous clamor.

And I'm here to remind you
Of the mess you left when you went away
It's not fair to deny me
Of the cross I bear that you gave to me
You, you, you oughta know

Alanis Morissette and the world had changed. The angry young woman and her disciples had come of age. As she explained when she spoke of her new acoustic treatment of the "explosive and rage-filled *You Oughta Know*, it's the underlying heartbreak that emerges."

Bobcaygeon

The Tragically Hip

Words & Music by Robert Baker,
Gordon Sinclair, John Fay, Paul Langlois,
Gordon Downie

© The Tragically Hip

I left your house this morning about a quarter after nine
coulda been the Willie Nelson coulda been the wine

In the summer of 1993, the Tragically Hip put together their own homegrown version of the alt-rock extravaganza, Lollapalooza, inviting Daniel Lanois, the Hothouse Flowers, Crash Vegas, and Midnight Oil to join them for a meandering music and arts festival that they called Another Roadside Attraction. By that time, grunge bands and alt-rock had revitalized the rock industry and Lollapalooza concert mosh pits had become danger zones.

"As early as Lollaplaooza '93, when the alternative rock culture began breaching the mainstream," Rage Against The Machine's Tom Morello points out, "there was an uncomfortable, violent tendency in the mosh pits at shows. It was kids who saw moshing on TV and decided it was a great opportunity to come down and kick somebody's ass." The first to quit the Lollapalooza pits were young women who could no longer count on not being groped while crowd surfing. Posing was out of the question in the overcrowded, testosterone rich throngs of angry young drunks who were more likely to puke on you than to return your smile.

when I left your house this morning
it was a little after nine
it was in Bobcaygeon I saw the constellations
reveal themselves one star at a time

But the Hip had something else going on. As Kieran Grant reported in her critique of a July 20, 1995 show at the Cayuga Speedway in Southwestern Ontario, "Another Roadside Attraction successfully offered a broad sampling of hip bands, without the overblown tendencies of Lollapalooza. The Tragically Hip can be held directly responsible for that, roping in a rowdy throng of over 16,000 for yesterday's Cayuga show." Grant, who was dispatched to the Speedway to provide *The Toronto Sun* with a preview of the Markham Fairgrounds show, could not resist adding a few, tiny barbs to her praise. "Led by the eternally eccentric Gord Downie," she continued, "the Hip rounded off the proceedings last night with a much-anticipated set that made a long afternoon of rain and cloud worth waiting out. What it is that makes the Hip so commercially popular, and only in Canada at that, remains an enigma. But one clue is that they're a superlative live act."

Drove back to town this morning with working on my mind
I thought of maybe quitting
thought of leaving it behind

The Tragically Hip didn't model their biennial festival on Lollapalooza. They got their idea while on the road in Europe, where they had performed before a festival crowd in Holland estimated at nearly 300,000. Their idea was to follow the European tradition of making their event a traveling music and arts festival, and call it "Heksenketel," the Dutch word for "witch's cauldron," but they were told that name was too obscure. They settled for naming it *Another Roadside Attraction*, the title of Tom Robbins' zany, *Second Coming* counterculture novel. For Another Roadside Attraction '95, the boys from Kingston chose cool bands like Inbred, Blues Traveler, Spirit of the West, and Ziggy Marley & the Melody Makers, providing a variety of musical genres and guaranteeing a spiritual celebration that no mere grunge fest could hope to muster.

In 1997, Sheryl Crow was added to a star-studded lineup that also included alt-country rockers Wilco, roots rock superstars Los Lobos, and young Kingston rockers Van Allen Belt. Her presence would coincide with a changing audience dynamic. As Michael Hollett observed, "Though the tour is just under way, it's clear the Hip's crowd is a little different. There are more women in the audience, and subsequent shows confirm this." The Tragically Hip had become the best rock band in the land. They had also mellowed some, and their new songs from TROUBLE IN THE HENHOUSE were already attracting more and more women to their shows before the traveling festival hit the road. "There was a time when we were categorized by the most vocal and marauding of our crowd, and they were up front," vocalist Gordon Downie admitted to Hollett, who had been invited along for a ride through the Rocky Mountains on their bus. "So, yes, we have enjoyed the reinvention of the woman at Hip shows and we're pretty proud of that."

went back to bed this morning
and as I'm pulling down the blind
the sky was dull and hypothetical
and falling one cloud at a time

Another Roadside Attraction '97 was a success on all fronts, but it would be their last of the old millennium. "There was a glut of festivals," the Hip's manager, Jake Gold, admits when asked about the demise of the biennial Roadside Attractions. He needn't point out that Lollapalooza '98 was also canceled due to lack of advance ticket sales. The Hip had entertained more than a half million Canadian fans and had introduced themselves to selected markets in the American northeast. The icing on the cake was that the Hip were heard for the first time by some of the American musicians they admired the most. Los Lobos' multi-instrumentalist, Steve Berlin, was so impressed that he agreed to co-produce their next album, PHANTOM POWER. "I had been aware of them for a number of years and knew three or four of their songs from the radio," Berlin admits, "but I didn't realize just how powerful they were until I got to see them play night after night. The connection they have with their audience is truly astounding. They just floored me. After that, I totally got it."

"The Roadside Attraction Tour was a pivotal point in the band's evolution," Downie notes, "because it opened up our eyes to the existing possibilities. Not only was it a challenge, but we realized there is a need for camaraderie amongst musicians. Oftentimes the music industry is founded on the idea of 'kill your neighbor' to get ahead. I saw cooperation among musicians. The tour showed us there are obstacles out there, but they are not each other." The most charming aspect of the Hip's roadside attractions was that, like Sarah McLachlan's Lilith Fair, they brought musicians together and led to many collaborations and co-productions further on down the road.

One of the most popular songs that the Hip performed during the summer of '97 was *Bobcaygeon*, a previously unrecorded ballad that contrasted the hectic pace of big city life with the laid back lifestyle found in smaller Ontario towns where you can see the stars come out at night. There were references to the checkerboard floor at one of their favorite Toronto haunts, the Horseshoe Tavern, and to race riots begun by Neo-Nazis that had marred the city's squeaky-clean reputation. An even more obscure reference was made to a band by the name of "The Men They Couldn't Hang." This band had been one of the groups that played Lee's Palace, a Toronto club that the Hip frequented and eventually played during the late '80s.

The song was characteristically non linear and as multifaceted as a crossword puzzle. The *Bobcaygeon* video contained more clues including an anti-hate message scrawled on the back of Rob Baker's acoustic guitar that read: "this machine kills fascists."

That night in Toronto with its checkerboard floors
riding on horseback and keeping order restored
til the men they couldn't hang
stepped to the mic and sang
and their voices rang with that Aryan twang

Obscure references seem to be rule of thumb for Gord Downie. He has been accused of overusing Canadian locations and Canadian heroes, like Terry Fox and Paul Henderson, when he could have sold more records to Americans if he had written about picking up groupies at truck stops outside Tulsa, Oklahoma, or guzzling one too many Lonestar beers in Austin, Texas. Instead, his songs are saturated with references that most Canadians would be hard pressed to decipher on their own. Nor do most of us need to know them all in detail to appreciate the Tragically Hip's performances. Downie's "twitchy madman" persona often takes off right in the middle of a song into even more obscure monologues that you have to be there to appreciate.

Of special note to the uninitiated is his casual reference to "the Willie Nelson." Willie is one of the best songwriters of the 20th century. But "the Willie Nelson" mentioned in tandem with "the wine" refers to both listening to Willie's mellow records *and* to Willie's favorite herb. As one tireless researcher of Hip lyrics notes, "the Willie Nelson" has become a "slang term the kiddies are using nowadays for the weed, the wacky tobacky, the hippie lettuce, the nonstop THC commuter train to Stonerville marijuana." Ironically, after recording the song for PHANTOM POWER, the boys in the band found themselves at Woodstock '99 on the same bill as Willie Nelson.

The Tragically Hip's Canadiana references are often used as cannon fodder for journalists' debates concerning the band's overwhelming acceptance in Canada and underwhelming achievements south of the border. "To me," Downie says in his own defense, "growing up listening to the Beatles or the Stones, they'd mention British places in their songs, places around London or Liverpool, and that made it more romantic to me. So, I always thought, why not write about Toronto or Winnipeg or wherever?" Coincidentally, Bobcaygeon, a small town in the heart of Ontario's cottage country, is home to the province's oldest fall fair, dating back to 1858, and is best known for hosting Canada's premier Open Fiddle & Step Dance Contest.

No doubt, Downie and the band worked up the number as some sort of quiet tribute either for their upcoming festival season or during the actual festivals themselves. It's just the sort of subtlety that he employs in reference after reference in his lyrics, the same sort of soft touch that a poet like Al Purdy might have made in one of his garrulous and often hilarious epics. Downie has published his own book of poems. Recognition for his literary skills was a long time in coming, but as producer Hugh Padgham has said, "Gordon's lyrics are his best strength, and they also read wonderfully well as prose. He is a writer, singer, performer, and poet, and that makes him pretty unique in the music business." Even though Gord Downie and Gord Sinclair write most of the lyrics for the band, they generously continue to share their songwriter credits with the other members of the band.

One of Downie's finest touches is the choice of that town's name for his gentlest of songs. There is a musical lilt to "Bobcaygeon" that stems from the days in 1615 when French explorer Samuel de Champlain was struck by the pastoral beauty of the local forests. He used the French word *beaubocage*, which refers to beautiful hedged farmland. Apparently, the Mississauga Indians took a fancy to his words. Two hundred years down the road, their "Bobcajewonunk" was derived from Champlain's eloquent Parisian French vocabulary. It had become an expression that referred to a "narrow place between two rocks where water rushes through" a physical description of the islands, rivers, lakes and canals that surround the town with the Anglicized Loyalist name, "Bobcaygeon."

Downie's masterful touch provides a repeated hook that identifies the serenity of the night sky in rural areas not polluted by electric lights, where the appearance of the stars provides rural dwellers a spiritual connection to the heavens that city dwellers no longer enjoy.

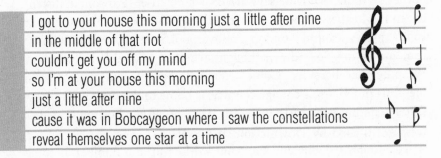

I got to your house this morning just a little after nine
in the middle of that riot
couldn't get you off my mind
so I'm at your house this morning
just a little after nine
cause it was in Bobcaygeon where I saw the constellations
reveal themselves one star at a time

The Tragically Hip began to jam and rehearse together in Kingston, Ontario, a city with a population at the time of 100,000 known for two different institutions, Kingston Penitentiary and Queen's University. The original lineup included sax player Davis Manning, who was replaced by rhythm guitarist Paul Langlois in 1986. Bass player Gord Sinclair and lead guitarist Rob Baker have known each other all their lives, growing up on the same block and beginning to jam together when they bought their first guitars at age 13. They met the others, including lyricist and vocalist Gord Downie and drummer Johnny Fay in high school. By the time that the four oldest boys were enrolled in classes at Queen's University, the band was eager to break out of the garage to play local gigs. "We played a lot around Queen's University,"

Rob Baker recalls, "Sweet 16 parties, high school dances, health clubs, a Jack & Jill party, biker's picnics — anyplace we could play." They soon secured house gigs at clubs like the Terrapin's Tavern and the Lakeview Manor, and began to branch out, making trips to Ottawa and Toronto. By December 1987, they were marketing copies of a self-titled EP, selling 2,000 discs in their hometown before Christmas.

When BMG began distributing THE TRAGICALLY HIP EP nationally, Canadians from coast to coast loved songs like Sinclair's *Smalltown Breakdown* and Downie's *Killing Time*, which have become concert favorites. The first hint of eclectic tastes to come was to be found in the name the boys chose to call their band. They had seen *Elephant Parts*, a video by ex-Monkee Mike Nesmith in which there is a skit that features people asking for donations to "the Foundation for the Tragically Hip poor, afflicted people in need of Jacuzzis, Lamborghinis, and cocaine." They took the name from Nesmith's skit.

A trip to New York City for the CMJ Music Marathon resulted in a Tragically Hip track being issued on a conference sampler, which encouraged MCA Canada president Bruce Dickinson to catch one of the band's sets at the Horseshoe in Toronto. He signed the band to a record deal, and soon after that they were hitting on the radio with *Blow at High Dough*. Their first full-length CD, UP TO HERE, also contained the dynamic *New Orleans is Sinking*, a song frequently used by Downie and the band to launch his eloquent, rambling monologues.

Like Rush lyricist Neil Peart, Gord Downie is well read and has crafted unique songs for his band. His method of composition owes far more to the Jim Morrison school of songwriting than to the usual manner of constructing verses and choruses to songs that have a beginning, middle and an end. He is known to jot down notes in a small notebook that he stuffs into his jeans and to refer to his notes while jamming spontaneously with his band mates. When this explorative process takes place during their live performances, new songs are sometimes born from old ones. While this can be confusing to the uninitiated, the Hip's fans have come to love everything that Downie does.

"It's a cool process we've got now," bassist Sinclair explains. "We gather and toss around ideas and start jamming, and develop songs in that way. Being together for so long, you just know someone's going to have a complementary part to what you're doing. Gord will sit in and basically rap on top, and the song will begin to take shape."

Tragically Hip fans are among the most dedicated rock fans on the planet, regularly using their net culture skills to keep in touch and up to date. When the band ventures outside Canadian borders, they can depend on legions of fans to show up at their concerts, whether they be in Sidney, Amsterdam, Vienna, Detroit, at Dan Aykroyd's Sunset Strip club or playing one of Bill Graham's venues in the Bay area. Their fans all declare that the Hip is the greatest band, ever; on their blogs, and in their posts they each boast of being the number one Tragically Hip fan.

The band members, it turns out, are not nearly as desperate as the Canadian rock media is concerning their so-called failure to achieve superstar stature in New York or LA. BMG had wanted to sign them to a record deal but had made some outrageous demands. "They told us they wanted us to dress up in fringe jackets and be a country rock band," Rob Baker recalls, "because that was the next big wave, so we walked away from that deal." After signing with MCA, they had been asked to change a lot of things, including their band name. But they hung onto their name and agreed, instead, to change the title of their second album from SASKAPHILADELPHIA to ROAD APPLES. The label executives liked "road apples" better, probably because no one told them that the term was a slang reference to frozen horse manure droplets that were used by rural lads as pucks in road hockey games.

"There seems to be some confusion about our name, about the kind of band we are," Langlois admits. "People either like the name, think it's clever and funny, or think it's a really pretentious, new-wave thing. We were billed in Germany a couple of times as an American Hip Hop band." Contrary to corporate opinions, the Tragically Hip's name did not become a stumbling block for rock fans in any country. Most people liked it, almost everybody on the planet except one man, which is why the Hip has never achieved every rock band's dream they have never made it onto the cover of *Rolling Stone*.

"The name cost us quite dearly in the States," Gord Sinclair revealed during an interview with *Ontario Golf*. "The guy who runs *Rolling Stone* magazine, Jan Wenner, came out of the closet as a gay man in the '70s, and the story we heard was that he played this charity base-ball game against Irving Azoff (the former chairman of MCA's Music Entertainment Group). Azoff showed up to the game and his team was named the Tragically Hip, apparently to sort of bug Wenner. The way we heard it was that Wenner thought we got the name from that story, which we didn't. But after 15 years and 10 records, you'll still never see a review not a mention of the Tragically Hip in *Rolling Stone*."

Sticking with their penchant for Canadian references to people like Canadian painter Tom Thompson, *Two Solitudes* author Hugh McLennan, and NHL hockey star Bobby Orr has made some of their best songs inaccessible to many Americans. *Wheat Kings*, with refer-ences to wrongly convicted Saskatoon, Saskatchewan, murder suspect David Milgaard, and a junior hockey team from Brandon, Manitoba, would nevertheless become one of the highlights of their live shows.

ROAD APPLES was followed by FULLY COMPLETELY and the mas-sively successful singles *Locked In The Trunk Of A Car, Courage, At The Hundredth Meridian,* and *Looking For A Place To Happen.* DAY FOR NIGHT took its title from Francois Truffaut's madcap 1973 movie about making movies and the cinematic process of filming night scenes at high noon. *50 Mission Cap* referred to 1950 Stanley Cup winning goal-scoring hockey hero, Bill Barilko. Barilko disappeared after board-ing a bush plane on a fishing trip the summer after the Toronto Maple Leafs won the cup. His remains were not discovered until the team won the cup again in 1962. Downie says he "stole" the story from a hockey card, which was issued by Pro Set in 1990. Canadians loved the song, especially hockey fans, and replicas of the "50 Mission caps" worn by Canadian bomber pilots during WWII began to appear at Hip concerts.

The band uses Kingston as an anchor to keep them all steady. As Gord Sinclair told *Queen's Journal*, "Kingston, for us, was always a jumping off point, where we were able to go into New York to play and go into Toronto to play, but have a place to come out of as well. At the time that we started playing music we were playing with a lot of different groups that moved to the Toronto area or moved down to New York or Los Angeles to seek their fame and fortune. At that time, a lot of those bands found themselves swallowed up by the city or by the music scene within the city."

Superstars in Canada, the Hip have played to smaller venues in the US, but nevertheless built a significant fan base in northeastern and southwestern states. They were, as Johnny Fay once quipped, "the world's tallest midgets." Hampered by lackluster support from Atlantic Records, they received national network exposure courtesy of Kingston resident Dan Aykroyd, who featured them as his guests on a 1995 *Saturday Night Live* show. They also toured their buns off. Gord Downie "is one of the most dynamic performers in the world," Dan Aykroyd told *MacLean's* magazine, "and the band is on a par with the Rolling Stones."

"The great thing about playing in the States," Downie says, "is that there are as many places to play as the rest of the world combined, probably. You gotta go there." They soon found themselves cast in an unfamiliar role, opening for other bands. "I liked it, and I didn't like it, to be honest," Downie recalls. "I definitely found it amazing that within the space of a month we opened up for the Led Zeppelin guys and the Stones. After doing the Stones, I couldn't help but think that it was very fateful, somehow, that some Jedi Master, somewhere, had decided that we needed this as the next stage in our education."

The band recorded at Daniel Lanois' Kingsway studio in New Orleans, in Memphis, and London, England, before putting together their "Bathhouse" facility in the tiny town of Bath, Ontario, near Kingston. Downie directed their videos. Other band members took on the responsibilities of selecting album cover art and tour logistics. Their decision to seek a deal with Atlantic seems to have been doomed from the onset. Simply put, Atlantic did not promote their singles or their albums in the same way that, say, Mercury promoted Shania Twain's THE WOMAN IN ME, or Maverick and Warner/Reprise promoted Alanis Morissette's JAGGED LITTLE PILL. Shania and Alanis had dumped their Canadian handlers and secured tough-nosed, experienced American managers, but the boys from Kingston stuck with the guy that had brought them to the dance, Jake Gold. Sticking to their guns has also provided serious advantages. As Sinclair points out, "We've been successful enough that the record company keeps us hanging around, but we've never been so successful that they wanted to meddle. It can be a funny business. You sell a million records and the record company's looking for you to sell 10 million next time out, and then if you sell two million, you're a failure. We've always been able to sell around 200,000 to 700,000 records enough to keep us in the black at the end of the year and keep the record company happy. We've flown fairly nicely under the commercial radar."

Gord Downie let it be known that they were sick and tired of answering questions about why the Hip were not superstars in the US. In an interview with Jane Stevenson, he turned the table and asked her, "Why isn't Canadian Film big down there? Is Paul Martin big down there? Margaret Atwood? Who are you comparing us to, the Barenaked Ladies? Our music is entirely different. Nickleback? Avril? Because of the people we are and the music we make, we get the success we deserve. Correct me if I'm wrong, and I know this is where I take it too far, but it's, like, 'Are we the only ones who have to bear this sort of national insecurity?' The whole country isn't doing good in America, and yet I just don't read [about] any other band taking this kind of flak."

"They have sold over 1,000,000 records in the States over their career and continue to build their live base every time they go on tour," Jake Gold points out. "Their last tour saw some of their biggest shows, ever, in a lot of markets. While they are not the Backstreet Boys in terms of popularity, they never wanted to be. They grossed more money in the States touring on the last album then any album before, and they did fewer shows."

"The only sort of measure we've ever had is 'Does everyone in the band like it?'" Paul Langlois told *Golf Ontario*. "If one or two are iffy, there's probably a reason for it." Sinclair agreed, adding, "That goes for everything we do the songwriting, the promotional aspect, the touring. If someone wasn't comfortable playing on the roof of a record store, we didn't do it. Business-wise, it's probably cost us in the short term. But, ultimately, it's the reason why we're still here, working on our tenth record." Sinclair and Langlois had taken up golf in the mid-90s and it had become a healthy diversion during their long stints spent on the road. "Most of us have families," Langlois points out. "We've grown together that way, which is good. Everyone has the same priorities."

1997's LIVE BETWEEN US was recorded at Cobo Hall in Detroit. Canadian critics raved about the entire set, singling out *Grace, too* for special recognition. Atlantic declined an offer to distribute the live album in the US and it was not available until a deal was signed with Sire Records, a Warner subsidiary.

1998's Phantom Power was the Hip's sixth studio album. Released in Canada on the Universal label due to MCA's restructuring, it was also released worldwide by Sire. The band's appearance at Woodstock '99 brought new interest to their albums. As the millennium ended, they released their seventh studio album, ninth overall, Music @ Work, before taking a well-deserved break from touring.

In 2000, Gordon Downie's solo album COKE MACHINE GLOW, produced by the Odds' Steven Drake and the Skydiggers' Josh Finlayson, was released on Rounder Records. The big surprise came when *Rolling Stone.com* posted a rave review by Richard Skanse. "COKE MACHINE GLOW," Skanse wrote, "may well be the most hauntingly beautiful album to come out of the Great White North since Neil Young's HARVEST." Skanse called the production "compelling" and singled out *Chancellor, Canada Geese* and *Lofty Pine*, which he said "boasted some of the finest melodies and lyrics Downie's ever come up with. This isn't an album you rock out to it's an album you reach for on a long drive."

When Nicholas Jennings took a ride through the coastal mountains on the band bus after a Rangers at Canucks hockey game and a Hip show in 2000, he was inspired to write an in-depth profile of the band. "Buddies since childhood," Jennings wrote, "the band members who include bassist Gord Sinclair and guitarist Paul Langlois still live in Kingston with the exception of Downie, who has moved to Toronto. They thrive on loyalty, blood ties, and hometown connections. 'We're very neighborhood connected,' says Sinclair. "Robby and I still live around the corner from each other and our kids go to the same school we did. Our parents, who are still together, raised us with similar values in a very stable environment. I guess that's made us who we are.'" Released in conjunction with a book of Downie's poetry, his first solo album did encourage some people to provide the Hip's front man with a little more respect. 2001's IN VIOLET LIGHT and 2004's IN BETWEEN EVOLUTION saw him reunited with his band mates.

On November 19, 2004, the Tragically Hip rocked the Saddledome in Calgary. In addition to chanting the usual "Hip, Hip, Hip," in anticipation of the band's arrival onstage, the crowd broke out into a spontaneous rendition of *Oh Canada*. "There's something about the Hip that just brings out the patriotism in humble Canucks," Sarah Kennedy reported in *The Calgary Sun*, "inspiring even restless fans to break out into our national anthem while waiting for them to hit the stage. Not even the Flames have that power in the dome, at least, not this season."

In their 20 years on the road, performing at clubs, theaters, arenas and festivals, the Tragically Hip have played thousands of gigs, but they are still the same five guys from Kingston. There are a few Canadian towns that they have yet to play, including Charlottetown, Prince Edward Island, for example. "Never played there," Downie admits. "A big oversight. We got drunk there on St. Patrick's Day once. The 'Saint Patrick's Day Massacre', we call it. We had played Summerside and had a layover in Charlottetown. We were pouring beer on each other's heads in a bar. It was awesome. What a night!" "We love and respect each other," he told Wendy Wallace. "The way we operate is democratic. We have faith and trust in each other, and we put the band first and foremost. We have very little else but each other."

"The Canadian music industry has changed substantially since we started," Downie claims. "At that time there was a mentality afoot that there were two kinds of bands: the good bands that were signed and the bad bands that weren't. You were only happy if you got a recording deal. And if you didn't get one, you were made to feel that you should quit music and do something else. I always thought that was criminal." The Tragically Hip's most recent album is IN BETWEEN EVOLUTION. On April 3, 2005, they were inducted into the Canadian Music Hall of Fame at the 2005 Juno Awards. Their star has been added to the Canadian Walk of Fame. At the Live 8 benefit concert, Dan Aykroyd joined the Hip on harmonica during their set. Their appearance onstage picked up the sagging concert energy.

Onstage at the Live 8 show in Barrie, Ontario, Downie's rage was channeled effectively, as he improvised a variation on the lyrics to *Ahead By A Century*, singing, "*you* should be ahead by a century," and putting real emphasis on the words "and the disappointment is getting me down." Downie's presence served to focus the performers' collective concern. It was not a time to deliver a mellow song like *Bobcaygeon*. Tragically, terrorist transit bombings in London during the G-8 summit that followed on the heels of the Live 8 concerts, deflected the worldwide focus that musicians around the globe had brought to pressing African issues.

> I got to your house this morning just a little after nine
> in the middle of that riot
> couldn't get you off my mind
> so I'm at your house this morning
> just a little after nine
> cause it was in Bobcaygeon where I saw the constellations
> reveal themselves one star at a time

In the new millennium, the band began working with Vancouver legend Bob Rock, who produced their critically acclaimed 2007 CD World Container and the follow up We Are The Same. The combination has turned out to be a winner. "I've met a lot of mystics and oracles of the production world," Downie told The Calgary Herald, "but I've never met anyone like Bob Rock." Sticking to their guns and celebrating their Canadian roots in their song lyrics has proven to be a winning formula for the Hip. Everybody loves them now, even Rolling Stone magazine, which has praised their "boundless ambition in making honest rock & roll."

The band performs Bobcaygeon during their shows to this day. Their music continues to be a uniquely Canadian musical treasure, and their fans show up at their concerts no matter how far from home they stray. For the boys from Kingston, entertaining has always been and always will be a two-way street. As Gord Downie told Michael Hollett in the summer of '97, "If you entertain people, people care about you. That's a new theory of mine, and it applies to everybody. What we get out of that is that it feels like magic sometimes — that's our end of the bargain."

The Hockey Song

Stompin' Tom Connors

Words & Music by Stompin' Tom Connors

© 2000 A-C-T Records

Hello out there, we're on the air,

It's hockey night tonight;

Tension grows, the whistle blows,

And the puck goes down the ice.

While he was on stage at Canada Day celebrations on Parliament Hill, the white-gloved custodians of the Stanley Cup surprised Stompin' Tom Connors. As Tom recalls in his autobiography, *Stompin' Tom & the Connors Tone:* "To an audience of thousands and a couple of million on television ... while I was singing *The Hockey Song*, a group of people from the NHL wheeled in a little table on stage behind my back which contained nothing less than the Stanley Cup itself. I signaled to the boys to keep on playing the tune as I went over and grabbed the cup and held 'er high . . ." The honor was well-deserved for the unofficial songwriter for Canada's favorite game and the outspoken champion of Canadian life, a stubborn nationalist who has gone against the grain of Canadian artists who have looked south to America to find fame and fortune. Stompin' Tom has persistently kept his eyes focused on his country of birth, castigating home-grown performers who have sold out, to the extent that he took a 10-year hiatus from receiving any music awards to register his protest.

Of course, there is nothing more Canadian than hockey, and when Tom wrote the *Hockey Song,* he stirred up a nationalist fervor among his fans and the fans of hockey in Canada. Tom sang about hockey with a passion that could be embraced by hockey players, hockey fans, hockey moms, and hockey coaches from pee-wee, bantam, midget and junior all the way up to the NHL level.

Oh the good old hockey game,
Is the best game you can name,
And the best game you can name,
Is the good old hockey game.

In the early '60s, when most Canadian recording artists were doing their level best to follow in the footsteps of teen idol Paul Anka and make it in the Big Apple and Vegas, Stompin' Tom emerged from the bush determined to make it in his home and native land. Since that time, he has issued 48 albums, none of them outside of Canada, and become known from coast to coast, despite receiving very little radio airplay. In fact, his records have seldom been cut with any attention at all paid to Top 40 trends or production values.

"They told me in 1964 I didn't fit the format," he has said. "They told me that in 1974. In 1984, they told me that again. I guess the format hasn't changed that much." Stompin' Tom has made a career out of being an outsider. He has epitomized the little guy, releasing his records on his own independent label.

The goalie jumps, the players bump,
And the fans all go insane,
Someone roars, Bobby scores,
At the good old hockey game.

Ever since Elvis bubbled up with his early hits on the small independent Sun Records label out of Memphis, the rock & roll era has thrived on indie releases. It has been a quick way to get noticed by the major labels. The Guess Who set the tone in the mid 1960s recording their hit *Shakin' All Over* at a local radio station and putting out a 45 rpm record on an indie label. Anne Murray began her career with an independent release on the Arc label before signing with Capitol. Thousands of Canadian 45s were issued in the '60s, '70s, and '80s, many of them by the artists themselves or by small, independent labels. Deejays and A&R label reps from RCA, Warner Brothers, Columbia, and Capitol listened closely.

Second period . . .
Where players dash with skates a-flash,
The home team trails behind;
But they grab the puck and go bursting up,
And they're down across the line.
They storm the crease like bumblebees,
They travel like a burning flame.
We see them slide the puck inside,
It's a one, one hockey game

Stompin' Tom's "good old hockey game" song is, incidentally, Neil Young's favorite hockey song. There have been others. In 1966, Douglas Rankins & the Secrets had a minor hit with the novelty song *Clear the Track, Here Comes Shack*, a tribute to the flamboyant Eddie Shack. Johnny Bower sang *Honky the Christmas Goose*, prompting many fans to regret that he ever retired from the Game. In 1967, the MacLaren Advertising Agency commissioned Vancouver composer Dolores Claman to write an instrumental theme that could be used during the CBC-TV *Hockey Night In Canada* broadcast. Her *Hockey Night In Canada Theme* went on to become the longest running theme song on a CBV-TV show before the network declined to pick up the option on a contract extension and the song was picked up like a waiver-draft pick by the rival CTV network. Released in '72 on Stompin' Tom's eighth album, *The Hockey Song* became a favorite in his live shows. Within a decade, hockey, like all professional sports, had become an entertainment spectacle, and rock anthems like Loverboy's *Turn Me Loose*, Queen's *We Will Rock You*, T-Rex's *Bang A Gong, Get It On*, and Steam's (Na-na-na-na, hey, hey) *Goodbye Song* were blaring out of NHL and minor league arena speakers along with a mix of Beatles' songs, Chuck Berry songs, and, in a few exotic locations, Stompin' Tom's *The Hockey Song*.

BTO's *Takin' Care Of Business*, Eddie Schwartz's *Hit Me With Your Best Shot* (sung by Pat Benatar), and Neil Young's *Rockin' in the Free World* all have a special appeal to Canadian hockey fans. Stompin' Tom's *Hockey Song* was played along with all the others. Over the years, many artists, including the Hanson Brothers, who also contributed their own composition, *I'm Gonna Play Hockey*, covered his song. The Shuffle Demons recorded that old favorite the *Hockey Night In Canada Theme* and began including it in their live shows. The Tragically Hip's *Fifty Mission Cap* paid tribute to Stanley Cup hero Bill Barilko, who died in a fatal bush plane accident during the summer after his heroic cup-winning goal. The Rheostatics' *The Ballad Of Wendel Clark Part I and Part II* was the third hockey song that paid tribute to a popular Toronto Maple Leaf player. The Zambonis took their name from the ice-cleaning machine and recorded a whole album of hockey songs. The Gear Daddies' *I Wanna Drive The Zamboni* appealed to the rink rats in the crowd. Tom Cochrane's *Big League*, and Jane Siberry's *Hockey* have also become favorites at rinks from coast to coast and from the NHL to junior ranks. Everybody, even Tommy Hunter, had a whack at writing a hockey song it seems, but Stompin' Tom's captures the immediacy of the crowd, the skaters, their sticks slapping at the pucks, the goalies, the ref's whistle, and the cheers and groans and gory glory of winning, best of all.

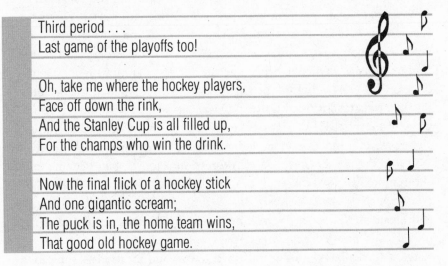

Third period . . .
Last game of the playoffs too!

Oh, take me where the hockey players,
Face off down the rink,
And the Stanley Cup is all filled up,
For the champs who win the drink.

Now the final flick of a hockey stick
And one gigantic scream;
The puck is in, the home team wins,
That good old hockey game.

Tom Connors was born in 1936 in Saint John, New Brunswick to an unwed mother who spent at least some of his early childhood in prison. By his early teens he had fled from foster homes and begun to seek his fame and fortune working as a merchant seaman, and then as one of the itinerant seasonal laborers that Ian Tyson sings about in *Four Strong Winds*. Tom hitchhiked from coast to coast many times before the modern highway system was built and eventually ended up singing for his supper, so to speak, in a bar in northern Ontario.

Legend has it that Connors' career got into high gear in '64 when he began a 14-month stint performing at the Maple Leaf Hotel in Timmins. A bartender gave him his "Stompin' Tom" nickname because he was always stomping his boot on the stage. After a while, he caused so much damage to one stage that he began carrying a board along with him to prevent damaging any more of them. When one curious reporter asked him about his stomping board, Connors replied, "It's just a stage I'm going through."

Tom cut his first independent single in '65 and followed it up with a steady stream of singles and albums on his own Boot Records label, which he also used to release and distribute records by new artists who needed a helping hand getting their careers jumpstarted. Tom's distinctive style won him an armload of Juno awards in the '70s. At the height of his career in the late '70s, he returned those trophies to the people who handed them out in protest of their encouragement to young artists to make it abroad and not in their home stomping grounds, so to speak.

After ten years he came out of retirement to perform his new song *Lady k. d. lang*, and his records were re-released on Capitol. He continued to put out new records and barnstorm his way across Canada, and penned a couple of popular biographies. Canadians who never attended a Stompin' Tom concert may have seen him on their TV, a tall, skinny man in a black hat and a red shirt stomping his foot and singing his songs to a barroom crowd of cigarette smoking, beer guzzling, working-class fans, all of them laughing and singing along on the full-length video *Horseshoe Tavern 'Across the Land' with Stompin' Tom Connors*.

By the early '90s, Stompin' Tom's 'cross Canada tours had become an annual event and his hockey song helped provide some of the controversy necessary to promote such extensive tours. The phenomenon gained momentum in the Ottawa Valley when the new Ottawa Senators franchise began to play Tom's song in their arena during NHL games and fans began to sing along. And when *Ottawa Sun* humorist

Earl McCrae wrote a controversial column about how some allegedly sophisticated visiting American sports writers attending a Senators' hockey game were "subjected to the horrendous caterwauling of that All-Canadian rube, Stompin' Tom Connors," Senators fans became incensed.

The columnist had already grabbed the attention of the thousands upon thousands of country music fans that live in the Ottawa Valley and surrounding area that were reading the daily newspaper that morning, but he continued to insult Tom, his song and Senators fans, writing: "As if this wasn't enough for those of us with taste and class, entire sections of hayseeds in the stands began undulating, clapping and singing along at the top of their lungs. They actually cheered the big, talentless galoot when the song was finished."

In some hockey markets this columnist's daily offering would have been regarded as lite entertainment, however, the very quote en quote hayseeds McCrae had cited in his tongue in cheek diatribe didn't find his efforts very funny at all. In fact, the mayor of Pembroke, one of the nearby communities McCrae had insulted, launched a class action lawsuit, and ticket sales to Connors' upcoming national tour soared. The lawsuit was eventually dropped but Tom's good old hockey song and the press that McCrae had generated for it spread like a virus through the NHL, first to nearby Toronto and then south of the border where Tom's records had never been played on the radio let alone at public events like professional hockey games.

Connors attributes his success to his down to earth attitude. "I never have been scared to make a fool out of myself," he said recently. "You know if you're down to earth that I've found people like a guy who's like that, sort of loose and I also like to see my audience. I like to see the faces! Once I play into that and they play into us guys, all of a sudden there is a rapport going. When that happens, the level rises a little more and a little more and the show goes on. We have a hell of a time." Connors' songs are unique and his approach to writing them low key. As he once said, "Some people like it and some people don't, but then what can you do, eh? I got a hell of a lot of songs about a lot of things . . ." Tom's "greatest hits" include *Bud the Spud*, *The Hockey Song*, *Big Joe Mufferaw*, *The Ketchup Song* and *Margo's Cargo*.

In 1996, during the days that led up to the Quebec Referendum, Tom hit the road in support of Canadian unity along with a number of popular Canadian acts. He was chosen to close the shows but he was an unlikely headliner. As he recalls, "They said, 'you're gonna have to follow, like, about six rock bands.' I said, 'I have no problem with that at all.' There was guys like Sloan in there and some other bands from the East Coast. So we go up there and we do the show and then low and behold they were mobbing the stage, and I don't know why, a 62-year-old fella. Why would anyone want to mob the stage? They are all from 18 and 19 right on up." That same year he was honoured when he was made an Officer of the Order of Canada. To this day Stompin' Tom has never ventured south of the border to perform his made in Canada songs. However, in 2004 when Conan O'Brien brought his *Late Night with Conan O'Brien* crew to Toronto for a week of taping, Stompin' Tom was invited to participate. And for the very first time since he first broke into show business 40 years before this at the Maple Leaf Hotel in Timmins, Stompin' Tom's lively wit was beamed across America on network television.

Oh the good old hockey game,
Is the best game you can name,
And the best game you can name,
Is the good old hockey game.

In this postmodern era of digital downloads and website sales, the days of mailing your independent 45s out to all the radio stations are long gone, and the gigantic record marts have gone the way of the dinosaurs, but Stompin' Tom soldiers on. In 2008, Tom chose to re-record *The Hockey Song* and some of his other early hits for his 48th album, *The Ballad Of Stompin' Tom Connors*, telling journalists that the original recording was "a little thin the first time I recorded it way back in '71 or '72." That same year, Tom performed his song at the NHL Awards Banquet and his son, Tom Jr., told the CBC that his dad was open to licensing it to the network to replace the *Hockey Night In Canada* theme. Tom later admitted that he was relieved because he probably would have had trouble coming up with a French-language version of his signature tune. His newly recorded digital version of the song has been used by Vancouver-based Electronic Arts to pro-mote their NHL 10 video game, and by NBC Sports to promote their NBC TV network broadcast of the 2012 NHL Winter Classic outdoor hockey game. Ironically, Stompin' Tom has become the soundtrack of hockey in America.

Listmania

We live in an age of lists, aligning and sorting the barrage of information we experience every day, a habit the invisible web masters at amazon.com have coined "listmania." Not only are our book buying habits and consumer preferences listed, our opinions are polled everyday by telemarketers and television programs. During the past decade in Canada, we've watched CBC-TV viewers help to compile a short list of the 10 greatest Canadians, with Tommy Douglas rising to the top of the list, almost like a pop star rising on the *Billboard* music charts. That is exactly what happened when CBC Radio set out to compile a chart of "50 Essential Tracks" by Canadian artists in a series of programs on "Q" hosted by Jian Ghomeshi. *Four Strong Winds* by Ian & Sylvia charted number one, with *If I Had a Million Dollars* by the Barenaked Ladies hitting at number two, *Heart of Gold* by Neil Young at three, *Northwest Passage* by Stan Rogers at number 4, and *American Woman* by the Guess Who holding down number 5.

But how were these lists compiled? What criteria were used to rank the 50 tracks? Ghomeshi and his cast of advisors established these criteria:

Does it woo you with words?
Does it move you with melody?
Does it have you from the hook?
Does it define a generation?
Did it create a musical revolution?

In choosing the Top 20 Canadian Rock, Pop & Folk songs, we have been a touch less impressionistic.

CHARTS

We have examined the *Billboard* and other industry charts to record how fast, how high, and how long the song appeared on the charts. In this category, Paul Anka's *Diana* hit number 1, only the first of many Top 20 hits during his long career.

SALES

We consulted sales figures monitored by SoundScan, *Rolling Stone*, *Cash Box*, and *Billboard*. In this category, Alanis Morissette has sold more than 35 million copies of JAGGED LITTLE PILL (equal to the population of Canada) followed by Shania Twain's two albums, THE WOMAN IN ME (20 million) and COME ON OVER (30 million).

AIRPLAY

RPM Magazine airplay figures are available for Canadian songs from 1964 to 2000 when this trade magazine stopped publication. In this category, we might be looking at Anne Murray who has criss-crossed the pop and the country charts and radio airwaves for decades.

EXPERTS

To select the Top 20, we read the opinions of our best music critics, such as Martin Meluish, Larry LeBlanc, Terry David Mulligan, Nicholas Jennings, Leah McLaren, Denise Donlon, Geoff Pevere, John Einarson, and Randy Bachman. These critics were consulted by CBC Radio while compiling their 50 Essential Tracks. Among these critics, there was limited consensus, other than to place *Four Strong Winds* at number one or number two.

POLLS

CBC Radio likewise polled their listeners, inviting them to call in and "pitch" their favorite song. We ran our own straw poll, soliciting opinions from family, friends, couriers, bank tellers — you name them. Facts and opinions began to give some songs momentum, like *Turn Me Loose* by Loverboy and *Bobcaygeon* by The Tragically Hip, bands that are stronger live than in the studio.

INFLUENCE

What about influence? Now we're talking about something that is visible, with an impact on the history of rock, pop, and folk music. Could the chart-topping American band called America have become a success if not for Neil Young's lyrics and melodies? What has been Neil's affect on Pearl Jam and grunge music? How many garage bands have cut their teeth on Steppenwolf's *Born To Be Wild*? How many drummers have found their beat in Neil Peart's solos?

COVERS

Singing covers is an even more visible form of influence. Think of who *hasn't* covered Joni Mitchell's *Both Sides, Now*? How influential has Ian Tyson been on Neil Young's acoustic career beyond his cover of *Four Strong Winds*? Barenaked Ladies reached back into Bruce Cockburn's catalog to cover *Lover's In A Dangerous Time*. Kris Kristofferson and Johnny Cash have both covered Leonard Cohen's *Bird on a Wire*. And so it goes.

REGIONAL HITS

Complicating the choice of the Top 20 songs is the regional appeal of some songs that were a hit on the East Coast but barely heard on the West Coast – and vice versa. For example, you will not find Chilliwack's *Lonesome Mary* or the Pointed Sticks' *Lies* on most retrospective Top 20 or Top 50 charts, but if West Coast residents were to select their own list, both of these tracks would probably make the cut. Ditto for *Doin' It Right On The Wrong Side Of Town* by the Powder Blues Band and at least one Doug & the Slugs favorite. Prairie fans would probably include records like Dick Damron's *Countryfied*, the Stampeders' *Sweet City Woman*, and the Great Western Orchestra's *Train of Misery*. Ontario fans would vote for Downchild Blues Band's *Flip, Flop and Fly!* Maritime fans would surely include Rita MacNeil's *The Workingman's Song* and *Flying On Your Own*.

NUMBER ONE

How can we decide what song is the greatest among the many great. This is not easy. Years ago Peter Gzowski on CBC *Morningside* called *Four Strong Winds* Canada's "second" national anthem, but a few years later he called *Northwest Passage* by Stan Rogers our "second" national anthem, showing the effects of hosting too many radio shows or, more likely, how difficult it is to select only one top song among such a wealth of great music.

Dueling Charts

Let's see what songs you would choose in compiling a Top 20 chart and what song you would rank as number one. We'll relist the chronological list of 20 songs we chose, let you rank them, and then compare your ranking with ours. Insert any song you think should be on the Top 20 list that we failed to chart.

CHRONOLOGICAL CHART

1957 *Diana* Paul Anka _____

1962 *Four Strong Winds* Ian & Sylvia _____

1967 *Suzanne* Leonard Cohen _____

1968 *The Weight* The Band _____

1968 *Both Sides, Now* Joni Mitchell _____

1968 *Born To Be Wild* Steppenwolf _____

1970 *American Woman* The Guess Who _____

1970 *Snowbird* Anne Murray _____

1972 *Heart Of Gold* Neil Young _____

1974 *Takin' Care Of Business* BTO _____

1974 *Sundown* Gordon Lightfoot _____

1980 *Wondering Where The Lions Are* Bruce Cockburn _____

1981 *Northwest Passage* Stan Rogers _____

1981 *Turn Me Loose* Loverboy _____

1982 *New World Man* Rush _____

1985 *Summer Of '69* Bryan Adams _____

1991 *If I Had A Million Dollars* Barenaked Ladies _____

1995 *Any Man of Mine* Shania Twain _____

1995 *You Oughta Know* Alanis Morrisette _____

2000 *Bobcaygeon* The Tragically Hip _____

Bonus Track: *The Hockey Song* Stompin' Tom Connors _____

MY CHART

Now grab a pen or a pencil (you may want to erase your choices) and rank these songs from one to 20 and create "My Chart." You can write in the name of the song or draw a line from the song title on the left to the blank spaces below. Be ready to defend your choices once your friends make their own ranked list.

List your number one pick first.

1. _____

2. _____

3. _____

4. _____

5. _____

6. _____

7. _____

8. _____

9. _____

10. _____

11. _____

12. _____

13. _____

14. _____

15. _____

16. _____

17. _____

18. _____

19. _____

20. _____

Bonus track. _____

OUR RANKED LIST

Here is how we ranked the top 20 songs. Ranking these songs from one to 20 involved some good old Canadian compromise. Challenge our selections, substitute other songs, and decide on different number one hits, as you see fit.

1. *Four Strong Winds* Ian & Sylvia _____

2. *Heart Of Gold* Neil Young _____

3. *Suzanne* Leonard Cohen _____

4. *If I Had A Million Dollars* Barenaked Ladies _____

5. *Any Man Of Mine* Shania Twain _____

6. *Takin' Care Of Business* Randy Bachman _____

7. *Snowbird* Anne Murray _____

8. *Both Sides, Now* Joni Mitchell _____

9. *Diana* Paul Anka _____

10. *You Oughta Know* Alanis Morissette _____

11. *Summer of '69* Bryan Adams _____

12. *Born To Be Wild* Steppenwolf _____

13. *The Weight* The Band _____

14. *American Woman* Guess Who _____

15. *Sundown* Gordon Lightfoot _____

16. *Bobcaygeon* The Tragically Hip _____

17. *New World Man* Rush _____

18. *Northwest Passage* Stan Rogers _____

19. *Wondering Where The Lions Are* Bruce Cockburn _____

20. *Turn Me Loose* Loverboy _____

Bonus track: *The Hockey Song* Stompin' Tom Connors _____

CBC RANKED LIST

Here is the list compiled by CBC Radio of Canada's best "50 Essential Tracks." The Top 20 included a few surprises:

1. *Four Strong Winds* Ian & Sylvia _____
2. *If I Had a Million Dollars* Barenaked Ladies _____
3. *Heart of Gold* Neil Young _____
4. *Northwest Passage* Stan Rogers _____
5. *America Woman* The Guess Who _____
6. *Canadian Railroad Trilogy* Gordon Lightfoot _____
7. *Both Sides Now* Joni Mitchell _____
8. *Suzanne* Leonard Cohen _____
9. *Big Yellow Taxi* Joni Mitchell _____
10. *Early Morning Rain* Gordon Lightfoot _____
11. *Lovers in a Dangerous Time* Bruce Cockburn _____
12. *The Hockey Song* Stompin' Tom Connors _____
13. *Life Is a Highway* Tom Cochrane _____
14. *Try* Blue Rodeo _____
15. *The Weight* The Band _____
16. *New Orleans Is Sinking* The Tragically Hip _____
17. *Summer of '69* Bryan Adams _____
18. *Takin' Care of Business* Randy Bachman _____
19. *Snowbird* Anne Murray _____
20. *Angel* Sarah McLachlan _____

WORST 10 CANADIAN SONGS

Just for fun, list the worst 10 Canadian rock, pop & folk songs.

1. _____

2. _____

3. _____

4. _____

5. _____

6. _____

7. _____

8. _____

9. _____

10. _____

Trivia

"The brain may die, but the compulsion for useless trivia lives on." — Molly Harper, *Nice Girls Don't Have Fangs*

If there is something we like more than lists, it's trivia. After reading the stories in this book, see if you can answer the 20 trivia questions posed in the following quiz. Test your friends. Show off how much you know. Make up your own questions and hints. You might even add these questions to that quintessesntial Canadian board game, Trivial Pursuit.

20 QUESTIONS FOR 20 SONGS

1. What Canadian singer-songwriter wrote the lyrics to Frank Sinatra's signature tune, *My Way*?
   Hint: He also composed the theme song for the *Tonight Show with Johnny Carson*.

2. What singer-songwriter was Ian Tyson responding to when he wrote *Four Strong Winds*?
   Hint: The answer is blow'n in the wind.

3. What Canadian folksinger posed as Kris Kristofferson when he met Janis Joplin in the elevator at the Chelsea Hotel in Greenwich Village?
   Hint: He called his fifth album DEATH OF A LADIES' MAN.

4. What song written by The Band is included on the soundtrack for the movie *Easy Rider*.
   Hint: The song is not *Life Is A Carnival*.

5. What song by Joni Mitchell hit number 7 on the *Billboard* Country charts?
   Hint: George Hamilton IV covered the song.

6. What name did Dennis Edmonton use after leaving Steppenwolf and writing *Born To Be Wild*?
   Hint: The red planet is on fire.

7. Where was Burton Cummings when Randy Bachman first played the opening chords to *American Woman*?
   Hint: Not on stage.

8. What Prince Edward Island singer-songwriter wrote the music and lyrics for Anne Murray's *Snowbird*?
   Hint: He was bidin' his time.

9. What artist performed with the Mynah Birds before heading out to Los Angeles driving a hearse?
   Hint: Everybody knows this is nowhere.

10. Who played piano on BTO's *Takin' Care of Business*?
    Hint: Pizza ordered by the Steve Miller Band was delivered to the BTO studio by mistake.

11. What Canadian singer-songwriter is infamous for staging elaborate parties following his annual concert at Massey Hall?
    Hint: Lots of people began hanging around his back door.

12. What label has Bruce Cockburn recorded on throughout his career?
    Hint: Ask Bernie Finkelstein.

13. What Canadian arctic explorer does Stan Rogers eulogize in *Northwest Passage?*
    Hint: He dies crossing the Beaufort Sea.

14. In what prairie city did Mike Reno first meet Paul Dean playing guitar in an abandoned Greyhound bus garage?
    Hint: Home of the band that charted high with *Sweet City Woman*.

15. What is the only song by Rush to rise to number 20 on the *Billboard* pop charts?
    Hint: The song was not *Tom Sawyer*.

16. Who co-wrote *Summer of '69* with Bryan Adams?
    Hint: He was the drummer for Prism and wrote the band's early hits.

17. What band is commonly inundated with packages of Kraft Dinner while on stage?
    Hint: That's almost 1,000,000 noodles so far.

18. What Canadian country artist supported her siblings by performing at the Deerhurst Inn in Huntsville, Ontario.
    Hint: She bared her midriff.

19. Just what was Alanis Morissette doing in the movie theater she mentions in *You Oughta Know*?
    Hint: Well ... you oughta know!

20. What band placed Bobcaygeon on the Canadian music map?
    Hint: It coulda been the Willie Nelson, it coulda been the wine.

21. What Canadian folk singer has hoisted the Stanley Cup above his head on stage at Parliament Hill during Canada Day celebrations?
    Hint: He performs with a board under his boot.

REFERENCES

BOOKS

Adams, Bryan. *Bryan Adams: The Official Biography*. Willowdale ON: Firefly Books, 1995.

Bidini, Dave. *Writing Gordon Lightfoot*. Toronto, ON: McLelland & Stewart, 2011.

Cockburn, Bruce. *Bruce Cockburn Songbook: All The Diamonds*. Montreal, Quebec: OFC Publications, 1986.

Dickerson, James. *Women On Top: The Quiet Revolution That's Rocking The American Music Industry*. New York, NY: Billboard Books, Watson-Guptill Publications, 1998.

Einarson, John. *Shakin' All Over: the Winnipeg '60s Rock Scene*. Winnipeg, 1987.

Einarson, John. *There's Something Happening Here: The Story of Buffalo Springfield*. Kingston, ON: Quarry Music Books, 1997.

Einarson, John with Ian Tyson and Sylvia Tyson. *Four Strong Winds: Ian & Sylvia*. Toronto, ON: McClelland & Stewart, 2011.

Gett, Steve. *Success Under Pressure*. Port Chester, NY: Cherry Lane Books, 1984.

Gnarnowski, Michael, Ed. *Leonard Cohen: The Artist and His Critics, Collected Essays, including* Frank Davey, "Leonard Cohen and Bob Dylan, Poetry and the Popular Song." Toronto, ON: McGraw-Hill, 1976.

Graham, Bill & Robert Greenfield. *Bill Graham Presents*. New York, NY: Doubleday, 1992.

Grills, Barry. *Snowbird: the Story of Anne Murray*. Kingston, ON: Quarry Press, 1996.

Grills, Barry. *Ironic: Alanis Morissette, The Story*. Kingston, ON: Quarry Press Music Books, 1997.

Gudgeon, Chris. *Stan Rogers: Northwest Passage*. Kingston, ON: Fox Music Books, 2004.

Jennings, Nicholas. *Before the Goldrush: Flashbacks to the Beginning of the Canadian Sound*. Toronto, ON: Viking Penguin, 1997.

Kay, John & John Einarson. *Magic Carpet Ride*. Kingston, ON: Quarry Press, 1994.

Luftig, Stacy. *The Joni Mitchell Companion*. New York, NY: Schirmer Books, 2000.

McDonough, Jimmy. *"Shakey:" Neil Young's Biography*. New York, NY: Anchor Books, Random House, 2002.

McGregor, Arthur, Ed. *All The Diamonds: Bruce Cockburn Songbook*. Ottawa Folklore Centre Publications, 1986.

Melhuish, Martin. *Oh What A Feeling: A Vital History of Canadian Music*. Kingston, ON: Quarry Press, 1996.

Meyers, Paul. *Barenaked Ladies: Public Stunts, Private Stories*. Vancouver, BC: Madrigal Press, 2001.

Nadel, Ira B. *Various Positions: A Life Of Leonard Cohen*. Toronto, ON: Random House, 1996.

Saidman, Sorelle. *Bryan Adams: Everything He Does*. Toronto, ON: Random House of Canada, 1993.

Shelton, Robert. *No Direction Home: The Life and Music of Bob Dylan*. New York, NY: Da Capo Press, 2003.

Tellaria, Robert. *Rush: Tribute*. Kingston ON: Quarry Press Music Books, 2002.

Van Ronk, Dave & Elijah Wild. *The Mayor of MacDougall Street*. New York, NY: Da Capo Press, 2005.

Woodward, Bob. *Wired*. New York, NY: Simon & Schuster, 1984.

Whitburn, Joel. *The Billboard Book of Top 40 Country Albums*. New York, NY: Billboard Books, 1996.

Whitburn, Joel. *The Billboard Book of Top 40 Hits*. New York, NY: Billboard Books, 1995.

Whitburn, Joel. *The Billboard Book of Top 40 Albums*. New York, NY: Billboard Books, 1995.

Whitburn, Joel. *The Billboard Book of Top 40 Country Hits*. New York, NY: Billboard Books, 1996.

Woodworth, Mark, editor. *Solo: Women Singer Songwriters In Their Own Words*. New York, NY: Delta Trade Paperbacks, 1998.

NEWSPAPER & MAGAZINE ARTICLES

Anderson, Joan. "Alanis Morissette revisits 'Jagged'." *Boston Globe*, Jul 17/05.

Anonymous. "Cockburn Speaks Out on Guatemala." *Billboard*, Mar 1978.

Anonymous. "Interview with Alanis." *Q Magazine*, 1996.

Anonymous. "Interview with Alanis." *Ottawa Citizen*, Jul 7, 2004.

Anonymous. "Interview with Jim Vallance." *Beatology Magazine*, Sep 1999.

Anonymous. "Questionnaire: Bryan Adams." *Q Magazine*, Nov 1991.

Barclay, Michael. "Rheostatics: Blame Canada." *Exclaim Magazine*, Nov 2001.

Becker, Tom. "Lionel Trains File For Bankruptcy." *Bloomberg News*, Nov 16, 2004.

Berger, John. "Paul Anka's Doing It His Way New Year's Eve." *Honolulu Star Bulletin*, Dec 28, 2000.

Bodony, Tim. "New Tragically Hip leaves much to be desired." *NY Times*, Oct 3, 2000.

Boettcher, Shelley. "Q&A With Bryan Adams." *Calgary Herald*, Dec 1999.

Bowman, Rob. "Life is a Carnival." *Goldmine*, Jul 16, 1991.

Brand, Stewart. "The Education of Joni Mitchell." *CoEvolution Quarterly*, Summer 1976.

Calhoun, John. "Tyson's River Road Flows Deep, Clear." *Toronto Sun*, Aug 11, 2000.

Cantin, Paul. "Rolling Stone Lauds Downie." Posted at jam.canoe.ca on Jul 10, 2001.

Chiasson, Paul. "Thousand Brave Wind and Rain to be with Queen in Edmonton stadium." *Canadian Press*, May 23, 2005.

Clark, Atlee. "The Hip Go Through An Evolution." *Queen's Journal*, Apr 1, 2004.

Clark, Larry Wayne. "Gordon Lightfoot – Portrait of a Painter posted at larrywayneclark.com.

Cockburn, Lynn. "Can't Fence Tyson In." *Calgary Sun*, Jun 29, 1996.

Conroy, Tom. "Good God!" *US*, Nov 1999.

Coppage, Noel. "Review: Sundown." *Stereo Review* 1974.

Cronick, Scott. "Paul Anka's Stellar Voice Dazzles Atlantic City." *Atlantic City Press*, Oct 11, 2004.

Crowe, Cameron. "Neil Young: So Hard To Make Arrangements For Yourself." *Rolling Stone*, Aug 14, 1975.

Crowe, Cameron. "Neil Young: the Last American Hero." *Rolling Stone*, Feb 8, 1979.

Daly, Sean. "Alanis Coy About Boy Toy." *Toronto Star*, 1999.

Deevoy, Adrian. "Q100 Interview: Bryan Adams." *Q Magazine*. January 1995.

Delaney, Larry. "Review: Stompin' Tom Connors & the Hockey Mom Tribute." *Country Music News*, Aug 5, 2005.

Druckman, Howard. "Under the Umbrella: the Hip." *North by Northeast*, Aug 1, 2005.

Drysdale, Rob. "Harvest: track by track." *New Musical Express*, Feb 12, 1972.

Dunstan, Robert. "Interview: Billy Talbot." *Rip It Up*, August 1996.

Elder, Ben. "Terry Clements: In the Lead." *Acoustic Guitar*, Jan 2000.

Elder, Ben. "What they play: Clements and Lightfoot." *Acoustic Guitar*, Jan 2000.

Elder, Ben. "Highway Songs." *Acoustic Guitar*, Jan 2000.

Ferguson, Jim. "Paul Dean, lead, Loverboy." *Guitar Player*, Mar 1983.

Ferner, Mike. "Interview with Bruce Cockburn." *Counterpunch*, Jan 27, 2004.

Frickie, David. "The News According to Neil Young: the rocker is angry with Bush and American Idol." *Rolling Stone*. Aug 21, 2003.

Gandee, Charles. "Joni Mitchell: Triumph of the Will." *Vogue*, Apr 1976.

Goldstein, Richard. "Village People: Beautiful Creep (a profile of Leonard Cohen)." *The Village Voice*. Deb 28, 1967.

Gordon, Dave. "Steven Page: Ladies' Man." *Lifestyle*. May 2003.

Grant, Kieran. "Another Roadside Attraction attracts 15,000." *Toronto Sun*, Jul 21, 1995.

Gray, Frank. "Folksinger's biggest wish." *Saskatoon Star Phoenix*. Feb 2, 1968.

Greenwald, Ted. "The Reinvention of Neil Young." *Wired*, Mar 2004.

Griwkowsky, Fish. "Lightfoot Thrills a sold-out Winspear Centre." *Edmonton Sun*, Nov 2, 1999.

Gunderson, Edna. "Taming Morissette's Restless Spirit." *USA Today*, Feb 3, 1999.

Hampson, Sarah: "The Hampson Interview: Paul Anka." *Globe & Mail*, Apr 27, 2002.

Harrington, Richard. "From Folkie To Rocker." *Washington Post*, Oct 19, 1984.

Harris, Ron. "Loverboy bass player swept overboard." Associated Press, Dec 2, 2000.

Herwald, Margi. "'Ladies' Man." *Cleveland Jewish News*, Oct 12, 2000.

Himes, Geoffrey. "Firey Folk." *Washington Post*, Oct 21, 1984.

Holden, Steven. "Review: Sundown." *Rolling Stone*, Mar 1974.

Hollett, Michael. "Inside Roadside." *Now Magazine*, Aug 6, 1997.

Humberstone, Nigel. "Medicine Man: Chris Fogel." *Sound on Sound*, 1998.

Inglis, Sam. "Elliott Mazer: Producer and Engineer." *Sound on Sound*, Feb 2003.

Jennings, Nicholas. "Portrait of an artist in her prime." *MacLean's*, Apr 4, 1988.

Jennings, Nicholas. "Rock with a Twist: Nothing but a Burning Light." *MacLeans*, Oct 1991.

Jennings, Nicholas. "From the Hip." *MacLean's*, Dec 14, 2000.

Johnson, Brian D., & Danylo Hawaleshka, Dale Eisler. "Joni's Secret Mother & Child Reunion." *MacLean's*, Apr 21, 1997.

Jones, Liana. "Ladies Men." *Onstage*, Mar 1, 2001.

Kava, Brad. "Alanis Morissette Kicks Off Club Tour." *Wall of Sound*, Oct 12, 1998.

Kennedy, Brendan. "Tragically Hip Are Coming Home." *Queen's Journal*, Sep 10, 2004.

Kennedy, Sarah. "The Hip Reigns Again at Dome." *Calgary Sun*, Nov 20, 2004.

Kent, Nick. "Neil Young at 50." *Mojo*, Dec 1995.

Kooper, Al. "Review: Music from Big Pink." *Rolling Stone*, Number 15, 1968.

Krewen, Nick. "Adams Promises Spanking New Show." *Hamilton Spectator*, Jan 11, 1995.

Krewen, Nick. "Bryan Adams' Life-saving Valentine." *Hamilton Spectator*, Feb 10, 1998.

Krewen, Nick. "Gord Downie Really Likes Hamilton." *Hamilton Spectator*, Jul 13, 1996.

Krewen, Nick. "Need to Know: the Hip and Rheostatics at Copps Coliseum." Dec 5, 1997.

Kubernik, Harvey. "Lightfoot: A Portrait of the Artist as a Mystery Man." *Crawdaddy*, Mar 1976.

Lanham, Tom. "Hello Mr. Soul: Neil Young Interview." *Pulse*, Apr 2002.

Laarhoven, Joyanne van. "Mariposa Folk Fest, Tudhope Park, Orillia, Jul 9-11.'" Posted at exclaim.ca.

Lawson, Steve. "Bruce Cockburn Interview." *Guitarist Magazine*, Nov 1999.

Lofaro, Tony. "Paul Anka Doesn't Live Here Anymore." *Ottawa Citizen*, Mar 10, 2000.

Lofaro, Tony. "Anka: It's Good to be Back Home." *Ottawa Citizen*, Apr 28, 2002.

Lofaro, Tony & Ron Eade. "What Does Anka Eat When He Visits Ottawa?" *Ottawa Citizen*, May 1, 2002.

LeBlanc, Larry. "Ian Tyson Travelling New Roads." *Country Music News*, Apr 9, 1905.

LeBlanc, Larry. "Tyson Album, Stage Show Draw On Her Life and Long Career." *Billboard*, Sep 9, 2000.

Leon, Alphonse. "Pretty Good Music, eh?" *Drop-D Magazine*, Jul 27, 1997.

Levitan, Corey. "Alanis Changes Her Tune." *Washington Post*, Sep 19, 1996.

Light, Alan. "Forever Young: Neil Young Has Turned the Clock Back." *Rolling Stone*, Jan 21, 1993.

Lima, O.J. "The Lady of Rage." *Seventeen*, Jan 1999.

McClain, Bruce. "Two Single Acts Survive A Marriage." *Detroit News*, Feb 1966.

Malka. "Joni Mitchell: Portrait of an Artist in Her Prime." *Maclean's*, Jun 1974.

Mansfield, Brian. "Twain's Greatest Hit — Her Stunning Success." *USA Today*, Nov 8, 2004.

Markle, Robert. "Lightfoot: A Friend's Portrait of the Artist at Work and Play." *Toronto Star Weekend Magazine*, 1977.

Maslin, Janet. "Review: Don Quixote." *Rolling Stone*, Apr 27, 1972.

Matteo, Steve. "A Rare Interview with Joni Mitchell, Jun 2005." Posted at insidecx.com.

Miller, Edwin. "Loverboy: Right Name For Rock Fame." *Seventeen*, Feb 1993.

Naglin, Nancy. "After Sundown: Gordon Lightfoot Makes Up for Lost Time." *Crawdaddy*, Apr 1975.

Nelson, Paul. "The Basement Tapes: Dylan and the Band." *Rolling Stone*, 1975.

North, Peter. "Lightfoot's Music Endures." *Edmonton Journal*, Nov 2, 1999.

Orloff, Brian. "Alanis Takes Another Look at 'Little Pill'." *Chicago Sun-Times*, 2005.

Page, Steven. "The Barenaked Truth about the Music Business." *Globe & Mail*, Apr 13, 2002.

Pareles, Jon. "Review: Jagged Little Pill." *NY Times*, Aug 1995.

Pareles, Jon. "Neil Young: A Believer in the Magic of Glitches." *NY Times*, Aug 11, 1997.

Pedersen, Andy. "Interview: Frank Sampedro." *Halifax Daily News*, Nov 11, 1996.

Perry, Steve. "Bruce Cockburn: A Voice Singing in the Wilderness." *Musician Magazine*, Mar 1978.

Pike, Lori E. "The Thinking Man & His Music: Bruce Cockburn Goes A Little Deeper." *Contemporary Christian Music*, Jan 1982.

Punter, Jennie. "Review: Ian & Sylvia's Moving On." *The Star*, Mar 25, 2000.

Pym, Michelle. "Bryan Adams: Nice Guys Finish First." *VOX*, Jan 1998.

Pynn, Larry. "Sudbury Saturday Nights Tom's Gift To Queen E." *Vancouver Sun*, July 16, 2001.

Quill, Greg. "Folk singer Sylvia Tyson Embraces the Present with a New One Woman Show." *Toronto Star*, Aug 6, 2000.

Ransom, Kevin. "The Band Interview." *Guitar Player*, May 1995.

Robbins, Li. "Four Strong Winds: Ian & Sylvia by John Einarson with Ian Tyson and Sylvia Tyson." *The Globe & Mail*, Sep 9, 2011.

Rockingham, Graham. "Lightfoot Returns to the Concert Stage." *Hamilton Spectator*, Nov 29, 2004.

Rockwell, John. "Neil Young As Good As Bob Dylan?" *NY Times*, Jun 19, 1977.

Rogers, John. "Paul Anka Does It His Way on PBS." *Associated Press*, 1990.

Rosebush, Jud. "Review: If You Could Read My Mind." *Rolling Stone*, Jul 23, 1970.

Roura, Phil. "Anka Swings, Baby." *NY Daily News*, Mar 6, 2005.

Ruhlmann, William. "Joni Mitchell: From Blue to Indigo." *Goldmine*, Feb 17, 1995.

Saidman, Sorelle. "Loverboy Bassist Presumed Drowned." Posted at mtv.com, December 4, 2000.

Seperounes, Sandra. "Tyson Tops ARIA Awards." *Edmonton Journal*, Jun 5/00.

Sevin, Joel. "And the Band Played On." *San Francisco Chronicle*, Nov 27, 1976.

Sharp, Keith. "Loverboy Turned Loose In America." *Music Express*, 1981.

Singer, Jonathan. "The Band: Where from here?" *Hit Parader*, Dec 1972.

Skinner, Ron. "Bryan Adams Interview: Finding the Right Studio." *Canadian Musician* Vol. 22. No. 2.

Slotek, Jim. "Stars Gather for Wall of Fame Gala." *Toronto Sun*, Jun 6, 2005.

Somnor, Jean. "Lightfoot: The Way I Feel." *Toronto Sun*, Nov 10, 1996.

Snyder, Julie. "So-called Chaos." *BAM*, Jul 20, 1995.

Spencer, Ruth Albert. "Interview: Richard Manuel." *Woodstock Times*, Mar 21, 1985.

Spencer, Ruth Albert. "Interview: Robbie Robertson." *Woodstock Times*, Apr 4, 1985.

Spencer, Ruth Albert. "Interview: Levon Helm." *Woodstock Times*, Apr 11, 1985.

Stetson, Nancy. "Anka a Versatile Survivor." *Naples News*, Jan 4, 2004.

Stevenson, Jane. "Night Out With The Ladies." *Toronto Sun*, Nov 20, 2001.

Stevenson, Jane. "The Hip Tired Of US Success Queries." *Toronto Sun*, Nov 2004.

Stevenson, Jane. "Rowdy Crowd Jazzed by Canada's Beloved Rockers." *Toronto Sun*, Jun 23, 2000.

Stratford, Chip. "Young Plays New Song for First Time in Vancouver," posted at *songfacts.com*.

Strauss, Neil. "John Lennon & Neil Young." *NY Times*, Sep 30, 2001.

Sullivan, Jim. "Neil Young interview." *Boston Globe*, 1990.

Takiff, Johnathan. "Bruce Cockburn: A Spiritual Believer Adrift In A Secular World." *Philadelphia Daily News*, Mar 3, 1978.

Talbot, David & Barbara Zheutlin. "Jack Nitzsche: Expecting to Fly." *Crawdaddy*, Nov 1974.

Tellier, Emmanuel. "Interview: Neil Young and Crazy Horse." *Les Inrockuptibles*. Jul 1997.

Timer, Tom. "Interview with Bryan Adams." *Top 40*, Nov 1992.

Todd, Douglas. "Belief Under Fire." *Vancouver Sun*, Nov 18, 1995.

Trafford, Tyler. "Ian Tyson and the Ranching Life." *The Canadian Cowboy*, Aug 2004.

Wallace, Wendy. "Get Hip: Canada's Hottest Band Celebrates 10 years." *See Magazine*, Feb 6, 1995.

Waters, Pamela Murray. "Bruce Cockburn: Heart of the Matter." *Dirty Linen*, Aug 2002.

White, Timothy. "Barenaked Ladies' Spectacle." *Billboard*, Aug 31, 1996.

Wild, David. "The Adventures of Miss Thing." *Rolling Stone*, Nov 2, 1995.

Wild, David. "So-called Chaos in the Studio." *Rolling Stone*, Dec 2001.

Williams, Rob. "Hip Down Memory Lane." *Winnipeg Sun*, Mar 28,2005.

Wyatt, Dale. "Interview: Gord Downie." *UWO Gazette*, Nov 5, 2005.

Young, Charles M. "Interview with Alanis Morissette." *Playboy*, Jun 1996.

OTHER SOURCES

Aligizakis, Irena. "The Making of an Authentic Poet: Ian Tyson Cowboy Poetry and Nature." Posted at irena.blackmill.net.

Ankeny, Jason. "Biography: Heart." Posted at allmusic.com.

Ankeny, Jason. "Bruce Fairburn." Posted at allmusic.com, June 14/04.

Anonymous. "Interview with Anjani Thomas on her work with Leonard Cohen." Posted at her web site: wundermusic.com.

Anonymous. "Alanis Morissette talks on going acoustic." Posted at SOFTPEDIA.net.

Anonymous. "Barenaked Ladies frontman Ed Robertson co-hosts 'Live! With Kelly'." Posted at winnipegfreepress.com."

Anonmyous. "Bryan's not lyin'." *BOP Magazine*. Posted at bryanadams-portal.com.

Anonmyous. "BBC radio interview with John Hammond and Leonard Cohen, Sep 1986."

Anonymous. "Bob Dylan and Neil Young." Posted at thrasherswheat.org.

Anonymous: "Neil Young & Pearl Jam." Posted at thrasherswheat.org.

Anonymous: "North American Dates announced for OLD IDEAS WORLD TOUR 2012." Posted at leonardcohen.com/us/news.

Anonymous. "Interview: Elliott Roberts." Neil Young Appreciation Society Newsletter, *Broken Arrow*, May 25, 1982.

Anonymous. "Bruce Cockburn's 30-year True North catalogue finds a home at Rounder Records." Press release, September 2002.

Anonymous. "Gord Lightfoot's Chronology." Posted at lightfoot.ca.

Anonymous. "Gord Lightfoot's TV Appearances." Posted at lightfoot.ca.

Anonymous. "History of Mushroom Studios." Posted at mushroomstudios. com.

Anonymous. "Interview with Bryan Adams." *Teenbeat*, posted at bryan-adams-portal.com.

Anonymous. "Interview with Mike Reno." Posted at melodicrock.com.

Anonymous. "Michael Moore Directs New Video of Rockin' in the Free World." Posted at thrasherswheat.org.

Anonymous. "Jim Vallance." Posted at thecanadianencyclopedia.com.

Anonymous. "Jim Vallance Interview." Posted at beatology.com, Oct 9, 1999.

Anonymous. "Ruth Lowe: the Sinatra Connection." Posted at cbc.ca, Sept 27/00.

Anonymous. "Mike Reno & Loverboy." Posted at rockforever.com.

Anonymous. "The Cockburn Project." Posted at cockburnproject.net.

Anonymous. "The People's Courtney." Posted at geocities.com.

Anonymous. "Interview: Langlois, Sinclair." Posted at golfontario.ca. June 2005.

Anonymous. "Saturday Night Live Transcript, Season one, Episode 21, Buck Henry, Gord Lightfoot, May 22, 1976." Posted at snltranscripts.jt.org

Anonymous. Barenaked stuff posted at bnlblog.com.

Anonymous. "The Hip FAQ." Posted at hipbase.com.

Anonymous. Everything you need to know about Stompin' Tom Connors. Posted at stompintom.com, a web site maintained by A-C-T Records.

Banasiewicz, Bill. "Excerpts from *The Official Biography*." Posted at Therushtribute@Cygnus-X1.com.

Barclay, Michael. "Singing For Supper." Posted at eyenet.com.

Barenaked Ladies' blog: bnl.blog.com.

Barsamian, David. "Interview with Bruce Cockburn." Posted at alternativeradio.com.

Bateman, Jeff. "Barenaked Ladies." Posted at thecanadianencyclopedia.com.

Bidini, Dave. "Interview: Gord Downie." Posted at hiponline.ca. March 2001,

Bird, June. "Interview with Bryan Adams." Posted at animal-lib.org.au.

Booth, Martin. "Alanis Morissette Rocks Philadelphia." Posted at earthtimes. org.

Breese, Wally. "A Conversation with Tom Rush." Posted at jonimitchell.com.

Breese, Wally. "A Conversation with David Crosby." Posted at jonimitchell. com.

Brittain, David & Don Owen, directors. "Ladies & Gentlemen: Mr. Leonard

Cohen." Documentary NFB film, 1965, 44 minutes. Home video release: 1994.

Brophy, Aaron. "Neil Young: Recovered and Recording." Posted at chartattack.com, May 11/05.

Brown, Mark. "Interview number one: Jagged Edge of Fame." Posted at geocities.com.

Cano, Theresa. "After 10 years fans still there for Alanis." Posted at azcentral.com.

Cantin, Paul. "The *Rolling Stone* lauds Gord Downie." Posted at JAM! Showbiz, July 10/01.

Dickie, Mary. "The Tragically Hip & By Divine Right." Posted at webeye.net, Feb 18/99.

Ferrin, Dave. "BBC Radio 2 Interview with Neil Young, June 5, 1987."

Fitzpatrick, Jamie. "Top 9 Hockey Songs." Posted at proicehockey.about.com.

Goddard, Peter. "Lightfoot at Massey Hall 1971." Posted at lightfoot.ca.

Graf, Christof. "Leonard Cohen's Chelsea Hotel At Midnight." Posted at leonardcohenfiles.com.

Grossweiner, Bob & Jane Cohen. "Industry profile: Jake Gold." Posted at celebrityaccess.com.

Halbersberg, Elianne. "Twain hits number one again." Posted at shaniaforums.com.

Halbersberg, Elianne. "Clean Sweep: Alanis hands over a hit." Posted at 4alanis.com.

Hannaham, James. "Alanis in Wonderland." Posted at geocities.com.

Harris, Michael. "Leonard Cohen: the poet as hero, a 1969 interview." Posted at medialab.chalmers.se.

Hoffman, Michael. "Mystic State Allusions in Rush Lyrics." Posted at egodeath.com.

Hoskyns, Barney. "Liner Notes for The Band 2000 Remasters."

Jorgensen, Julie. "Barenaked and heading for Hollywood." Posted at CNN.com.

Kelly, Jim. "Hip 'n' Divine: on the road." Posted at chartattack.com, 1999.

Kingsmill, Richard. "ABC Radio Australia: Interview with Neil Young, Nov 20/03. Posted at thrasherswheat.org.

Kruger, Debbie. "Interview with Graham Nash, Nov/99." Posted at debbiekruger.com.

Laman, Rob. "Gord Downie stretches his wings." Posted at papmag.net. Apr 2001.

McGrath, Rick & Mike Quigley. "Scotch & Pretzels, an interview with Gord Lightfoot." *Georgia Straight*, Oct 21, 1970.

Matteo, Steve. "Interview with Joni Mitchell." *Inside Connection Online*, Oct 2000.

Marsh, Dave. "Clear Channel Bans John Lennon's Imagine." Posted at john-lennon.com., Sept 19/01.

Mayer, Andre. "Canada's Live 8 Concert." Posted at CBC.ca, July 5/05.

Mazer, Elliott. "The Mix Files, May 1/01: Neil Young's Heart of Gold." Posted at computersandmusic.com.

Mettler, Mike. "Tragically Hip Bio." Posted at maplemusic.com.

Osborne, Doug. "MultiMAX helps Chris Fogel." Press release, October 21, 2002.

Pemberton, Jane. "Bachman-Overdrive Inspired Elvis to Take Care Of Business." Posted at spinner.ca on June 15, 2020.

Reesman, Ben. "Glen Ballard: the heart of the song." *Mix Online*, February 1/99.

Roberts, Alex. "Magically Hip: Summer nights at the Pier, Seattle." Posted at hipbase.ca. Aug 22/04.

Saunders, Kate. "BBC radio interview with Suzanne Verdal McCallister, June 1998."

Scoppa, Bud. "Interview with Bob Rock." Posted at addictedtonoise.com.

Simmons, Silvie. "Interview: Jack Nitzsche, June 1981." Posted at spectropop.com.

Stenger, Richard. "BNL Battle Napster with Trojan Downloads." Posted at CNN.com.

Stewart, Robert. "Smith ordered to stand trial, *LA Times*, Nov 25, 1985.

Sward, Robert. "Leonard Cohen Interview, Montreal 1984." Posted at cruzio.com.

Twigg, Alan. "Famous Visitor interviews with Leonard Cohen." Posted at ABCBookWorld.com.

Unterberger, Richie. "Sylvia Tyson Interview part one and two." Posted at richieunterberger.com.

Vermille, John. "Interview with Bruce Cockburn." WUSB Program Guide, Fall 1985.

Viney, Peter. "The Weight." Revised version of *Jawbone* article, posted at the-band.hiof.no.

Warburton, Nicholas & John Einarson. "Three's A Crowd: bio." Posted at canoe.com.

Whibbs, Shannon. "The Hip Hijack Canada Day." Posted at chartattack.com. July 5, 2004.

White, Pamela. "His Heart Rocks: Bruce Cockburn." Posted at BoulderWeekly.com.

Wolf, Charles. "Unpublished Interview with Bruce Cockburn at the Old Waldorf." Posted at Bruce Cockburn Pages: www.kingfield.com.

Zimmer, Dave. "Neil Young Biography: the Godfather of Grunge." Posted at thrasherswheat.org.

Zollo, Paul. "Closer To The Light with Bruce Cockburn." *SongTalk*, Vol. 4, issue 2, 1994.

Note from the Author

Songwriters are a rare breed, indeed, as I have learned in my lifetime association with some of the best. I have enjoyed a professional acquaintance with several artists profiled in this book, notably Ian Tyson and Sylvia Tyson, Leonard Cohen, Joni Mitchell, Randy Bachman, and Shania Twain. During my time spent in the trenches of the Canadian music industry, I have also met songwriters Ron Irving, Patricia Conroy Lindsay Mitchell, Linda Kidder, Sue Medley, Bill Henderson, Gary Cramer, Bing Jensen, Charlotte Diamond, Raffi, Roy Forbes, Shari Ulrich, Billy Cowsill, Cindy Church, Laura Vinson, Wykham Porteous, Tom Phillips, Sue Foley, Mike Shellard, Mike Plume, Doug Bennett, Beverley Elliott, Tom Lavin, Gary Cramer, Valdy, Rick Scott, Joe Mock, Michelle Wright, Russell de Carle, Joan Besen, Kelita, and Dick Damron, among others. Dick helped me make the transition from publicist to writing pop and country music histories and celebrity biographies, including *Country Women in Music, Shania Twain: Up and Away,* and *Dick Damron: The Legend and the Legacy.*

In the late 1980s, I hosted a Rogers Kitsilano Cable TV show called *Intimate Evenings with Songwriters.* The first shows featured my friends Gary Fjellgaard and Patricia Conroy, along with the wandering Willie P. Bennett. Canadian-born, Nashville-based, Ralph Murphy (*Half The Way, He Got You, Seeds*) dropped by to tape a show, bringing his pal Bobby Wood, the Memphis songwriter and piano player who backed everybody from Elvis to Garth Brooks. The *Intimate Evenings* programs were the first unplugged TV show that I know of, preceding MTV's by a few years.

I had met Ralph Murphy before at a SOCAN event in Vancouver, where I handed him my *West Coast Song Book,* the first collection of Vancouver songs, ever, and when I went to Nashville to tape interviews for my book *Country Women In Music,* Ralph took me to lunch with Harlan Howard, the guy who wrote *Heartaches By The Number* and coined the phrase "three chords and the truth."

On another memorable occasion, I was invited back to a bar at a Vancouver hotel, where Murray McLaughlin and Denise Donlon were bivouacked while hunting talent for an early Bluebird North songwriter showcase. Hands down Vancouver's longest-running talent show for songwriters, Bluebird North is now hosted by Shari Ulrich and billed as the show "where writers sing and tell."

In the mid-1980s, I began working full-time as a music journalist, publicist, producer, and "Jack of all trades." I produced a radio show pilot and 20 shows for poets and songwriters called *The Poem Show*, accepted a position as editor of *The Rana Review*, a West Coast country music quarterly, and began a ten-year stint as West Coast columnist for *Country Music News*, Canada's national country music newspaper.

At the 1987 Canadian Country Music Awards, Ian Tyson won Album of the Year for COWBOYOGRAPHY. Next to Billy Cowsill's stage shows, Tyson's were the best in the West, and I attended as often as I could, once writing an article about his terrific band, the Chinook Arch Riders. On one occasion, after he headlined the JR Country FM Festival in Fort Langley, Ian had his manager invite me to dinner at his hotel. "You can come and eat unlimited shrimp with Ian and the boys in the band," his manager, Paul Mascioli, told me. At that time, Paul was also the president of the Canadian Country Music Association. "But everything Tyson says is off the record."

Later that night, the boys in the band kidnapped me and took me deep into the Fraser Valley to a remote farm house, where Ian's band members swapped songs until the wee hours of the morning with members of a young Saskatchewan band that called itself Blue Rodeo. Their harmonies were sweetened by a couple of female vocalists. This was a very special moment in my life, I realized, as I sat there listening to young songwriters letting it all hang out long after midnight when the paying customers have gone home. It has not been a life without rewards.